To Kristy, Wishing you a wild & precious life! Hugs, Cynder

MY WILD &
PRECIOUS LIFE

A Memoir of Joy, Grief and Adventure

By Cynder Sinclair, Ph.D
Editorial Services by David Wilk

MY WILD & PRECIOUS LIFE

A Memoir of Joy,
Grief and Adventure

By Cynder Sinclair, Ph.D
Editorial Services by David Wilk

Cover photography by Kurt Koenig
Cover Designs by Rodrigo Aguillar, Hudio, Inc.
Foreword by Ken Saxon

Foreword

Imagine arriving at 75 years old with bountiful physical and mental energy, a 100-megawatt smile and a stand-out laugh, and still engaging each day to its fullest.

Cynder Sinclair is such a person.

I've had the privilege of knowing and working with countless community and nonprofit leaders over the years in my work. Cynder stood out from the moment I met her - with her bold red hair, her dynamic personality, and her willingness to take risks and try new things.

One might think that for someone to be at the privileged place where Cynder is at in her life, that she had it easy, and that she has had the benefit of little misfortune and not much stress. But you'd be mistaken. Cynder has been through more than one life's full of challenge and adversity.

In his book <u>David & Goliath</u>, Malcolm Gladwell writes about how adversity and trauma do crush some people, but they make many others stronger. Cynder's story is one of resilience, learning and adventure. And in her last chapter, she mines some life lessons that are a great list of mindsets that can help any of us find more resilience in our lives.

Take the time to read Cynder's story - through opportunity and adversity, through love and loss, through nonprofit and business, through travel adventure and spiritual search, and through a life filled with service to her fellow man —

and will find a compelling life's journey and also connect with some of what has allowed her to grow into her shining presence.

Cynder adores poetry, and her book and life story bring to mind such a poem I love by William Stafford. It's called "Silver Star."

Silver Star

To be a mountain you have to climb alone
and accept all that rain and snow. You have to look
far away when evening comes. If a forest
grows, you care; you stand there leaning against
the wind, waiting for someone with faith enough
to ask you to move. Great stones will tumble
against each other and gouge your sides. A storm
will live somewhere in your canyons hoarding its lightening.

If you are lucky, people will give you a dignified
name and bring crowds to admire how sturdy you are,
how long you can hold still for the camera. And some time,
they say, if you last long enough you will hear God;
a voice will roll down from the sky and all your patience
will be rewarded. The whole world will hear it: "Well done."

— *William Stafford*

When I got to the end of her book, I was moved to respond to Cynder with a hearty "Well done." But then I remembered that Cynder is anything but "done." I imagine her putting out a second edition someday, with additional chapters to come. Cynder's "Carpe Diem" attitude propels her forward, and the rest of us are left to shake our heads in admiration and wonder.

–Ken Saxon

(Following a successful entrepreneurial business career, Ken Saxon co-founded Leading from Within to invest in and nurture social sector leaders, who play such a critical role in the health of our communities. Ken was awarded the 2012 Man of the Year Award by the Santa Barbara Foundation for his significant and positive impact on the local region. He is an alumnus of Princeton University and Stanford's Graduate School of Business.)

My Wild & Precious Life

Preface

*"So tell me, what is it you plan to do with
your one wild and precious life?"*
−Mary Oliver

Every time I wrote down my bucket list, writing a book was at the top. I always thought it would be a book about nonprofits since most of my career has been in the social sector. I never dreamed it would be about my life story. But while I was engrossed in searching for my birth father, a process you will read about in chapter three, I gained new insights into the importance of learning more about one's parents and family. I began to feel drawn to the idea of writing my autobiography for the benefit of my many dear children, grandchildren and great grandchildren.

But how should I start? I had no idea. One day I was looking through our local newspaper and, for some reason, a tiny classified ad caught my attention. It said David Wilk was an editor who helps people write their memoirs. I noticed that he lived nearby in the sweet town of Ojai. I contacted him, we met for coffee in Carpinteria and we began working together to write this chronicle of my life. With his diligent guidance I was able to write this book you are about to read — and in so doing, check it off of my bucket list.

I began to think about the nature of memory as I began writing. How would I know if my memories were accurate, especially since I am now almost 75 years old? I did a little research on the topic and discovered that there are three important aspects of memory: encoding, storage and retrieval. Encoding is how we get information into the brain, whereas storage is how we retain information over time and retrieval is how we get information out of the brain. Differences in each or a combination of these aspects influence the similarity or discrepancy of memories from one person to another.

I decided to focus my writing on truth that is singularly my own, since there seems to be no such thing as an absolutely accurate memory, unless it is recorded by a camera. Three people in the same family can have the same experience, yet each one would write about it differently. The subjectivity of our lives is immense, so this book will reflect my own personal memories and my emotional responses to these occurrences. Events I describe here may not be what someone else remembers, but I do my best to adhere to my own truth and my own memory.

These three things I hope for the reader: that you are inspired by what is possible even in the face of adversity; that you are moved to write your own memoirs someday; and that you are encouraged to become the best version of yourself possible.

For myself — I am grateful for my unfailing resilience.

Chapters

Introduction

I have never written a book before and even though this book is about my own life, I had no idea where to start. Thankfully I identified an excellent book editor, David Wilk, shortly after I decided to write my memoirs. David recommended that I start by writing a chapter about a project or creation that I am particularly proud of or that brought me joy. My first thought was my work in Kingsburg, California, in the late 1970s and early 1980s, which ultimately resulted in founding the Kingsburg Community Assistance Program and Highway City Ministries.

So the first chapter, *In Service to Others*, tells about how I became a Christian and how that decision resulted in the creation of multi-faceted organizations to serve the farmworker families in California's San Joaquin Valley. I'm proud to say that these two nonprofits were the first winners of World Vision's Mustard Seed Award for the most innovative ministries to the poor in the country.

The second chapter, *The Power of Resilience*, highlights my early years in Alabama and Florida and then my move to southern California during the third grade. It contains some interesting stories about my family's frequent moves from Manhattan Beach, California, to Vestal, a tiny town in upstate New York, and back again every two years.

Chapter three, *Searching for Father*, is still an amazement to me and a source of great joy. When I was 16 years old, I discovered that the man who I thought was my father was actually my stepfather. I assumed that I would never find my birth father or even know my actual maiden name, since my mother was never forthcoming with his name (as it turned out she probably never even knew it). This chapter tells about the process of actually finding my father and getting to know what he was like.

Adventures in Child-Rearing, chapter four, describes how I met my first husband and, at 19-years-old, began raising his three children and then the two children I gave birth to. Interesting stories about our life in Fresno, Kingsburg, and then living on a sprawling ranch with all kinds of animals fill this chapter.

A New Lease on Life, chapter five, talks about my tangle with the FBI, the end of the 25-year marriage to my first husband and the beginning of my life with my second husband.

Chapter six, *Befriending the Outcasts*, relates my move to Stockton, California, my work with the San Joaquin County Child Abuse Prevention Council and my adventures in the men's prison, Duel Vocational Institute.

The seventh chapter, *Adventures Galore*, tells about my move to Santa Barbara, California, to serve as CEO for the Girl Scout council serving the central coast, imparts several exciting stories about my work at Girl Scouts (like the time I encountered a large mountain lion while alone on top of a mountain) and recounts the traumatic brain injury I received while cycling in Ireland. This chapter also describes the beautiful wedding to my third husband at Santa Barbara's Old Mission, which some people still refer to as "the party at the Mission."

Chapter eight, *Courage is the Key*, is appropriately named as it describes some of my kayaking and cycling adventures, taking my son, Matt, from the Fresno County jail at midnight to enter the Santa Barbara Rescue Mission's rehab program, arranging for Child Protective Services to rescue my two young granddaughters from their mother's meth house, my intimidating visit to my birthplace — Selma, Alabama — when I turned 60 years old, starting a new job at Santa Barbara Bank & Trust, writing my doctorate and serving as CEO for Santa Barbara Neighborhood Clinics.

In chapter nine, *Focusing on my Purpose*, I talk about starting my consulting business, Nonprofit Kinect, serving for six months as interim CEO for the Girl Scout council in North and South Dakota (including a scary run-in with Homeland Security), my work as CEO of Community Action of Ventura County and my retirement which began with an emergency appendectomy.

Chapter 10, *Overwhelming Grief*, relates going through the dying process with my oldest son, Rick, while providing key support to my family with the help of Hospice of Santa Barbara. This is a sad but uplifting story of my family's journey through the grief process.

In chapters 11 and 12, *Finding my Soul Mate* and *Traveling the World*, I tell about how I met Dennis Forster, my life partner and the love of my life, and I describe our amazing travels through 27 countries in five years.

The final section, chapter 13, is a compilation of 10 lessons I have learned through my life journey — Persistence Pays Off, Continuously Choose Joy, Find Others' Unique Gifts, Build Others to Their Highest Potential, Find Ways of Adding Value, Focus on the Positive, Always Create Beauty, Show Up and Pay Attention, Find Your Heroes, and Trust Your Own Wisdom. My hope is that these lessons will enrich the life of the reader.

–Cynder Sinclair

Dedication

To my life partner, Dennis Forster, for his constant encouragement and support in writing this book . . . and in life.

I would like to further dedicate this book to:

- Dr. Dora Johnson, my Doctoral instructor who inspired me by believing in my potential.
- Helen Cummings, my dear friend who taught me to walk closer to God and how to achieve my goals with grace.
- My birth father, Cmdr. Harold Allan Hall, from whom I inherited so many positive traits.
- David Wilk, my intrepid editor, without whom I would never have been able to write this book.

CHAPTER ONE
In Service to Others

Go to the people. Live with them. Learn from them.
Love them. Start with what they know.
Build with what they have.
But with the best leaders,
when the work is done, the task
accomplished, the people will say
'We have done this ourselves.'
— Lao Tzu

    The idea first started coming to me when I was volunteering as a teacher's helper in the small farming town of Kingsburg, California. Since I spoke Spanish, the professional teachers put me in charge of small groups of Mexican children. I began to notice their threadbare clothing and tattered shoes, especially because it was so cold outside. None of them knew

English. None of the children were acquainted with their peers or knew anything about classroom procedure. Each one seemed to feel completely lost, as if they had no idea what to do or say.

They also seemed hungry. I later discovered that since it was not harvest time, their parents were no longer receiving their usual wages for picking crops. So with no money for food, these children's diets consisted of squash and whatever their parents could grow near their little huts.

I especially remember a first grader named Pedro. He was slight in build and very quiet. His dark hair needed a good washing and a haircut. But his brown eyes were clear and observant of everything going on. Like the others in this group, he rarely made eye contact and his head often drooped as if in embarrassment.

Pedro's parents had journeyed from a small town in Mexico to find a better life for their family by picking Thompson Seedless grapes in the summer months, through early September. But come October as the temperature fell, the need for field workers dried up leaving his family without employment. They weren't documented migrants, so they stayed in their tiny shack and planted squash in the dirt nearby, hoping to survive until the next growing season.

Pedro's clothes were dirty, way too big for him and had several tears. He never had a coat to keep him warm in the chilly, foggy valley days. He was quiet at first, but as we began to talk more in our small group he seemed to perk up. He was smart, eager to learn and once he got over his shyness, he caught on to the lessons quickly. As I watched Pedro and his peers slowly emerge from their shells, I welcomed every day I spent with them.

So now it was the mid-1970s and I was raising my five children in Kingsburg, a small farming community in the San Joaquin Valley. I wanted to be helpful to the teachers in my children's grade school classrooms. When I offered my services to be a helper, the teachers were eager for my assistance.

Kingsburg was a small agricultural town with a population of about 3,000. The townspeople prided themselves on being a little Swedish community, complete with Dala Horses on the lamp posts along Draper, the main street.

In later years, every May I sewed costumes for myself, each of my kids and my oldest granddaughter so we could participate in the Swedish Festival. One year I even had our old doctor's buggy refinished to a brilliant black and red sheen and trained our old black mare to pull the buggy in the parade with my son Matt, granddaughter Stephanie and me at the reins.

Another year, we entered our authentic 12-passenger stagecoach – packed with several of the children from our Sonshine Learning Center dressed in Swedish costume and pulled by our horses.

Bright flowers filled this little town's stores and vendors served yummy fruit soup and crispy Ebelskivers. The main industry was farming with hundreds of acres of row crops, fruit orchards and grapevines. There was also a large cotton seed oil plant with a distinctive but not unpleasant odor that permeated the countryside.

My family lived in a relatively large house in the middle of town with expansive picture windows and three beautiful willow trees in front. Every day, after I took my older children to school, I would put my two-year-old son Baird in the child seat on my bike and pedal over to my neighbor's house where several moms joined together for morning coffee. I enjoyed getting to know all of these neighborhood ladies and soon felt like I belonged.

My daughter Pam, who was about 12 at the time, was full of energy and really liked helping others. She was a cheerleader at school and belonged to the Tri Hi Y club, which was part of the YMCA. Since I was trying to find a way to help the Mexican children in my son's classroom, with whom I was building sweet relationships, it suddenly occurred to me that I could start with a clothing drive. Pam's club was looking for a worthy project and this would be perfect. After explaining the children's need for warm clothing, the girls enthusiastically agreed to this new venture.

I was hoping to use this project as a way for our Tri Hi Y girls to practice thinking strategically and to create an action plan. We all met in one of the junior high classrooms after school and began to make lists of what we would need. The lists included clothing drives in the schools and churches, flyers to get the word out, a way of picking up the donated clothes, a place to sort and store them for distribution, tables, hanging racks and clothes hangers and then a way of inviting the families to pick up clothes.

I remember the day I met with Robin Petersen, the principal of the elementary school, to ask if he would approve conducting a clothing drive at his school to benefit some of the students. He was a really nice man and I knew him fairly well, since my children had attended his school for a few years. Still, I was a little nervous about asking for his help because the school hadn't had a clothing drive before.

I was relieved when Robin quickly replied, "Sure. I'm glad to participate. I think this will help our families a lot." I also met with three pastors of local churches to ask if their congregations would contribute to the clothing drive. They agreed, partly because some of the girls in the Tri Hi Y club attended their churches.

We created handmade flyers and passed them out at the school and churches, with each girl taking and distributing a stack. We had no idea how many donations we would receive but we knew we would need a place to sort and store them. So we made arrangements with one of the girls' parents to rent a garage they owned that wasn't being used. It was a good size but it was full of dust and cobwebs and was located at the end of a dirt road.

The girls jumped in and we all began to clean the dirty old garage. My sons, Rick and Mike, ages eight and 10, even pitched in to help. Next we arranged some donated clothing racks from a newly renovated store and put a big plywood table (borrowed from one of the girls' garages) in the middle of the room for sorting. We all chose the day to pick up the rented U-Haul truck—the enclosed kind with doors that shut. We had no idea how many clothes were awaiting us at the various sites but we wanted to be prepared.

On the appointed day, I picked up the truck and several girls squeezed into the front seat with me. We were excited! After picking up clothing from the grade school and four churches, we could hardly shut the truck door. We all spent the rest of the day unpacking the truck and finished about dusk when we returned the U-Haul truck. We were all tired and dirty but really happy with our day's work.

We agreed to meet back at the garage the next day and start sorting the treasures. Since the girls had to go to school until mid-afternoon, a few of their moms agreed to help me. It took two months of continuous sorting, organizing and washing before we were ready for families to come by to choose their favorite clothes.

But how would we invite the families? I didn't even know where to find them. All I knew was their children went to school with mine and they were in need of basics.

I decided to find a way to introduce myself to these families and gain their trust so I could invite them to visit our very full garage. I went back to Robin and asked him for a list of families he thought were poor. I was surprised when, without a word, he swiveled in his desk chair, looked in his file drawer, and quickly pulled out a paper with several names and addresses. He handed me the list and said, "All of these families live way out in the country and it might be hard to find some of them. So good luck."

I have to tell you that I have always had a bad sense of direction and, of course, this was before the days of GPS. So, finding these families (and finding my way back home) was a challenge. But I was determined.

So, one morning I set out to find my first family. Driving along the dusty country road lined with rows and rows of lush grapevines with the principal's list in hand, I realized I did not know exactly where I was going or, for that matter, even where I was. I tried to make mental notes about where I was and which direction to turn so I could find my way back home later. My head was spinning with worry about getting lost. At the same time, I wasn't even sure what I would say to the families once I found them. I began to rehearse in my head what I would say to them once I found someone home.

I was thrilled when I located the first house. It was actually a square hut built of two by fours with no windows and an old sheet hanging on a curtain rod over the doorway. As I walked up to the door, a woman named Maria came out to greet me. I smiled and mustered up my courage and greeted her in Spanish.

As a bit of background, during the summer between my junior and senior year in high school, I was a foreign exchange student to La Paz in Baja California. Since this was 1963, La Paz was very underdeveloped. I was the only person there who spoke English, so in order to communicate I had to use the Spanish I had learned in my high school classes. At first, I was tentative, but there was no time to be embarrassed, so I plunged right in. I was surprised that before long I was completely fluent. After three months living among these friendly families and being immersed in their loving culture, I felt right at home conversing in Spanish. I continued to study Spanish when I went to college.

"Some of the nice people in town would like to bring your children Christmas presents," I said. "Would that be okay?"

Instantly, Maria lit up and smiled. After telling me her kids' ages and sizes, she invited me inside her humble dwelling. She quickly retrieved a tattered broom and swept the dirt floor until it looked tidy. She smiled as we sat on two rickety old wooden chairs and talked about her children. She said her family came here two years ago to try to make a better life. Her husband was working in the field and she was home because her daughter was sick with the flu. She seemed happy to have someone to chat with, since it was so lonely out there. As I turned to leave, she said I was welcome to come by anytime.

I felt a great sense of relief that the first visit went so well and began looking for the next address. After some searching, I found the mother of the next family in a converted chicken coop in the middle of a dirt field. I had to duck down to enter and walk around inside. We sat on slanted wooden slats that used to host chickens. The wire mesh and feathers were still present. But the woman seemed happy and glad to have company. As she nursed her baby, we talked about her family and what her children would like to receive for Christmas. After a while, I forgot we were sitting crouched over in a chicken coop because our chat was so engaging.

After several weeks of visiting families and building rapport, I began to invite them to visit our little clothes-filled garage. Typically they would arrive in a borrowed pick-up. The father drove with the mother in the front seat and the kids scattered throughout the truck, depending on their age. I watched out the garage's side window as each family drove up to the dusty driveway alongside the building. I noticed the father would keep his head down looking somewhat embarrassed. The mother would come into the little shed with kids trailing behind. She seemed a little uncomfortable, which puzzled me since I was always there to help them navigate the racks of clothing.

Pretty quickly I realized something wasn't right. The families seemed glad for the warm coats and clothes, but they appeared self-conscious about receiving the gifts. It dawned on me that this process undermined their dignity. Receiving charity like this made them feel inferior.

I began to dream of a way for them to obtain the garments in a manner that would affirm their dignity. I decided the only way was to start a thrift store where the families could choose their own clothes at a price they could afford. Since raising children was my only experience at this time, I had no idea where to start. I had never worked in a store, much less started one.

One day, I was discussing my dilemma with a society lady sitting next to me at a chamber of commerce meeting, when the gentleman sitting next to us overheard our conversation and said, "What about my building?"

"Henry, I didn't know you had a building," I said.

He invited me to tour it right after the meeting. He carefully unlocked the small door to the site which was located right on the main street. We climbed the long, steep staircase through the dim light and arrived at a maze of long-abandoned insurance offices.

Still not knowing what I was doing and lacking any type of plan, I said, "This is perfect, Henry! I'll take it." At $50 monthly rent, I was in business. Now what? How do I start a "sort of" business?

To provide some more background, in 1975 I was a new Christian. Becoming a "believer," as my friends called it, was an interesting and unlikely process for me. Shortly after I moved from Fresno to Kingsburg with my husband and four children, I began to meet some of the local moms with kids that attended school with my kids who were now one, six, eight, and ten. Later, my son Matt was born at Kingsburg Hospital.

From the time I was a grade schooler moving from coast to coast, I have intentionally angled a way to fit in with people wherever I lived. So when some of my new friends invited me to attend their Bible study, I agreed in an effort to seem like "one of them." I attended several of these weekly meetings. I always politely paid attention and nodded at the right times, but inside my head I thought, "I hope these people don't think I really believe this stuff about Jesus being the Son of God." But, on the outside, I tried to appear as if I believed and fit in.

One day, as I was driving along taking care of some mundane errands in town, a vision of my high school geometry book appeared out of nowhere in my mind. I always liked geometry and I remembered the lesson often said something like, "Given: All sides of an isosceles triangle are equal. Problem: Side A is one foot long. How long is side B?" I thought it was strange to see my geometry book in my head, but there it was.

Next, I had the vivid thought, "Given: Jesus is the Son of God. Now solve the problem." My first thought as I drove along on this very mundane shopping trip was, "Well I guess I can think about this as a hypothesis rather than a fact or a belief. If it were true that Jesus was the Son of God, what would be the answer to the problem?" Thinking about this in an abstract, theoretical sense was very different than actually believing it.

But a crack of light had opened in my brain and it began to shine into my heart, without me consciously being aware of it. When I returned to the next week's Bible study meeting, I could take in the information and discussion in a very different way. Now it was relevant and I didn't have to pretend to be a believer. I could feel that, somehow, things had shifted in my spirit and now I was actually a believer. I never told anyone of this internal struggle, but later a couple of the women commented that they could tell something was different about me.

These wonderful ladies continued to minister to me, teach me about the scriptures and show me how to apply these verses and stories to my life.

So now that I had made this important decision, I needed to know what it meant for my life. Always being a bit of a linear thinker, I looked up "Christian" in the dictionary. It said, "A follower of Christ." I figured if I was going to be a follower of someone, I should know what their priority list looked like so I could pattern my life accordingly. I started by reading through the Gospel accounts of Jesus' life. When I quickly realized the poor were at the top of his priority list, I wondered how I could follow this example.

Even though my husband was gone every day, working at his office, he began to notice me reading scripture and attending Bible study. He became angry and condescending. He said things like, "I never wanted to be married to a Christian." I began hiding my scripture reading and Bible studies by engaging only while he was gone. Still, he continued to deride me about this.

One day as I was leaving for Bible study, he said, "You're going to have to choose between me and God. When I get home tonight, I want to know your answer." I knew I was in for a rocky road and I also knew I would not choose him over God. When he returned home from work that day, he seemed to have forgotten his threat. So I didn't bring it up but I continued my journey.

I thought that since my new project was a Christian endeavor, I would be able to find ladies in the churches to volunteer to help. I met with a few groups of women, explained the project, and asked for their assistance. Most of them declined, saying they preferred to conduct their spiritual walk through Bible study rather than work. I was pretty disappointed and somewhat confused— because it made logical sense to me to put one's beliefs into action to benefit others. But two of the women from Henry's church, Elaine and Carolyn, agreed to help. So, the Tri Hi Y girls and these two ladies helped me clean up the rooms.

It proved to be quite a big project. We swept the floors, washed the windows and cleaned the walls. One of the volunteers made cute little curtains for the windows. We all agreed we wanted this to be a clean, well-organized store rather than a dusty, messy one. Just because it was a thrift store with donated merchandise did not mean it had to be junky looking.

I wanted to remind everyone who came into the store, especially those who volunteered, exactly why we were doing this. So, I found a nice piece of large, white cardboard and wrote the scripture verse that guided me through this process from the beginning:

"I was hungry and you fed me, naked and you clothed me, thirsty and you gave me water, a stranger and you invited me in, sick and in prison and you visited me. What you did for the least of these, you did for Me." -Matthew 25:35-40.

I nailed it high up on one of the walls for all to see. Even though my handwriting was a bit crooked it got the message across.

Now it was time to transfer the clothes from the little garage to the newly spruced up store. We first moved the large wooden table from the garage. We borrowed pickup trucks from a couple of the girls' parents and gradually carried load after load up the steep stairs, placing them on the big table so we could come back later and organize them. It was hot, tiring work, made more challenging by all of the stairs we had to climb with heavy loads of clothes. Finally, we brought the clothing racks over and placed them throughout the little rooms. Most of the clothes were clean and in good condition, but I took the dirty ones home to wash. I was so proud of our crew for working so hard for this selfless cause.

It took about four weeks of diligent work, but finally everything was organized and we were ready to welcome our "guests." So, I once again began my treks out to the fields, little shacks and chicken coops to invite the families to visit the store.

Most were wary and a little uncomfortable with the idea of coming into town, since they were used to spending their days in the fields and they viewed town as a place for the wealthy. These families weren't used to going into a real store, let alone on the main street.

But little by little, they began to make their way. Soon, the word was out—this was a place where they could choose clothing for their families at a price they could afford.

Their transformed demeanor amazed me. No longer were their heads bowed with embarrassment. Now they smiled and chattered happily as they found just what they needed.

Local church members gladly contributed a steady flow of excellent clothing. We called the store Kingsburg Community Assistance Program, or KCAPS for short. I think I called it KCAPS instead of KCAP because I thought it sounded better and because I had a sense we would create more programs.

Soon everyone in town was talking about KCAPS as though it had always existed. Volunteers began to show up to offer their services and families gradually became more comfortable coming into town and making their way up the steep stairs. Activity grew slowly but steadily.

To help attract families, I arranged for the Fresno County Public Health Department to send healthcare providers to the store every Thursday morning to give well-baby checkups, immunizations and other basic healthcare services. The stairs added to the complexity of this project because we had to carry all of their equipment up the stairs. We cleaned off a couple of the tables and covered them with clean tablecloths and hung curtains for privacy in the "exam rooms." As an added incentive, I brought coffee and donuts for the providers so they would feel more welcome.

This service was important for the families because they had no other place to go for this type of care. It worked very well, served as an attraction for families and provided a needed service. Once the families got into the store for their healthcare, they realized they could come back to shop there.

After about a year of operation, I began to realize we needed a larger space preferably located on a side street rather than on the main street. I found my mind absorbed with how to help these unfortunate families. I got the idea to start a food bank so we could collect and distribute food to these conscientious farmworker families. When the picking season was over, the families had no income and usually lived on squash or whatever they could grow in the dirt by their house. So the winter months brought many challenges for these folks.

I talked about the need for a larger space with whoever would listen to me. Then one day Elaine, one of the volunteers who was especially committed to putting her faith to practical use said she owned a large empty building on one of the side streets. This 5,000 square foot structure used to house their family's heating and air conditioning business before she and her husband, Archie, retired. Now it sat empty. I was beyond excited.

After discussing all of the details, I agreed to rent the building for a modest stipend each month. By now we had accumulated quite a large group of volunteers, most of whom were from the local churches. As it turns out, a couple of the more committed volunteers had explained to their fellow church members why it was important to put their spiritual beliefs into action by serving the poor through KCAPS. So, this army of volunteers moved all of the clothing down the stairs of Henry's building and into the new building. It took several weeks, but the store was finally open for business. We even had a donated cash register and fixtures.

As soon as the new store was up and running smoothly with volunteers taking daily shifts, I began to plan for a food bank. Our neighbors were scrounging for food, severely undernourished and always hungry. I needed a way to collect the food and a place to store and display it. I arranged to meet with a few of the pastors to ask if their congregations would join in a food drive. Ultimately, six pastors agreed to invite their parishioners to contribute to a food drive.

I was a bit dismayed when one pastor said he heard that we were telling people about Jesus at KCAPS. He said he didn't like us doing that and I told him I would let the volunteers know he said this but I was careful not to promise any changes. As a new Christian, I was confused by a pastor expressing these sentiments since I thought that putting one's faith into action and sharing the Good News of the gospels was the whole point. But I politely (and a bit stubbornly) kept my focus on our goals of serving the poor.

Soon, thanks to the church food drives, a steady stream of donated canned and dry goods flowed into KCAPS. We also gained access to the government cheese donations.

But I had no place to stack and arrange the food. I needed shelves, lots of them. I identified just the right place to build the shelves, with a wall separating the food bank from the thrift store area. One day I stood in the cavernous building alone. I brought a hammer, nails, and some wood from home and was determined to make some shelves. As I stood there, with hammer in hand, I was befuddled. I had a frustrating realization: I had no idea how to build shelves or even go about making this project a reality.

At that moment, I glanced out the expansive windows fronting the street and miraculously saw my friend Archie walking along. I immediately realized this was my answer. Archie and his family owned the building and I was sure he and his many buddies were experienced with carpentry. Archie's wife, Elaine, was one of our most dedicated volunteers, so I knew them well. I hurried through the store, opened the heavy glass front door, and hollered out to Archie. When he stopped and turned around, I rushed over to him and explained my dilemma. He came inside and I showed him my idea of where to build the shelves and the wall. He said it would be no problem and within a few days, Archie and several of his friends were sawing, hammering and building our food bank shelves.

After about a week, the food bank area was complete and the volunteers stacked and organized all the donated food. It felt like a miracle. Our little town of Kingsburg was responding resoundingly to the challenge of helping others who were less privileged.

I remembered the lesson I learned earlier about affirming rather than undermining dignity and I wanted to find a novel way of distributing the food to the farmworker families. The food was all donated and I would not charge the families for the food because I knew that they couldn't afford to pay anything at all during the winter months when they needed it most. But what could I tell the families that would make them feel like they had somehow "earned" the food?

Luckily, my husband Larry and I were friends with many of the large farmers, so I paid them all a visit. I reminded them that the farmworkers they depended upon to harvest their orchards, vineyards and fields lived in our town with their families year-round. I suggested it wasn't right that they eat only squash and whatever else they could grow themselves during the off-season.

My first meeting was with Don Jackson who was one of the biggest farmers in town, farming hundreds and hundreds of acres of row crops and vines. I knew he depended heavily on these families to pick his crops. He knew about KCAPS because his wife, Pat, was a dedicated volunteer and very involved in one of the churches. But he didn't know about the new food bank project. When I explained about the living conditions of the families who served him and why they needed food in the winter, he quickly agreed to do all he could to work with other farmers to contribute large amounts of dry pinto beans and rice.

Their help, together with the church food drives, filled the foodbank shelves. But now I needed to get the news out to the families and invite them to come choose their food from our shelves. In order to affirm their dignity, I drove out to each of the families' home to tell them the good news about the food bank.

When I pulled up to the first family's residence, I noticed several men gathered around a small campfire. There were also several dogs roaming around, children playing and one of the moms bustling around. I felt a little nervous, partly because I wasn't sure how the men would receive me and partly because the dogs looked scary, but I mustered my courage, climbed out of my car and walked over to them as if it was the most natural thing to do.

They all turned to look at me with a bit of suspicion on their faces. This, of course, made me even more nervous. Even though I had met the mom earlier, these men had never seen me. As I greeted them, they seemed confused that someone that looked like me (red hair and freckles) was speaking Spanish to them.

I explained that the farmers and others in town appreciated their work during picking season and they had collected food to give them as a bonus to their salary. Some of them already knew about the KCAPS thrift store because they had purchased clothing there. When I told them about the food bank and how it was located inside the thrift store, they all seemed surprised but happy, no longer suspicious.

That arrangement suited everyone just fine. The farmers and townspeople were happy to contribute and the families felt they had earned the food they received.

Another thing I noticed while serving as a teacher's helper in my children's classroom was that many of their classmates were not prepared for school. They didn't know English, they weren't acquainted with their peers, they lacked understanding of classroom procedure and they felt inferior to the other children.

So, about a year after finishing organizing the food bank, I decided it was time to start a pre-school. Back in those days, only wealthy families could send their children to pre-school. But I was determined to find a way for these little Mexican kids to build self-esteem by being properly prepared for their school career.

I knew nothing about education or how to run a school, but I knew I had to find a solution. One morning, while pushing my grocery cart through the aisles of our local grocery store, I saw my son's pre-school teacher. I stopped in my tracks and knew I had the answer. As we both picked out our produce, I said, "Janet, I want to start a pre-school in town to prepare the children from farmworker families for kindergarten, but I have no idea how to do it."

She said, "If you find a place and furnish the supplies I need, I can put this together for you." Since I was so impressed with her teaching talent, I agreed on the spot.

First we needed a place to hold class. I had been attending Bible study with some ladies from the Evangelical Covenant Church, so I told them about my dream of starting a pre-school. I needed a space for this unique pre-school. This school would be open to all kids, wealthy or not, regardless of their primary language. Tuition collected from the ones who could afford to pay would help offset the costs for the less affluent. English would be used for most communication so the young Mexican children could become bilingual. But the English-speaking children would also be learning some Spanish in the process.

The ladies became excited and said they would speak with the pastor to see if I could use one of their Sunday school classrooms. Within a month, we had a signed agreement. There would be no rent to pay, just upkeep of the space. The church would consider this as a "local mission."

Ladies in the church sewed cute smocks for each child so they all looked alike. That way, no one could distinguish the kids' income level by their clothing. We named the school Sonshine Learning Center. Since it was in a church, the "Son" referred to Jesus shining down on all the children.

Once again, I drove out to the homes of the farmworker families to tell them about the pre-school and invite them to attend. When I went to the first home, the mom was happy to see me as always. When I told her about the school and how her young children could attend at no charge, she smiled but looked a little concerned. She said she was excited about her kids getting ready for kindergarten and learning English, but she would need to discuss it with her husband. I arranged for interested parents to tour the facility and meet the teacher.

Ultimately, after many conversations, all of the families with pre-school age children agreed to give it a try.

I knew I had a transportation problem, so I talked to Robin, the school principal, to see if he had a suggestion. He told me about a small, old yellow school bus they weren't using. I agreed to purchase it for $1,000. Fortunately, my husband Larry was willing to supply the funds.

Next, I learned that the driver would have to have a certain license to drive the school bus even though it was small. A retired school bus driver heard about my dilemma and offered his services for a stipend. By now the thrift store was producing revenue for KCAPS, so we used those funds to pay the driver and the bus expenses. I explained that he would be going around to all the homes in the countryside and picking up the kids who had no way to get to school.

I was glad I had spent so much time visiting with the families and establishing trust, but I knew that sending their young children off in a bus with a stranger would be challenging for them. So, the first week I rode in the school bus to each family's home, greeted the parents, and walked with each child onto the bus, assuring them we would deliver their child home in a few hours. I even introduced them to the bus driver. I told them there would be no fee but if they wanted to give $5 per month when they had the funds, it would be appreciated. Many of them contributed, feeling good about doing their part for the project.

Years later, Robin, the same long-time school principal who gave me the list of poor families, told me something that warmed my heart. Kids that came to kindergarten from Sonshine were very well prepared for school, unlike their older siblings who did not have that privilege (since there was no pre-school for them at the time). As my own children grew and went through the upper grades, I paid close attention to the kids who had attended Sonshine. Most of them earned top grades and were excellent students.

I remember one child in particular, Manuel, who seemed to be bright and full of energy. He eventually graduated at the top of his class at Kingsburg High School and went on to attend Fresno City College and then Fresno State University. Several of his friends attended college with him. I have no doubt they are all leading successful lives today.

Eventually, Sonshine Learning Center became its own nonprofit organization with its own board of directors. But it still kept the same mission of serving God by serving the poor.

During several of my earlier home visits, the mothers would tell me they wanted to attend Spanish church services. They had tried to attend the local Catholic Church, but the pastor didn't speak Spanish so they gave up. I asked each of the many churches in Kingsburg if they would be able to hold a service in Spanish. Not one had a pastor who could do this.

It was about this time that I met Carlos at a neighbor's house. His employer, who owned a dairy and was a strong Christian, had invited Carlos to attend the weekly Bible study in his home. This is how I learned that Carlos worked at this nearby dairy where he milked cows. I was impressed with Carlos as he told me about his sincere desire to preach the Word to Spanish-speaking people who worked at the dairy. I remember feeling almost giddy as I realized he might be the answer to my plan to start a Spanish-speaking church.

I told him about my dream of creating a place where the farmworker families could come to worship God in their own language. His eyes lit up at the thought of being part of this dream. But since he had four children and a wife to support, I knew I would have to find a way to pay his salary. I was determined to make this dream a reality. I told him to have faith and to pray that I could find a way to pay his salary so he could bring the gospel to the families instead of milking cows.

By now our family had moved a little distance from town into a sprawling 6,000 square foot home, nestled in 120 acres of manicured Thompson Seedless grape vines. The expansive grounds hosted horses, cattle, pigs, sheep, chickens and peacocks. A large riding arena, grassy pastures, a huge swimming pool, tennis courts and an enormous barn we used for charity fundraising events filled the five acres closest to the house. It was so beautiful that travelers along our country road would often park in our driveway and picnic on our front lawn because they thought it was a park.

One day, I invited 12 of our local pastors to come to my beautiful ranch house for lunch. I was eager to tell them about my idea of starting a Spanish-speaking church. All of these pastors had already been participating in food and clothing drives and promoting Sonshine Learning Center, so they were familiar with KCAPS.

Remember, I was still a brand new Christian with no understanding of denominational differences, much less variances in theology. So, inviting all of those pastors to lunch to discuss starting a new church made perfect sense to me. After lunch was served at my over-sized round oak table, I told them about my dream of hiring Carlos to preach to these families in Spanish. I suggested that each of them could contribute to a fund at KCAPS to pay for Carlos' salary.

I had no idea what a naïve idea this was until later when I learned about denominational differences and how each church liked to do things their own way. My thinking was simply, "We all love Jesus, so let's get out there to preach about Him to people in their own language."

Much later, I discovered that each church has its own particular denominational view of scripture and protocol. So, given the variety in denominations represented around the table, I was foolish to think an idea like this would fly. Looking back, I remember lots of stunned looks and clearing of throats because they were not in the habit of working together, certainly not when theology was involved. Since I realized everyone was uncomfortable with my idea, I felt pretty silly and a bit confused, not knowing where to take the conversation next. So, I suggested they take the idea back to the appropriate committee at their respective churches and we could discuss it later.

I tried to be patient, but I felt pretty anxious as I waited week after week with no communications. I even made an appointment with one of the pastors to ask for his feedback on the idea. I was floored when he said, "Is Carlos going to talk about being born again? Our folks don't go for that kind of talk, you know."

I tried to remain composed but I was thinking, "I thought it was Jesus who talked about being born again." I told the pastor, "Gosh, I'm not sure but I will ask Carlos and get back to you. In the meantime, will you please consider supporting this project?"

Finally, after several long weeks, seven of the churches agreed to form the Kingsburg Coalition of Churches, with KCAPS as the lead. We met faithfully for a few months to work out all the details and then we hired Carlos. He was ecstatic.

Now I needed to build a bridge of trust between Carlos and the farmworker families. So, I drove us around to all of the rural homes to introduce him to the families and explain the plan for a church. While in each home, Carlos would pray a bit and tell a Bible story or two and then we would move on to the next place, usually two or three miles apart. Each family seemed genuinely excited about the idea of being able to worship in their own language.

Once we had established trust between Carlos and the families, Carlos began going out to the fields and homes to preach alone. After nearly a year of Carlos' itinerant preaching, we found a large, abandoned grocery store that would later serve as a place where everyone could congregate. The original owner had passed away and his son now owned it and attended one of the churches who had agreed to participate in this project. The son was eager to be part of our new church, so he agreed to rent the building to us if we paid the maintenance fees, insurance, and property taxes. Once again, the thrift store provided some of the funds for this, but this time we had financial help from the seven churches who were part of the Kingsburg Coalition of Churches, too.

The building was over 5,000 square feet with high ceilings and old linoleum flooring. Volunteers from the seven churches and others in the community found folding chairs and someone even donated a simple pulpit and a rickety piano.

Carlos was now on his own with the families, so he enthusiastically invited them to the first church service. I was nervous wondering about whether people would actually come. But, sure enough, when the doors opened over 100 people flowed through the door to take their seat on one of the donated folding chairs. I was glad to see that a few representatives from some of the coalition churches were there too. Carlos stepped up to the front and began the service in Spanish as if he had been doing it all his life. Later he admitted he was nervous, but he sure seemed calm and sure of himself.

I remember our first Thanksgiving service very well. After the service they had planned a potluck dinner. I didn't attend the service, but I came to the dinner and brought a salad to contribute to the meal. There was a buzz of activity with the adults chatting in small groups and organizing the food while the kids ran around playing various games. Carlos quieted everyone so he could say the blessing over the meal and then everyone got busy filling their plates with the delicious food.

A couple of guys brought guitars and everyone enjoyed the lively Mariachi music. As the evening wore on, I became tired and found myself wishing it would end so I could help clean up and go home to bed. I was glad everyone was having such a good time, but I was really tired and weary.

Right when I thought Carlos was going to wrap up the festivities, he gathered everyone for another sermon and prayer. I thought to myself, "Oh come on Carlos, it's time to go. It's so late and I'm sure the people want to leave. Nobody wants to listen to yet another prayer."

As I stood there with my tired head bowed dutifully in prayer, I peeked out of one eye and was astounded by what I saw. Kneeling down in front of Carlos were at least a dozen fathers with their older children kneeling next to them, all praying together. Carlos placed his hand on each head as he walked through the group. The scene took my breath away and I felt a little embarrassed that I was in such a hurry to end the service. Finally, it was over. We all cleaned up the food and everyone filed out into the chilly night happily chatting among themselves.

The church continued to grow and eventually became one of the largest churches in town. Years later the Mennonite Church took this church under its wing. I was surprised when, the next year, I was chosen as Kingsburg's Citizen of the Year. What a humbling experience.

Three years after starting KCAPS, Bufe Karraker, who was the pastor of the church I was attending (Northwest Baptist Church), asked me if I would start a similar program in Highway City, located in what was at the time a very poor area of north Fresno not too far from our church. I agreed and got busy getting to know the community, meeting farmworker families, and looking for a suitable place to start a thrift store and food bank. This time it was a lot easier to find volunteers because they attended my own church. Since the pastor was promoting the work, many people wanted to help out. This program, which we called Highway City Ministries, soon began growing as it met the needs of the local families.

By now it was the early 1980s and I heard about something called the Mustard Seed Award, being given by World Vision, the largest Christian ministry in the world. They had two categories: multi-church and single church. They were looking for projects that started with a small idea and grew into a larger entity that had the potential to be replicated. This concept was based on the parable of the mustard seed from Matthew 13:31-32 where Jesus says, "The kingdom of heaven is like a grain of mustard seed that a man took and sowed in his field. It is the smallest of seeds, but when it has grown it is larger than all the garden plants and becomes a tree, so that the birds of the air come and make nests in its branches."

The prize was $5,000 to each first-place winner. I had never written a grant before but thought I could figure it out. I carefully filled out all the paperwork and submitted two applications: one for KCAPS as a multi-church entry and one for Highway City Ministries as a single church entry.

I'll never forget the day I received a phone call from a secretary at the World Vision headquarters. She said both projects had received first place over the entire country as the most enterprising and innovative ministries to the poor. She said she didn't realize that both were started by the same person until she went to type up the award letter. We were both astounded. Since then, KCAPS has continued to grow over the years and has spawned similar programs throughout the San Joaquin Valley.

In the late 1970s, I heard a guest speaker at our church in Fresno whose message completely inspired me. I sat riveted listening to his story about how he was beaten almost to death and thrown in jail during the civil rights era in Mississippi. John Perkins told us about how he decided to respond with love rather than anger by starting Mendenhall Ministries in the middle of one of the poorest neighborhoods in Mississippi.

After devouring his book, *Let Justice Roll Down*, I knew I had to go there to see his work for myself because he seemed to have the same heart for the poor as I did. I was so impressed by his work because he had done some of the same things I dreamed of doing in Kingsburg. I needed to find out how he did it and see it with my own eyes.

Even though I was busy raising five children and my husband wanted me to stay at home and tend to the family (unless I went to the grocery store or some other household errand), I was determined to go to Mississippi. I'm still not sure how I convinced him to let me go, but after making preparations for childcare and meals, I packed a small bag and traveled to Mendenhall. John met me at the airport and, over the few days, gave me a tour of his work there.

At least a dozen volunteers from all over the country, who had also been inspired by John's message, lived for several months at a time in the humble houses nestled together on the compound. Walkways between the houses and the front and back yards were dirt mixed with an occasional bit of grass. Yet it was beautiful to my eyes.

John, his wife Vera Mae and their crew ran a small thrift store, led the local children and some adults in Bible study and held tutoring sessions for the youngsters in the neighborhood. John named his main call to action *The Three Rs: Relocation, Redistribution, and Reconciliation*. This concept, along with his strong commitment to sharing God's love with his neighbors was the key to the success of his work: Mendenhall Ministries.

He advocated relocating to a community of need, redistributing talents and skills by teaching others and reconciling the races and all people to each other. He encouraged all those who mastered these skills to remain in the community to teach others rather than to move away to a nicer area.

I returned home after four days with John and his team with renewed energy and a clearer vision of what was possible in my little farming town. I was also surprised and energized to see John's work at Mendenhall Ministries because when I heard him speak at my church, it sounded like his project was very large and elaborate. It was actually focused on a small neighborhood. I quickly realized that even a small effort could touch lives of disadvantaged families in profound ways. My trip to Mississippi renewed my commitment and clarified my vision of the way forward.

The more I got to know John and Vera Mae, the more I realized we were kindred spirits. More than once they visited as guests in our home, bringing many of the kids from their ministry with them. Eventually, John and Vera Mae moved to Pasadena to a neighborhood that had the highest daytime crime rate in all of California. They started the Harambe Center to serve the neighborhood children with Bible study and tutoring. Later they started the John M. Perkins Foundation for Reconciliation and Development and my husband and I agreed to serve on their board of directors.

I was so impressed with the impact John's work had on at-risk communities that I began to urge him to form a national foundation to serve as a model for other communities throughout the country. Many of his other colleagues were giving him the same message. Finally, he started the Christian Community Development Association. I served as the first executive director and organized their first two annual conferences, hosting over 300 attendees in Chicago. I also traveled around with him presenting the concept of Christian community development to many Black churches. I have always been proud of being part of that effort. Thankfully, it continues to grow and is larger and stronger than ever today.

The more lowly your service to others, the greater you are.
To be the greatest, be a servant.
Matthew 23: 11

Scenes from the KCAPS thrift store we founded in Kingsburg
Photos courtesy of HansfordSentinel.com

The KCAPS thrift store today; Girls in midst of a clothing drive

KCAPS crew expressing appreciation; (below) Fans of KCAPS

National Winner

KCAPS earns honor for helping Kingsburg needy

The Kingsburg Community assistance Program, Inc. (KCAPS) was recently awarded $5,000 and chosen as the top program in the United States for its innovative work with a community of need.

KCAPS works in partnership with 10 Kingsburg churches serving local families in need.

The award, cosponsored by the Mustard Seed Foundation and Love, Inc. a division of World Vision, was established to recognize the organization with the most enterprising outreach to the poor. Criteria for the program was based on the program's innovativeness, use of volunteers, demonstrated results, long-term focus, sound management and capacity to be duplicated or adapted by other churches.

World Vision and Love Inc. will make a formal presentation of the award at a joint church evening service on Sunday, Feb. 10. The location and time will be announced at a later date.

KCAPS and Kingsburg churches were highly commended for their innovative program.

"We are committed to the families living in the Kingsburg area," said Cynder Rocker, ministry founder. "Our work here is evidence of the power of Jesus changing lives. We feel extremely honored to receive this award from World Vision."

The selection committee was most impressed with Kingsburg's united comprehensive approach and specifically with the concentration on children.

KCAPS opened its thrift store in September 1978, using store revenues to help serve local families in need. Over 100 local volunteers donate their time to this ministry, working at the thrift store, distributing food from their food bank, helping tutor children, working with youth programs, assisting with the emergency services program and giving their time for special holiday projects.

KCAPS also sponsors children at Sonshine Learning Center, a Christian preschool founded by KCAPS in 1980, and is a cofounder and continuing supporter of the Kingsburg Hispanic Church, *Iglesia Del Pacto*. KCAPS aims to provide opportunities for local families to improve their own lives with a strong emphasis on fostering self-esteem in youth.

"We always want to be available to local families in need," said Sharon Melcher, executive director of KCAPS. "We have a great bunch of volunteers who are making a positive difference in the lives of the children here." Melcher said that anyone interested in helping is welcome to volunteer.

National publicity is a part of this recognition. The work at KCAPS will be featured in several national and local media including *World Vision* magazine and David Main's "Chapel of the Air."

World Vision is a Christian relief and development agency with approximately 5,200 projects in 89 countries. In October 1988, World Vision formed a partnership with Love Inc. to help serve the poor in the United States. Founded in 1981 in Holland, Mich., Love Inc. operates as a network which links people in need to church volunteers. It now has over 75 active and developing programs in 25 states, mobilizing volunteers from 1,800 churches from at least 50 denominations.

The Fresno chapter of Love Inc. is one of the largest and most active in the country, working together with over 170 churches in thee Fresno area. "I have been encouraged by KCAPS work for many years," says Alan Doswald, executive director of Fresno's Love Inc. "KCAPS is an excellent example off local churches taking responsibility for the needs and suffering in their own community. This is the driving philosophy behind Love Inc., matching needy families with local churches."

There are two divisions of the Mustard Seed Award, the single church category and the multiple church category (won by KCAPS). Finalists in each division received $5,000 for the highest criteria ratings, $1,000 for the second and $500 for the third. KCAPS' sister ministry, Highway City Ministries (HCM) founded by Rocker in 1983, was honored with the first place award for the single church category. HCM is an outreach ministry of Northwest Baptist Church serving Highway City families in need. Kingsburg's First Baptist Church founded Northwest Baptist Church over 25 years ago.

MUSTARD SEED FOUNDATION
1990 PARTNER CHURCH MINISTRY AWARD
FIRST PLACE
KINGSBURG COMMUNITY ASSISTANCE PROGRAM
KINGSBURG, CALIFORNIA

(Previous page) Reprint of a story from the Selma Enterprise
announcing our winning of the Mustard Seed Award;
(above) The award.

John Perkins was an activist minister from Mississippi whose efforts on behalf of poor families were a huge inspiration to me. Later he founded the Harambe Center in Pasadena, CA. (below) meeting with John and his associates in Mississippi.

CHAPTER TWO
The Power of Resilience

She stood in the storm and when the wind did not blow her way, she adjusted her sails.
— Elizabeth Edwards

Cross country treks, multiple school changes and always being the "new kid" characterize my childhood. On one hand it was character building; on the other hand it was a constant source of anxiety. I choose to acknowledge the latter but focus on the former because, as a result of this experience, I am now comfortable with any person, in any group, at any location. That ability has served me well over the years.

I was born in Selma, Alabama to a single mom and we lived with my grandmother in a large white house with a wide veranda. My grandmother wasn't particularly wealthy, however many houses in that area looked like this. It was a little run-down but looked beautiful from the street. Not that I remember the house, but I traveled to Selma to see my hometown when I was 60 years old.

According to my mother, a Black nannie would rock me in a rocking chair on most days—once again, not because my grandmother was well-to-do, it's just the way things were done in the Deep South at the end of WWII.

I was fortunate to have a very close relationship with several of my cousins while growing up in Alabama. Even after we moved to California we continued to visit each other often. To this day I am grateful to share the special connection and memories with my cousins Sandra Laughlin, Bonnie McDonald, Michael and Marc Moulton and Andy Stahl.

My grandfather died when my mother was only eight years old. So my grandmother was forced to raise her six children alone for many years, with my mother being the youngest. I learned that just before I was born, my grandmother left the family home in Pensacola to marry a paint salesman named Roy Harris who had left his wife with five young children. The marriage didn't last long and soon my grandmother divorced the paint salesman and moved back to Pensacola where my mom and I moved with her. The paint salesman returned to his wife and five children. Interesting stories like this seem to be relatively common right after the war.

When I was a year old, my mother married a man named Raiford. They had one child, my brother Kipling West. As the story goes, my mother left him while my brother was only a baby because Raiford was a mean man with a hot temper. I have no memory of Raiford. When I was two years old and Kip was about a year old, maybe younger, my mother married Douglas Fouse, whom she met in Pensacola. Doug was an officer in the

Navy and Pensacola was a big Navy town. As it turns out, my mother and her sister were very popular with the naval officers.

Doug was the only father I knew as a little girl. I called him Daddy. He was born and raised in Ambridge, a small steel town near Pittsburg, Pennsylvania. He was finishing up his engineering degree at Dartmouth and living with his parents. By now, my grandmother had moved to Miami, Florida, so my mother, brother and I moved in with my grandmother while Daddy finished his schoolwork.

After graduation, Daddy moved in with us in Miami and he got a job at Foremost Dairy delivering milk and other dairy products. In those days, milk came in glass bottles and was delivered right to a family's front porch. One of my fondest memories is when Daddy let my brother and me ride in the back of the milk truck while he was on his route. This, of course, was not allowed by the dairy officials. My brother and I were so worried because someone would see us that we hid in the back of the truck squealing with excitement as we took turns peeking out the small oval window in the back door while we drove along.

One day Daddy's boss invited me for a tour of the dairy. I was thrilled as he escorted me through the immense freezers filled with ice cream and dry ice. I felt like I was the luckiest girl in the world.

Foremost Dairy's main competitor was Borden's Dairy. Daddy would often tell us kids about how Foremost was far superior to Borden's. One day when I was about four years old— dressed in a frilly white polka dotted dress my grandmother sewed for me and sporting the long red curls reaching past my shoulders which she carefully curled every day – the boss asked if I wanted some ice cream. Of course! I was tickled at the prospect of enjoying my favorite dessert.

He sat me on a chair at a small round café-type table and sat a dish of vanilla ice cream in front of me with a spoon. I was relishing every bite, when Daddy, who was standing by a large camera off to the side, asked me, "Susie, what kind of ice cream are you eating?" I looked up and enthusiastically replied, "Foremost." Even though this television commercial did not have sound, Daddy and his boss were thrilled that viewers could easily read my lips. I continued to finish off my delicious treat.

Even though I was young, I have several memories of the strange racial times back then. I remember one time my mom, my brothers and I were walking along the side of a road. I saw several Black children playing in the grass near us, so I ran over to play with them. My mother was not happy and gave me a spanking for playing with "those children." I also remember feeling puzzled whenever I saw the "white only" and "colored only" signs by the bathrooms. One time we got on a public bus with my mother holding my hand and carrying my baby brother, Rick, who had dark skin because he tanned easily. The bus driver made us sit in the back of the bus. We were all quite confused.

Years later when I was a junior in high school in upstate New York, the teacher gave the class an assignment of writing an essay about segregation. Even though in my heart I didn't believe it was right to separate people according to the color of their skin, I wanted to get a good grade on my essay. While growing up I always heard my parents, my grandmother and my aunts talk about how the "colored" should stay away from us because they were dirty and messy and didn't take care of things. So, my essay gave all these reasons for why segregation was good. I was sure my paper would earn me a good grade even though I didn't believe it myself.

Imagine my embarrassment when my teacher held up my essay in front of the class and said I was the only one who said segregation was good. I was confused and mortified. Looking back, I realize how the values were so different in the south and the north. I was glad to discover that others shared my secret instinct that segregation was wrong, even though I was afraid to voice my real opinion in that essay. I guess I was always trying to keep everyone happy because I knew there would be terrible consequences otherwise.

So I wrote what I thought was the "right answer" based on my upbringing. I learned an important lesson that day. There is a fine quote about this, from the great congressman John Lewis, that I discovered later: "You cannot be afraid to speak up and speak out for what you believe."

After a couple of years living with my grandmother, who I called Nannie, my mother and Daddy bought a cute three-bedroom house in Miami, a short bus ride away from where Nannie lived. Since she didn't drive, Nannie often visited us by bus. She doted on us kids, especially me. She loved sewing frilly dresses for me and wrapping my long red hair around her fingers with a wet hairbrush to make long ringlets. When we lived with Nannie in Miami, I got to sleep on her big Murphy bed in the living room. I was always intrigued and a little scared of the big dark closet we pulled the bed out of each night.

Sometimes my parents would be angry with me and send me to bed without supper. Whenever that happened, Nannie would sneak in with some treats and say, "Shhh, don't let anyone know, Susie." I always felt like I was her favorite grandchild.

Nannie was a great cook and a hard worker. I remember her spending long hours in the kitchen preparing meals for us. One of my favorites was chicken gumbo. I remember trying unsuccessfully to make it for my family years later. I didn't know much about the ingredients, but I wanted to get some of those round green vegetables I remember being in it. So I went to the grocery store and asked the clerk where I could find gumbos. When he looked puzzled, I said, "You know—gumbos—those round green things in chicken gumbo." He laughed and took me to the produce section where he pointed out okra. The end result wasn't even close to my grandmother's version.

Three years after I was born, my mother and Daddy had a son, Frederick Ernest Fouse. Daddy raised "Rick," Kip and me as if he was our father. And, in fact, we didn't know anything different. He was a very good father to all of us—an excellent provider with a great sense of humor. He and my mother were very affectionate with one another. Over the years, he took great pride in my high grades and generously helped me with my homework. He would also time my 60-yard dash practices with his stopwatch when I was in junior high school. I ended up setting a record at that school for the 60-yard dash.

Unfortunately, my dad also had quite a bad temper. It seemed that my brother Kip and I got the worst of it. When he was angry, his face would turn red and he would pull his belt off of his trousers and yell at me to come to him. Whenever I saw his face get red, I knew I was in for trouble. I never knew what made him angry, I just figured it was my fault somehow. He would hold one of my wrists with one hand and beat me on my bare bottom and legs with his belt. Always yelling something angry.

One time I overheard Nannie tell my mother that she had taken the bus to visit us, but she turned around and went home because when she walked up to the screen door, she saw him beating me with the belt and she didn't know what to do. Nannie had a thing about never interfering. Eventually, I got pretty good at always reading Daddy's nonverbal mannerisms so I would know when to stay out of his way.

Every afternoon, when we lived with Nannie, I would watch expectantly out the front porch screen. As soon as I saw a certain twosome, I would call out to my mother, "My lady friends are here and they need me to walk with them!" I would hurry across the street to the sidewalk where my two friends stood waiting for me. I always thought of them as older women, but they were probably in their 30s or 40s. They seemed to love having me walk around the block with them. I felt special—almost like my presence made them happy. Actually, for me it was a welcome respite from the unpredictable environment at Nannie's house.

When I was in third grade, we moved to Southern California, landing in a small coastal town called Manhattan Beach. I know it's very upscale now, but it was quite humble in the 1950s. Most of the houses were small single story homes made of wood. Kip, Rick and I used to love to play on the nearby sand dunes. We rubbed surf wax on big pieces of cardboard we found in the trash, climbed all the way to the top of the dunes, squealing with delight all the way on our fast descent. We didn't have a television set yet, so my brothers and I would walk to the nearby appliance store and watch their TV through their large front window. I remember that being pretty exciting.

One time when I was about 11 years old, I decided to make my own skateboard. Back then, roller skates had two parts that slid together to make the skates, and we used a special key to tighten them to fit. I found just the right size of wood, pulled one of my skates apart and nailed one part to the front and one to the back. Then I told Kip to go down to the bottom of a steep hill that emptied onto Manhattan Beach Boulevard and yell if he saw a car coming. I would climb on the skateboard and ride it all the way to the bottom of the hill, usually falling a couple of times and skinning my knees. I sure had fun and, thankfully, there was never a car coming when I got to the bottom of the hill.

My dad was happy to put his engineering degree to use in his new job as an aeronautical engineer with North American Aviation, which years later became Rockwell. When I asked about his job and where his office was, he always replied with a finger to his lips, "Shhh, it's top secret." Of course, that made me even more curious. Years later, after his death, I was sorting through his work papers and came across several folders with documents that used to be top secret but were now declassified.

I wouldn't say my dad was a hoarder, but he sure didn't like to throw anything away. After he passed away and I was going through some of his things, I found a black marker pen in its original package. But it had obviously been opened. There was scotch tape holding the plastic piece to the cardboard backing. Looking closer, I noticed that the marker was dry. And then I saw he had written "dry" on the outside of the cardboard. He just couldn't bring himself to throw it away.

When we first arrived in California and I went into my third grade class in the middle of the school year, I remember being very embarrassed. My classmates had heard that the new girl had come from a school called Little River School. They wanted to know what kind of a fish I was. I don't know why it embarrassed me so much, but I sure remember the feeling as if it just happened. But I also remember my mother bringing homemade cookies into my third grade classroom for all the kids to enjoy. She had a cute dress on with an elastic belt tightened at the waist. All of the kids said I was so lucky to have such a pretty mother.

There was a big difference between my life in Miami and in Manhattan Beach. Miami felt like a little cocoon with Nannie always doting on me and some of my aunts and cousins also living nearby. I loved being a Brownie Girl Scout, with my mother serving as our troop leader. I especially enjoyed wearing my special brown beanie, uniform dress and even special dark brown shoes and socks.

But when we moved to California, everything was different. Everything seemed bigger and more spread out. There were just my parents and brothers and we didn't know anyone else. Being the new kid in school—the one with the bright red hair and freckles—I was pretty self-conscious. Eventually I made some friends, but it took a while.

I joined Girl Scouts in Manhattan Beach and my mother again was our leader. I have so many fond memories of that time period. My friends all thought my mom was cool because she took our Girl Scout troop camping all the time. She also helped each girl work on the badges we chose as a troop. Two of my particular favorites were the outdoor cooking and camping badges.

I remember one time when my mother took our troop camping over the weekend at nearby Alondra Park. She showed us how to collect pine cones and put them under our sleeping bag to make a mattress (this was before the days of blow up mattresses). Then, after erecting our tents, she showed us how to dig a ditch around the outside of our tent so the inside didn't get wet if it rained (this was before the days of "leave no trace"). We made a big campfire and cooked our one-pot dinner over it.

The next morning, it started to rain. A Boy Scout troop was camping near us and when it started to rain, they quickly packed up everything and left. My mother, however, said, "Now you girls can practice all we've learned from working on our outdoor camping badge." She was pretty proud of us and we all laughed at the scurrying Boy Scouts.

I especially liked selling Girl Scout cookies because I noticed everyone was always happy to see me. I became quite the good salesman. In fact, I was so good that when my brother

Kip wanted for us to get fishing poles so we could fish at the pier, I decided to sell the all-occasion greeting cards that were advertised on the back of the comic books we read. I said, "If I can sell Girl Scout cookies, I'll bet I can sell these cards so we can get the prizes." We set our sights on selling enough cards so we could get two fishing poles, two reels and a sinker maker. In no time, I sold enough cards.

I remember how excited we were the day the fishing poles arrived. We put them together and then went up and down the alley looking in trash cans for bits of lead so we could make weights by melting them in our new sinker maker. Happy was the day when we marched down to the beach with our poles in hand. We actually caught a fish off the pier that day and cleaned it in the special sink. But when we got home, our mom said we were too stinky with fish smell and she washed us off outside. Still, it's a wonderful memory!

My brother Rick was not as adventurous as Kip. He was quiet and sort of kept to himself. So my escapades mostly included Kip. Rick was usually too young to go. Kip and I loved to go up and down the alleys behind our house picking up pop bottles we could turn in at the neighborhood market for cash. He also liked picking through everyone's trash for "treasures." We got a nickel for every large size bottle—just enough to buy a piece of chunk chocolate at Joe's Candy Cottage. When I saved up enough, I would spend it on Elvis Presley's latest 45 speed record. I had quite the collection.

I loved Elvis! I had his fan magazine pictures plastered all over my bedroom walls when I was a teenager. We had a rumpus room behind our house in Manhattan Beach that was "my room." I had the kind of record player you had to wind up. I would wind it up with gusto and dance to the songs like "Dance with me Henry," "Rock Around the Clock" and "Jailhouse Rock" for hours. Of course, after a song or two, I had to hurry over and wind up the record player again. But then I would go back to my dancing. What fun that was.

Unfortunately, my dad continued to abuse me not only physically, but also sexually. I don't remember a lot of detail from this period, but my mother says that when I was four years old I came into the living room of my grandmother's house and announced, "We have to go to Burdine's to get a new daddy because I have a bad daddy." And then when I was in fourth grade, I said to my mother, "Please don't leave me alone with Daddy because when you're gone, he breathes real hard and he scares me." It's interesting that my mother remembered these instances, but nothing ever changed. I learned to live with the ambiguity – not understanding the significance of it all.

When I was in the sixth grade, my dad announced his job was requiring us to move to New York. I felt like my world was collapsing. I finally felt like I fit in at my school in California, and now we were moving away — away from all my friends. Kip and Rick were pretty upset too — they were in fifth and third grades. It turns out that North American had a contract with IBM in upstate New York and my dad was the representative for a project to build bombers for the Air Force. So, they loaded our belongings and all three kids into the family station wagon and we headed across country to a very small town near Binghamton, called Vestal.

This was the first of several trips across the country from California to New York and back the other way. Each time it was a terrible disruption of my childhood. Every time we traveled across country we would stop in Ambridge (Pennsylvania) so we could visit my dad's parents, Grandma and Grandad Fouse, for a week or so. Ambridge was the small town near Pittsburg where my dad grew up. I learned later that Ambridge was short for The American Bridge Company, which built the Golden Gate

Bridge in San Francisco. Back then, steel mining plants employed most of the work force.

My grandparents lived in a large brick house with a wide swing on the front porch. I always looked forward to these visits with them because my grandad loved fudge cycles. My grandma didn't like him to eat them because she said they made him fat. So my grandad and I would sit outside on the front steps and he would say, "Susie, go in and tell grandma you want two fudge cycles." She always gave them to me, although my guess is she probably knew one was for my grandad. And then I would walk with him around the corner to downtown where he would introduce me to all his friends, all the while eating our fudge cycles.

I would sit for hours with my grandad listening to the Pittsburg Pirates play their baseball games on the radio. One time I heard an advertisement on the radio about something called Man Tan. Supposedly it would give you a beautiful golden tan in just a few hours. I was so excited because I had always been embarrassed that my skin was so white, when so many of my friends at the beach had nice, tanned skin. I asked my grandma to help me get a bottle of the magic potent and she did. I covered my body with the clear liquid before going to bed that night. The next morning I couldn't wait to look in the mirror at my gorgeous tan. I was shocked! Instead of seeing a nice brown tan, every inch of my skin was streaked with orange. I stayed inside and scrubbed my skin for days.

I remember one time when I was about 14, during a visit to Ambridge, I was so upset about having to leave my boyfriend in California that I moped and pouted the entire visit. Everyone was sitting at the dinner table in my grandparents' dining room and I refused to eat or talk. Finally, I got up, excused myself from the table and walked out of the room so I could be alone with my grumpy thoughts. I overheard my grandmother asking my parents, "What's wrong with Cindy?"

It was well into the school year when we moved to Vestal, so just like when we moved to Manhattan Beach, I was the "new kid." My classmates loved calling me "red" or "carrot top" which made me feel even more embarrassed and odd. Years later when a friend looked at some of my school photos from that time, he said, "You look like you could have been Alfred E. Neuman's sister." He was right. I had bright orange-red hair and a face full of freckles. It's no wonder they made fun of me.

After a while, I got used to the name-calling and not quite fitting in and began to find ways of becoming part of the group. I got pretty good at it. I learned to make friends easily because even though I always felt on the outside, I knew how to make it seem like I was on the inside—one of the group. I developed instinctive strategies of becoming "popular" by watching what each person liked and trying to mimic that. One time, I noticed that a girl I wanted to be friends with took great pride in her creative hairstyles. So I asked for her help and before long we were both known for our elaborate beehives and twisty pony tails.

Another good example of this was when I was in high school. My house was the place where everyone wanted to hang out, especially before big parties like the prom. This was partly because every Friday before a big event my mom would send me to school with a shopping list where my friends would all write down what kind of alcohol they wanted to drink at my pre-party. My mom would purchase the booze and mixers because she said she wanted us to drink at home instead of driving around. Of course, this would not be acceptable now, but at the time I was the one with the "cool mom" and everyone wanted me to be part of their group.

High school was also when I had my first real job (besides babysitting). I was hired as the ticket taker at the La Mar Theater where I sat in a glassed-in booth near the sidewalk. I was thrilled with my job, but I would be a bit envious as my friends walked by on their way to the beach. Still, I was glad for my new paycheck.

The fact is my fair skin wasn't suited to the beach anyway. My friends would mix iodine and baby oil, slathering it all over their body and lying in the sun for hours. When I tried the same thing, I ended up with a terrible sunburn which infuriated my mother. She made me wear a straw hat when she knew I was headed to the beach. But I always stashed it behind a bush because only tourists wore hats like that and I wanted to fit in. When I would arrive home after a day at the beach (picking up the hat and putting it on my head before I got home), she would take one look at my sunburned face and angrily exclaim, "Your face looks like a baboon's fanny!" She would then proceed to gently dab cotton balls soaked in cold vinegar to relieve the pain.

High school is also where I had two teachers who made a difference in my life. Nellie was my typing and shorthand teacher. She was so strict that many kids tried to avoid taking her class. But I loved it because I was good at typing and I could tell she liked me because of it. I credit her with my superior typing ability serving me so well over the years.

Homer was my social studies teacher. Lots of kids made fun of him because he was a little different; but I loved to listen to his stories about politics and history. He taught me how to keep my mind open to different ways of looking at the world. One day he took me into his office and with a very serious look on his face said, "Cindy, I want you to know that you can be anything you want to be because you are so smart." I thanked him and smiled politely but I really didn't know what he was talking about because I had no idea what I wanted to be.

During the summer between my junior and senior years of high school, I had the honor of being an exchange student to

La Paz, Mexico in Baja California. It's a tourist destination now, but back then there wasn't even a road connecting it to other towns. No one spoke any English, so I had no time to be embarrassed about speaking rudimentary Spanish. I had to dive right in and use the Spanish I learned in high school. I caught on quickly and it was a wonderful experience. I have a couple of memories that especially stand out for me.

I lived with a lovely family named Aramburo. They owned the local pharmacy and were considered well-to-do. Maria Elena, the daughter of the family and I were the same age, so she introduced me to all of her friends. They had never seen someone with red hair before, so they took me to the nearby beauty parlor and asked the operator to look at my hair and tell them if it was "real." They were pretty amazed at the answer!

There was a young man who took a liking to me and one night I was awoken by a guitar playing outside of my bedroom window. I immediately jumped up, turned on the light and went over to the open window. My host sister came into my room right away and told me to get back in bed. She said this young man and his friends were serenading me and the proper response was to lay in bed, turn on the bedside nightlight and enjoy the music. I followed her instruction and it was quite delightful.

Another young man, Gustavo, took a liking to me and gave me a tour of his ranch. While there, he pulled up a bucket filled with water from his well. He filled a dipper with water from the bucket and gave it to me to drink. He said, "If you drink from my well, you will return some day." Of course I drank the cool water. It was so romantic!

I spent the whole summer there enjoying every day and meeting lots of townspeople. My Spanish became quite fluent very quickly since I was the only person in the town that spoke any English. Every day my host family members, along with everyone else in town, took a siesta from noon until 2:00 or so. The stores were closed and no one was on the streets. I've never been good at napping, so I used the time every day to read the book I brought with me, *The Agony and the Ecstasy*, the enchanting biography of Michelangelo by Irving Stone. I was glad it had so many pages because it took me all summer to finish reading it.

In eighth grade we moved back to Manhattan Beach. There I was again trying to fit in with the same kids as before. After two more years, we moved back to Vestal where I had to adapt to the new environment. We were back in California for my last two years of high school, where I graduated with honors from Aviation High School. Moving around so frequently taught me how to make friends quickly, how to adapt myself to the norms of a group, how to see change as normal, how to let nothing rock my boat and how to think and act quickly.

Life in Vestal was so different than in Manhattan Beach. The little California beach town was so casual with all the kids going barefoot and spending time at the sunny beach. My mother was constantly complaining about us kids tracking sand into the house and make us wash off with the hose before we came inside. She was good natured about it, but it kind of bugged her.

In Vestal, her complaint was when we tracked snow into the house. Everything there was a lot more structured and the activities were so different. I learned how to make snowmen and ice skate on the abundant backyard frozen ponds. One time my date refused to go out with me because when he came to pick me up I wasn't wearing any socks. That was the normal way in the beach towns, but in upstate New York white bobby socks were expected at all times.

Wherever we lived, our parents always took us three kids to Sunday school while they would attend church, usually a Presbyterian or Methodist church. My mom would dress us all up in our Sunday best. And then my dad would want to take pictures of everyone. All that was very sweet, but it took a long time so we were often late to church. Once again, I was the new kid who didn't fit in, walking into Sunday school late, and standing out like a sore thumb because of my hair and freckles.

Finally, one Sunday I hit on a brilliant idea. I told my brother, Kip (who also didn't like being the new kid who was late) that I had an idea that would save us from the embarrassment. I said, "Here's the plan: when they drop us off at Sunday school, we'll walk through the halls pretending we are headed to the bathroom. Then when Sunday school is over and all the kids get out of class, we'll meet mom and dad outside the church and let them assume we actually attended class. When they ask us what we learned in class, we simply say that we learned about Jesus." It worked like a charm.

Later I discovered that the reason we moved so often was because whenever Secretary of Defense, Robert McNamara, changed his mind about how many bombers we were going to build, my dad was transferred since he was Rockwell's lead representative on the project.

The moves were always challenging for my brothers and me because we never knew when our dad would come home and say we were moving across country again. But there were also some bright spots in the moves. We would drive on Route 66 to get from one coast to the other and always drove through Las Vegas where we would spend the night so we kids could swim in the pool. It was delicious to frolic in the cool water when it was over 100 degrees outside. My dad would carry me on his back while he swam across the pool and I would squeal with delight, afraid he would duck me under the water.

I was 16 years old when I discovered my dad was not my father, nor was he Kip's father. I'll never forget the Saturday my mom was getting ready to go to the store. She had her back turned to me as I sat on her bed. She was reaching into her closet for just the right purse to go with her outfit. I asked if I could go with her to the store. She said, "No just stay here." I asked again and when she said no again, I said, "Please don't leave me home with Daddy." She immediately turned around with a look on her face I'll never forget and demanded to know why. I remember being so afraid that I had said the wrong thing and now I was in big trouble. I tried to change the subject, but she insisted I tell her. So, I said, "I don't like what Daddy does to me when you're not here."

The fact was my dad had been molesting me for several years. I had tried to tell my mom from time to time but I was too afraid of getting in trouble and it seemed like she didn't really want to hear it. I didn't want him to be angry with me, wanting to avoid a beating with his belt. I didn't want any of my friends to ever find out what he was doing to me because I was too embarrassed. I thought it was my fault. So I made sure our family always looked perfect to anyone looking on from the outside. I became a master at this deception. Actually, I felt that since I was the oldest, it was my responsibility to make our family look good to others.

My mother's response to me on that Saturday morning was, "Oh well, he's not your father anyway." Which is how I found out he wasn't my birth father.

I was stunned but I knew better than to comment or ask questions because it would set off my mother's temper (which I always tried to avoid). But if Daddy wasn't my father, who was my father? If he wasn't my father, then who was I really? I always had a feeling there were lots of secrets in our family, I just didn't realize I was one of them. My mother was obviously the keeper of this secret, yet I didn't see even a glimmer of remorse or any sign of concern for me. She only seemed upset that now a big secret was out in the open.

She made my dad leave the house and move into a motel, but after a short time he returned. Thankfully, he never touched me again.

Daddy passed away from a heart attack in 1998. When I think of him, I am thankfully able to hold both realities simultaneously: he was a good father in many ways; he also did some things to me that were absolutely not good. I guess one thing I learned from that experience is that people can have both positive and negative aspects to their personality and behavior. It's always best to focus on the positive.

My memories of the sexual abuse are pretty foggy. In fact, I didn't even remember it at all until I was in my early 40s. Like many victims of abuse, I had blocked it out completely. Thankfully, once the memories started to return, I was able to get some counseling and therapy to deal with it. There I learned that it was not my fault. He had a severe character flaw and I was just in the wrong place at the wrong time.

But it has definitely had an impact on my life as an adult. For years, I had no self-confidence. I didn't often voice an opinion about anything unless I thought it would be accepted by others. I never wanted to rock the boat or be around anyone who had a temper. I knew that anger meant I would get hurt. I'm sure another significant impact is that I've always had trouble establishing genuine intimacy, especially with a husband. Thankfully, I think I'm now past that.

So there I was without a legitimate last name. I was raised believing Fouse was my last name. I never knew what name was on my birth certificate because my parents always made up an excuse to the school authorities who asked for it. I guess they wanted us to think Daddy was our real father. When I did find out the name on my birth certificate from Selma General

Hospital, it was Horten. But I also discovered this was the name of the man my mother married when she was 16 and that they divorced after two years, which was two years before I was born. She probably used Horten on my birth certificate because she really didn't know who my birth father was. She told me a long, convoluted, and (as it turns out) untrue story about how my "father" had died in a fiery plane crash in the war.

Eventually, I figured I would never know my real birth name so I made up my own last name, Sinclair, because it was of Scottish origin and was an alliteration with my first name. My mother says she named me Cynder Sue because my hair was bright orange and reminded her of red, hot cinders. As a kid, I was embarrassed by the name Cynder and wouldn't let my parents tell anyone my name. Instead I went by Susie, and then Sue, and then Cindy. I finally grew into using Cynder when I was in my 30s.

While in high school, my best friend was Julianne Gillespie. She was cute and fun and we always hung out together. In our senior year, she asked me if I wanted to go to college. I had never thought about it and my parents had never mentioned it. So, I said, "Sure." She said her sister was going to college and that I would like it.

Then she asked, "Do you want to go to UCLA? My sister is going there and you'll like it." I said, "Sure." Next, she asked, "Do you want to join a sorority?" When I asked what a sorority was, she said, "My sister is in one, you'll like it." So we both applied for and were accepted into UCLA and joined the Alpha Chi Omega sorority (just like her sister). We lived in the sorority house for two years.

Unfortunately, I eventually lost track of Julianne even though I tried many times to find her. Of course, I didn't know it was considered hard to get into UCLA. I was just lucky that I had good grades.

My parents paid my tuition and the fees for my sorority house, but I felt a little bad about that (even though back then the tuition and fees were very low compared to today). So I was really excited when I happened to read that there were scholarships available for tuition reimbursement if one's father had died in the war. I quickly sent away for the required paperwork. I was thrilled when it arrived in the mail a few weeks later because I thought it would be a way for me to relieve my parents of the burden of my school expenses. I filled out as much of the paperwork as I could, leaving just a few blank spaces for my mom to fill in with information like my father's date of death and place of service.

I called my mother on the phone and excitedly told her about this wonderful news. She was clearly upset. I was confused. She began to stutter and appeared to search for the right words. I had learned that this was typical behavior for her when she was about to tell a lie. She quickly said, "We can't fill out that form because he never knew I was pregnant and I never told him before he died in the fiery plane crash." She went on to add details like my father had never wanted children but she did so she secretly left her diaphragm out one night and that's how she got pregnant. When I asked about his parents and siblings, she quickly said, "They're all dead."

I had a strong feeling she was lying about some or all of this, but I was afraid to challenge her or even ask questions because I knew it would make her angry. So I just stayed quiet and left it alone. I felt betrayed and insignificant. Did I not matter enough for my own mother to tell me the truth about my very existence? I had always lived in a state of not knowing the truth and pretending to believe her stories, so I gathered the bits of myself I could find and kept moving forward with my life.

Since I had always been an overachiever, I thought it made perfect sense to take 21 units, work part time as a sales clerk at May Company and fulfill my sorority duties. I majored in Political Science and minored in languages—taking French, Spanish and Swahili simultaneously.

I wanted to work for the State Department so I could "save the world," so I thought I should start with Africa. I decided that if I was going to Africa, I should know the language. This is why I signed up for Swahili. I took Spanish because my dad always wanted me to continue learning this language; I took French because I always loved it.

Life settled into a routine but very full schedule. Up early for classes, lots of time doing homework and studying for exams, dinner at the sorority house, and then I rode the public bus to May Company each evening, returning to the sorority house at about 11:00 p.m. I loved the Greek life and certainly enjoyed the plentiful fraternity parties.

I remember when I got my first tax return check from my job at May Company. It was $50 and I was pretty excited. I immediately went to town and spent the entire check on fancy undies, bras, and garter belts (yes, we were still wearing garter belts then). Soon after I purchased them and folded them perfectly in my lingerie drawer, I came home from a date one evening and my sorority sisters had strung them up on clothesline all over my bedroom. Everyone got quite a kick out of that little prank, even me.

At the end of each semester, the fraternities would host TGIO parties (Thank God it's Over). During my second year at UCLA, I went with a date to a TGIO party at the SAE (Sigma Alpha Epsilon) fraternity house. Like all fraternity parties, there were beer kegs galore. I walked over to a keg to fill up my cup with beer. As I leaned over to pull the lever, I looked up into the smiling, handsome face of a guy I had never met. "Hi, I'm Rick

Bishop," he said. I politely told him my name, noting how good looking and charming he was.

Later I went to the ladies room. No sooner had I entered the main door when he appeared in the doorway holding the door open. He refused to leave the ladies room until I gave him my phone number. I was so flustered that I gave him my home number rather than the sorority number.

That night, about 3:00 in the morning, he called the number I gave him. My mother answered drowsily. "Is this Cindy's sorority sister?" he asked. "No, this is her mother," she said grumpily. As you can imagine, my mother loved telling that story for years.

Shortly after that, Rick and I started dating.

(Above) My parents with me and my brothers Rick and Kip
(below) Me with my parents in 1982

My mother, Betty Fouse, in 1942. Sadly, mom passed away just as we were going to press with this book. She was 94. I really miss her sweet spirit

My mother at Christmas

My grandmother, Nettie Brown. I called her "Nannie"

Nannie at age 20 in 1916 and as I knew her

Here's me at four months and one year old

Four years old; (next page) I'm 9 (top) and then 11

My brother Kip holds the swing for me so I can climb to the top at our Nannie's house in Miami

My high School graduation photo

With my parents at my college Sorority Presents event

CHAPTER THREE
Searching for My Father

Belonging has always been a fundamental
driver of humankind.
— Brian Chesky

Never in my wildest dreams did I think I would ever find my father, or even discover his name. Of course I wanted to know, but since I had absolutely no information about him, I never gave it much thought. Not even when I received an email from Karen Ramsdell who was board president for the Santa Barbara Genealogy Society.

I knew Karen from my Girl Scout days. She was the general manager of the Santa Barbara Airport and we honored her as a Woman of Distinction in 1998. Karen said she heard that I facilitated nonprofit board retreats and wondered if I would consider leading the planning session for the Genealogy Society.

I was thrilled at the idea of working with Karen again and honored that she would ask me to help. I quickly agreed even though I knew nothing about this organization, or even that they existed.

On January 12, 2020 I arrived at their beautiful facility on Castillo Street, fully prepared for the retreat. I thought I wouldn't know anyone there except Karen, but I looked around the room and I recognized almost half of the 22 attendees. Since I had been involved in nonprofits so long, I knew many of these folks from their service on other nonprofit boards.

We went through the day, often breaking into smaller groups, and I found the discussions fascinating and the passion for genealogy impressive. These people genuinely relished digging into their past to discover tidbits about their ancestors. During the break, one of the ladies asked me if I had ever done any work in genealogy. I admitted I didn't know much about my family history and nothing about my father. Karen was intrigued. I assured her it was a lost cause because I had no information to go on.

A week later, as I was presenting the final report from the retreat, Karen mentioned that a couple of the board members were professional genealogists. I couldn't resist asking her for the names and contact numbers. I actually reached out to Nancy Loe, one of the professional genealogists that Karen told me about, a few weeks later. I figured it was futile to follow through with this idea, but I couldn't help myself.

Nancy was a bit incredulous when I told her I had no information about my father, not even a name. But she was undaunted. She told me to request DNA kits from four sites: 23andMe, Ancestry.com, My Heritage and Family Tree DNA. I didn't hold much hope but followed her instructions. While we waited several weeks for the test results, we exchanged emails about the maternal side of my family. Nancy did some research on my mother's side, but I figured it wouldn't help at all with finding my father, especially since it appeared that my mother didn't even know who he was.

Her process was fascinating, even though much of it seemed to be in a different language – with terms such as segments, thru lines and centermorgans. The benefit of having information from my maternal side became quickly apparent when she found a match with a distant relative, Bruci Hall. Nancy compared Bruci's DNA with my maternal side and there was not a single match. This indicated to Nancy that Bruci was the first link to my paternal side. If I shared DNA with Bruci and there was no match between Bruci and my maternal side, Bruci had to be a link to my paternal side. I was beyond thrilled and amazed! All of a sudden, a crack of light of possibility pierced the dark unknown.

I discovered some interesting things about my mother's family during this genealogic search. Some of her family's records date back to earliest days of the Old South, when Georgia and Alabama were colonies of British America. The family of Ernest Brown, my mother's father, not only had a tradition of service in the Navy in more recent times, but also stretches back to North Carolina in the years just after the Revolutionary War.

My grandmother, Nettie Kennedy Brown, claimed Irish heritage through her Kennedy family. The Kennedys arrived very early in Connecticut Colony, British America, but by the end of the 18th century, they were living in Georgia. The Gardiners also are a prominent family in my maternal tree. My great-great grandfather, James Thomas Gardiner, Sr., was born in Alabama in 1824. He had 14 children with three wives, including his third and last wife, Emma Louise Harris, my great-great grandmother.

Perhaps the most is known about Emma Louise's father, my great-great-great grandfather Myles Green Harris, and his third wife, my great-great-great grandmother, Lucy Elizabeth M. Wingfield. Their marriage united two wealthy and powerful slave-owning families in Greene County, Georgia. The Harris family moved to Greene County from the Province of Maryland; the Wingfields came from the Province of Virginia, both British American colonies at the time. The Harris house on the Oakland plantation still stands near Sparta, Georgia.

Finally, all of my DNA results were in and Nancy went to work with her intensive research, even enlisting the help of a veteran colleague. One of the many emails we received along the way was from Darren Swolley, a paternal relative we met online during the search. Darren was related to my father's aunt and he was actively involved in genealogy. His interest was piqued and he seemed to enjoy giving us lots of help.

Nancy called me on May 22, 2020, after four months of research, to say she found my father. I was beyond astonished and over the moon with joy! How could this be true? After 74 years, I finally had a real last name—my father was Harold Allan Hall.

I caught my breath as I looked at the image of him on Ancestry.com. His hair was red, his eyes blue and his cheekbones and chin looked just like mine. It was like gazing at a missing piece of myself. I halfway thought I might hear him speak at any moment. I had seen his likeness in my own face every time I looked in the mirror, I just didn't know it until now.

I had always wondered why I was so different from my mother. Some of our physical features are similar (we both have red hair), but our personalities are very different. I believe we inherit our temperament, our basic nature and our way of looking at the world. Mine was different from my mother and I always wondered why.

I used to make up stories in my head describing my father's traits and ways of being. After hearing stories about him, I can see that I inherited my focused determination to achieve my goals, my intellectual curiosity and my high energy level from him. It all made sense to me now.

I also learned that I now had seven new half-siblings. Harold and his wife, Berta, had seven children in 10 years. Even though no one knew, I was the oldest of Harold's eight children.

Nancy had already gathered the names and contact information for each of the seven siblings. But now what? My father had passed away in 1998 from a rare form of cancer, but I dearly wanted to contact his children—my new half-siblings. Darren and I were still emailing back and forth a bit so I told him about my trepidation in contacting my siblings. What if they thought it was a hoax or that I was a fake? What words would explain who I was and how we were related after all these years?

Darren offered to contact them for me. I felt excited and relieved at first, but then worried that his presence might complicate matters. So I arranged to have a phone conversation with Darren the next morning. I wanted to hear his voice and how he presented himself. After I hung up from the call, I felt reassured and agreed for him to call my half-brother, Dan, since Darren thought that was the best choice. Darren said he would call Dan in the next few days, but a couple of hours later, while I was out for my daily hike, Darren called to say he had contacted Dan. Yikes! I wasn't prepared for this.

Later that day Allan, who is our father's oldest son, called me. He explained that when Dan spoke with Darren, he thought it was a hoax and expected Darren to ask him for his credit card, so he had referred Darren to him.

I had given Darren my website address so that if anyone wanted to find out more about me or even see a photo of me, they could easily do so. I wanted my new family to know that this person claiming to be so closely related to them was not a crazy person or someone after their money. She was a responsible upstanding citizen with an honorable life's work and an impressive amount of talent and accomplishments.

Allan told me he had looked at my website and done some research on me before calling. He said that as soon as he saw a picture of me on my website, he knew I was part of the family. He explained that our father had red hair and blue eyes just like mine. Allan and I had a delightful conversation. He ended by saying, "I want you to feel welcome to our family and know that we love you." I was thrilled! I never expected anything like this in a million years.

All of a sudden, the missing pieces of my life seemed to be magically coming together in a way I had never even imagined possible.

A few days later, Dan called me and explained about the call from Darren and why he had passed it off to Allan. He said that he and Allan had discussed my appearance with some of their siblings and also with their mother. He said they agreed to welcome me to the family.

I routinely open my iPad every morning to read the local online newspaper, check in with Facebook, and look at a few emails. On May 29, I was excited to see a long email from another of my new siblings. The email said that Dan had called to relate the new information and several of them had been discussing my appearance for the last few days.

Apparently, my mother met my father, Harold Allan Hall, when he was stationed in Pensacola in April 1945 – where he had just returned from a stint in the Pacific during World War II. I was conceived in June of 1945 and, just 30 days later in July 1945, my father's orders took him to Banana River Naval Air Station in Cocoa Beach about five hours drive from Pensacola. It appeared that neither he nor my mother knew she was pregnant. They quickly lost contact with each other.

He met his wife, Berta, in nearby Orlando in October of 1945. They were married on March 10, 1946, which ironically was the day after I was born. It was obvious to all of us that my father did not know about my mother's pregnancy.

I was still reeling from the shock of finding my father and all of these new siblings. I'd never felt so accepted and included before.

About two weeks later, I received an unexpected phone call from Andy, another sibling. He said, "I understand you have spoken to some of my siblings. I wanted to call and introduce myself to you. My name is Andy and I want to welcome you to our family and tell you that we love you." I was being completely buried in love and acceptance when I was so worried I would be shunned and mocked.

What a gift! I now had the last name of my real father and the true story of his life—not to mention the acceptance and love from some of my new siblings. I was overwhelmed. I felt like I fit in somewhere for the first time in my life. I always felt like I never quite belonged to any group and went to great lengths to create the illusion that I was a part of a crowd or a family. I was always on the outside looking in, whether it was in my quasi-birth family, or trying to make friends in various schools or even within the family I raised.

A sense of belonging was a powerful new feeling for me. I had become so accustomed to pretending I belonged and trying to convince others it was true. Now here I was — surrounded by people from my actual family who really loved me.

Some of my siblings explained that our father was a real hero — an exceptionally conscientious, kind and loving son, husband and father. He was an honorable person and was an example to all who knew him of how to live life with grace and good humor, despite what life threw his way. It makes me sad that I never got to know him in person.

91

I'm writing this in 2020, the year of the COVID-19 virus pandemic. To date (December 2020) the virus has infected 16.5 million people in the U.S. and 300,000 have died from it. Most people are abiding by the regulations which call for wearing a face covering (even during long plane rides), staying six feet apart from others (except in your own household) and sheltering in place as much as possible. Patrons are not allowed to eat inside restaurants — only at outside tables. All stores must limit the number of people who are allowed to be inside at one time. Other businesses like gyms, nail salons and beauty parlors remain closed.

Each year the Hall family convenes in Florida for their family reunion. I was thrilled when several of the siblings invited me to attend. Unfortunately the annual family reunion planned for early November of 2020 will be postponed until there is a vaccine for the virus. I sure am looking forward to meeting my new family in person! In the meantime, I am enjoying connecting with some of my new siblings by phone and email. I appreciate those who are sharing stories about our father's life.

Here is a summary of what I have learned from military records and other public information about my father's life.

The doctor arrived at my father's family home near Kennebec, South Dakota, October 28, 1921 to deliver him. He popped out with bright red hair, blue eyes and freckles. As a child he quickly realized he needed to ignore the kids who called him "red or carrot top" because he couldn't do anything about his hair color anyway. (I love that insight into him because that's exactly how I handled being born with red hair and freckles.)

My father and his family lived a very simple, rural life with no running water or electricity. Since they had no well, they had to haul water a long distance from a creek using a horse drawn wagon. He and his siblings walked the 10 miles to school every day and he graduated high school with top honors.

As the story goes, my grandfather, Frank W. Hall, was on a cattle drive in Winner, South Dakota, when he ate some bad beans. The doctor was called and they put him in a room behind the shed where he always played guitar with the Indians. Ultimately, he died of botulism when my father was just 12 years old.

My father knew from doing all the hard labor on his family's farm with his brothers that he didn't want to be a farmer. His mother suggested he borrow some money from the local banker and go to Spearfish Normal College. (A "normal college" was the old name for a teacher's college.) So, at 19 years old in the midst of the Great Depression, he borrowed $35 and left for college to train to be a teacher. He got a job at the nearby lumber mill to pay his expenses and enrolled in the college where he studied English and music, preparing to be a teacher.

One day, during his second year of college, he was standing around talking with his buddies when a small plane landed out of nowhere. The pilot hollered, "I'm looking for volunteers! Who wants to go for a ride in my plane?" Intrigued, my father jumped at the chance, climbing into the two-seater small plane with an open cockpit. From then on, he was hooked on flying and his life was changed forever. My father began to squeeze money from his lumber mill job to pay for flight instruction. He stayed in college but his courses changed from teaching preparation to analytical and aerial geometry, trigonometry and navigation.

In the fall of 1941, after Pearl Harbor, the U.S. government paid for his lessons in Civilian Pilot Training where he earned his pilot license. "From farm boy to air pilot in 10 months," my father was reported proudly exclaiming. He was on his way to becoming a naval air pilot. After graduation from the two-year college, he went to Iowa City for pre-flight courses in Navy lore and regulations, then to Minneapolis to what was known as the "elimination base." "Nobody's going to eliminate this farm boy!" vowed my father. Pensacola was the last step to earning his commission, September 3, 1943.

My father was right where he wanted to be. After two months of flying submarine inshore patrol from San Diego, California, my father was stationed at Guadalcanal as a carrier aircraft test pilot — not a safe or easy job, but he loved it. He stayed there until the end of the war. After stints of duty in Pensacola, Panama and Banana River he was released to inactive status in 1947.

He retired after 25 years of service with the rank of commander. After that he established a thriving real estate business in central Florida.

His children describe our father as a brave, kind, gentle, hard-working guy whom everyone loved. He made everyone feel safe because they knew he was so dependable and fair. Our father loved playing golf and always kept his 6'2" body in good shape.

He worked hard in real estate after he retired from the Navy. My father's motivation wasn't to make large sums of money, but rather to help people find a home they would love.

In 1972, the stiffness he had noticed in his left leg and hip turned out to be cancer. His operation at Shand's Hospital in Gainesville took 12 hours and 26 pints of blood. The cancer was removed but so was his whole hip joint. Only wires kept his leg bone attached to his pelvis.

My father's surgeon said he would never walk again. But he had kids to put through college and a lot of living to do, so he was not about to give in to being an invalid. It wasn't long before he was walking unaided, running his real estate office with the help of two of his sons, driving his car and playing golf. He also took time to visit the hospital to encourage other cancer victims.

He was a walking inspiration, a winner, and he always will be. Harold Allan Hall passed on January 17, 1998.

My paternal lineage features colonists and citizens of the Old South, pioneers in the Plains states and Cornish immigrants. The paternal side of my tree features the surnames Hall, Whitford, Keast, Lunsford, Miller, Welker and Manuel. My father's paternal line has been traced to John Hall, born about 1824 in Wise County, Virginia, and his wife, Malinda Miller. Their oldest child, Greenup Edward Hall, was born in Greenup County, Kentucky in 1852. They had 11 surviving children; Frank Washington Hall was their sixth child, third son and my great-grandfather.

Frank's wife, Susan Lunsford, was born in 1857 in Wayne County, Virginia. Six years later, that section of Virginia broke away, formed the state of West Virginia and stayed with the Union during the Civil War. The Lunsfords were an old Virginia family. It is believed that the Lunsfords arrived in Virginia between 1610 and 1653. If correct, this English Lunsford line extends from the present back 30 generations to 1057 in Sussex, England.

My grandmother, Anna Lucille Whitford's ancestors are Cornish. The Whitford line hails from Saint Agnes and the Keast line from Liskeard in Cornwall, western England. My great-grandparents, William Whitford and Mary Keast immigrated in 1885 to Nebraska. About 1907 they moved to South Dakota. William and Mary raised 10 children, all of whom lived to adulthood.

To be able to write all of this information about my father and my paternal ancestry fills me with joy and wonder. In all of my life I never thought I would discover this missing piece of myself.

My handsome father, Harold A. Hall in 1960

Posing with his "Darling Dottie," and as a cadet

My father, Commander Harold Hall, in 1967

CHAPTER FOUR
Adventures in Child Rearing

*A mother is not a person to lean on, but a person
to make leaning unnecessary.*
– Dorothy Canfield Fisher

His clear, crystal blue eyes captivated me the instant I saw him as I leaned over the beer keg to fill my cup. My eyes traveled down to take in his engaging smile. He said, "Hi, my name is Rick Bishop." I told him my first name, filled my cup and hurried over to rejoin my date — feeling a little shaken and off balance.

I was attending Sigma Alpha Epsilon's (SAE) *Thank God It's Over* party held at the end of each semester at UCLA where I was just completing my freshman year. I went to the party with a date along with several of my sorority sisters from Alpha Chi Omega and their dates. We were all making the rounds that evening on June 10, 1965 — visiting several fraternity parties.

I walked down the short hallway to use the rest room and that's where I encountered Rick again and gave him my phone number. Shortly afterward we started dating.

I began attending UCLA in September of 1964, right after graduation from Aviation High School in Manhattan Beach. My good friend, Julianne Gillespie, had encouraged me to enroll in UCLA and join a sorority together. Since both of us had top grades we were easily accepted, but the class schedule was rigorous and sorority life took many hours. I also chose to work part time at May Company department store in Westwood while taking 21 units with three separate foreign languages. I seemed to thrive on a busy schedule.

My family home in the "tree section" of Manhattan Beach was a 30-minute drive from campus, so I visited my parents often on weekends. Rick began to pick me up there and take me on dates. He charmed my mother as well as me. One of our first dates was to the spectacular Host restaurant in the flying saucer-themed building at the Los Angeles Airport. It's closed now, but back then it was pretty fancy. We also went to movies and to nightclubs like the Lighthouse, where we once saw Dizzy Gillespie. It was a whirlwind summer for me. I was completely head over heels in love with Rick.

Toward the end of the summer, my world began to crumble little by little without me even realizing it. It started when we were sitting on my parents' living room couch. Rick handed me a letter to read, addressed to Larry Rocker. I was confused and didn't understand why he would show me a letter addressed to someone I had never heard of. He said, "That's me." I was so befuddled by this revelation that I didn't know what to say.

A week later as we sat at my parents' kitchen table Larry (formerly known as Rick) further revealed, "I want to be honest with you and let you know that I have been married." I was surprised but thought to myself, "Well he is six years older than I am and I've heard of people getting married young." I responded, "Oh, but you're not married now, right?" He said he wasn't. Larry said he lived in Fresno with his mother and helped take care of her. (After this strange turn of events with Larry I could never again seem to call him by his name.)

Larry visited me often and one time he took me to Ventura. It was so beautiful there and I had never seen this part of the coast before. I remember feeling so grown up, taking a car ride with him to another city two hours away. While we were there he said, "Do you remember I told you I had been married? Well, there was a child." I was surprised but thought to myself, "Well, I guess people have babies when they are married." But I responded, "But she lives with her mother, right?" Larry assured me she lived with her mother in Fresno.

By the end of the summer Larry revealed to me that he actually had two children, not one, and not long after he clarified that it was actually three. Both revelations absolutely astounded me. In retrospect, I should have walked out the door and never spoken to him again. What's the future with living with a liar? Amazingly I absorbed that information and did not object. At any rate, he went on to assure me they all lived with their mother.

In September I returned to my life at UCLA and the sorority house. Larry and I continued to date. I invited him to be my date for my sorority's winter formal on December 9, 1965. It was a fancy affair and so much fun. At the end of the evening he said he had to go to Fresno because his mother was sick in the hospital. Larry asked if I would go with him. I agreed but since the sorority rules did not allow members to enter after 2:00 a.m., I had to climb up the trellis onto the balcony, pack an overnight bag, and climb back down to his waiting car. Of course, this only added to the excitement of the evening with this charming guy.

After checking into Reps 41 Motel on Blackstone Avenue in Fresno, Larry left me in the room while he went to the hospital. He said he felt so bad for his poor mother because she had just made new curtains for his room and now she was sick. Years later I discovered that it wasn't his mother who was in the hospital, but the mother of his children. She was there having their fourth baby!

We continued to date during the following months and one day in June of 1965 Larry asked if I would leave school and come live with him in Fresno. He said I could finish up my schoolwork at Fresno State University (I actually graduated from Fresno State University with my Bachelor's degree in 1974, which was 10 years after I graduated high school and started at UCLA). I agreed to go with him because I was so in love. It felt like a grand adventure to start a life like a real adult.

Of course, my parents were not thrilled with my decision and urged me to complete my college degree. But I gathered my things from the sorority house and off I went with my new found love to Fresno.

We located a small but adequate apartment above a garage, and we carried our few possessions up the steep stairs and settled in. We made it our own by pasting a wild wallpaper over the large kitchen cabinet. Thankfully, the landlord liked it.

One evening we had just returned from a drive-in movie when I heard footsteps coming up our stairs. I was puzzled, wondering who it could be since it was dark outside and we didn't know anyone in town. Then came a knock at our door. We didn't have a porch light, so when I opened the door I could hardly see the people standing there in the dark.

The two women marched briskly into our apartment. One said, "Hello, I'm Mrs. Rocker." The second one said, "Hello, I'm Mrs. Rocker." They explained one was Larry's mother and the other was his wife. Larry brought in two chairs from the kitchen and invited them to sit down. I was speechless but stood calmly by the wall heater in the chilly little room trying to appear non-judgmental. They proceeded to take turns saying what a bad father and husband Larry was and how he should be ashamed. Towards the end of the visit, they even had a few choice derogatory words for me. Eventually they left in a huff.

Larry was such a smooth talker and good salesman. He knew what to say to convince me that things were not as bad as they had described. He said he hadn't lived with his wife from the day he and I moved in together. He explained that she had mental health issues and that his mother had a hot temper.

I have no clear idea why I didn't run home or back to UCLA. Maybe it was because I was young and in love. Maybe it was because I was used to accepting and dealing with change and difficult situations—like my father's abuse or our constant moves across country or dealing with never fitting in. Whatever the reason, I remember feeling like I could handle any challenging situation and make the best of it. So I somehow chose to believe him. I stayed.

One day Larry announced that he had found a house for us to rent and his two sons would be coming to live with us (Rick was five years old and Mike was three). He said it would relieve some of the stress from their mother and that the oldest child, Pam, who was seven years old, would come frequently to visit us. Since Larry presented the plan by saying these poor little children needed a stable family environment, and since I have such a high level of responsibility for others, I was eager to do what I could to help. So at age 19, I was now a "mom." I knew I had a lot to learn but I willingly jumped in to do what I could.

The simple two-bedroom house had a large front yard, a garage, and a sizable back yard. Rick and Mike loved the bunkbeds we installed in their bedroom. We didn't have much money at all, but we did what we could to make it comfortable and homey. Larry went to work as a salesman for Sentry Insurance. While the boys were in school during the day, I attended Fresno City College so I could work toward eventually completing my Bachelor's degree. Since my goal was no longer to work for the State Department and save the world (as it was when I started UCLA), I changed my major from Political Science to Home Economics. I hoped that I could learn something about raising children and caring for a family.

Eventually, Larry and I were married. Larry and his first wife, Margaret, divorced on July 16, 1966 and Larry and I were married on June 29, 1967, a year after I first moved in with him.

One day when Pam was visiting us, our milkman Randy, knocked on the screen door and then brought several large bottles of milk into the house and placed them in our refrigerator, which was his weekly routine. Randy knew the boys but had never met Pam. So I said, "Randy, meet Pam. She is Larry's daughter." As soon as Randy was back in his milk truck, Pam started crying. Through her tears, she asked me, "Why did you say I was Larry's daughter? Why didn't you say I was your daughter?" I took her in my arms and held her close. From that day on, I thought of Pam as my daughter just as I thought of the boys as my sons.

Pam would often ask Larry why he picked the boys to come live with us but not her. After we had been in the house for nearly two years, Larry asked me what I thought about Pam coming to live with us. He said, "One more won't make that much difference." I said it sounded like a good idea. But I remember after the first week of caring for all three kids, I was sitting on the couch, exhausted, and Larry said, "See I told you three wouldn't be any more work than two." Of course, I was glad Pam was living with us, but caring for the three kids took a lot of my energy.

My mother taught me to sew when I was young, so it felt good to sign up for a pattern-making class at Fresno City College. I enjoyed making most of Pam's clothes and a lot of my own. I was even hired by my sewing teacher to tailor some clothes for her—and she was very particular. A few years later I designed and made fancy, long velvet dresses to sell in a shop in Manhattan Beach to make a little extra money

We didn't have much money to buy furniture, so we shoved two chests of drawers together and put a single mattress on top for Pam's bed. She loved it because it had a ladder on the end so she could climb up and gain ready access to her drawers. All three kids had lots of friends in the neighborhood and would play games like "Statue" and "Hide and Seek" each day until it got too dark.

One day Larry told me he would like for me to have a baby so we could have a more complete family. I felt like I had my hands full with three children, but since I always saw him as being in charge of things, I agreed. I stopped my birth control and soon I was pregnant. I didn't gain much weight, so I felt pretty good most of the time.

I would often take Rick and Mike to the nearby park so they could play and run off some of their energy. As we were walking across the large expanse of lawn on the way to the park one day, I began to feel a pain in my side. I thought it was just some gas but I had to stop every few steps to wait for it to pass. The boys kept shouting impatiently, "Come on Mom, hurry up!" Baird wasn't due to be born until June 5 and this was June 2 so I thought I just ate something wrong.

That evening we had dinner with another family in their home. I have always been a fast eater — and I've often been embarrassed about it. That night I finished eating my meal before anyone else and when I realized it, I tried to cover it up. But Mike, who was about six years old, sat up tall, looked around the table at everyone's plate and exclaimed with a very loud, very proud voice, "Well I guess the fastest in our house is faster than the fastest in your house." I was really embarrassed then!

I kept feeling little pains as I was eating dinner, similar to what I felt earlier in the park. Without my realizing it, Larry had been timing the pains. When dinner was over he asked if the other couple would watch Rick and Mike because he thought it was time to take me to the hospital. Baird was born that night.

My only mode of transportation was a used bicycle. One day I decided I wanted to get a new curtain rod for over the bathtub because the old one was bent and ready to fall apart. I was about eight months pregnant but it made perfect sense to me to ride the bike to the hardware store while the kids were at school to buy the curtain rod, which cost $6.00. Once I purchased it, I asked the store clerk to help me tie it to my bike. I was riding along feeling pretty good about my ingenuity and thinking how surprised and happy Larry would be when he got home and saw my purchase.

I hung the shower curtain on the new rod and waited for him to come home. The first thing he said when he walked in the door was, "What in the world were you doing riding your bike down Shields Avenue today?" I could tell he was angry but I didn't know why. I soon learned that he was driving in his car with his sales manager and when the manager saw me he exclaimed, "Hey look at that pregnant woman riding a bike with something strapped to the frame!" Larry said he felt humiliated and couldn't bring himself to tell his boss that that lady was his wife. It didn't dampen my spirits—I still felt pretty proud of myself even though I tried to appear remorseful.

Soon after Pam came to live with us, Douglas Baird Rocker was born on June 2, 1968. Pam loved helping me take care of him. My parents also came to visit us to help with his care. In fact, my mother took him back with her to Manhattan

Beach for a couple of weeks because I was recuperating from a bad case of hepatitis which sapped all of my energy. I had prepared myself to nurse Baird, but the Fresno hospital nurses hurried him off to the third floor isolation unit when they realized I had hepatitis. So, I was forced to feed him with bottles instead.

Later, when Baird was old enough to eat baby food, I decided to make my own because I read that jarred baby food had too much sugar. I bought some extra ice trays, blended all sorts of cooked vegetables, fruits and meats together and filled the trays to the brim. I would take out the frozen squares of food, warm them up and feed Baird. Thankfully, he liked it all.

I was determined to do the best job of parenting I could for Baird. So I bought a book called, *Give Your Child a Superior Mind*. The idea was to expose the child to all sorts of textures, shapes and sounds. Larry thought it was kind of silly, and maybe it was, but I was pretty committed to following all of the instructions.

About a year after Baird was born, Larry announced he had found a home for us to purchase in Kingsburg, a small farming town about half-hour drive south of Fresno. I had no idea how we could afford to buy a house since we lived so frugally. But, as usual, I went along with the plan. We were all excited about this darling two-story house perched on a small hill in the middle of a nice neighborhood. Each of the kids had their own bedroom. It had a good-sized backyard and a walkway lined with flowers, curving through the front yard under three elegant birch trees. We even got a cute little rat terrier that we named Jigger who was constantly running all over the place.

We raised the kids in this sweet house for about 10 years. I enjoyed making sure all three of the older kids took turns helping with dinner, setting the table and washing the dishes. I wanted to make sure they would be self-sufficient when they got older. I also wanted to ensure they all ate healthy, well-balanced meals. But when the three older kids began to participate in team sports, each one had a different schedule. So I decided to make my own frozen dinners for them.

I had a friend who used the Swanson TV dinners. Even though I would never think of buying such things, I asked her to save the empty tin dinner trays for me. Every Sunday I would cook two or three entrees — chicken, pork chops, meatloaf — and fill each tray with one entrée serving, some frozen vegetables and tater tots. I covered each one with tin foil and added a piece of masking tape listing the contents so they could choose whatever they wanted for dinner. I placed them all in the freezer. One time I counted 50 dinners stacked up. This was before the days of microwaves, so each of the kids would choose their dinner and put it in the oven for 30 minutes. This worked like a charm — the kids got to choose their dinner and I knew they were eating well balanced meals.

One of the children's favorite meals was what we called *must-goes*. We usually enjoyed this delicacy on Sundays because the name came from the idea that everything in the refrigerator must go before we start a new week. So I would gather all the left-overs and make a stew or a soup or lay out an array of dinner choices. I often heard from one of the kids, "Mom can we have must-goes?" Whenever someone outside the family heard this plea, they would be intrigued about the ingredients in such a dish.

The three older children had lots of friends at school and in the neighborhood. Pam was a cheerleader starting in junior high school and Rick and Mike played football and basketball and were on the wrestling team. All three kids were on the swim team. I never missed a match or a game, including Pam's cheerleading events.

As I related in Chapter One, it was during our time in Kingsburg that I founded the Kingsburg Community Assistance Program (KCAPS). So in addition to raising three adolescent kids and a youngster, I was quite busy with all the various KCAPS programs: the thrift store, food bank, pre-school, and church. I seemed to thrive on being busy.

For four years, while we were still living in Kingsburg, we owned a beautiful home in North Lake Tahoe where we enjoyed skiing at Homewood Ski Resort and boating on Lake Tahoe. We kept our cabin cruiser boat tied to a buoy not too far from our dock. It was a five-hour drive from our home, but we always enjoyed every minute when we were there. One time my parents came up to visit and I wanted them to enjoy a boat ride on the lake. Larry didn't come with us and he was always the one who drove the boat. But I thought I could figure out how to do it.

I told my parents to wait on the dock while I went to get the boat and then pick them up for a fun ride. I climbed into the dingy like I always saw Larry do and paddled out to the boat which was fastened to the buoy with a large rope connected to a substantial hook. I noticed that the wind had picked up and the waves were getting bigger. I wasn't sure if I should unhook the big boat first and then attach the dingy to the buoy or do it the other way around. I tried detaching the big boat first, but the wind began to drag the boat away from me. I was petrified as I realized I could easily lose the boat.

I pulled it back with all my might and prayed hard that I could reattach it to the buoy. It worked, but now I was still puzzled about how to get myself out of the dingy and into the big boat. So I attached the dingy to the buoy and then climbed up the thick rope until I was hanging onto the boat. I climbed into the boat and then hung over the side to detach it from the buoy. I successfully started the boat and maneuvered it over to the dock, picked up my parents and we all went for a really nice ride through the wind and waves. Thankfully I was able to bring them back to the dock, reconnect the boat to the buoy and then climb into the dingy and paddle back to shore. I felt lucky to have successfully navigated all of this.

Our years in Kingsburg were pretty idyllic. The kids did well in school, I enjoyed being involved in their activities and my work with KCAPS and Larry was relishing his work. One Saturday when Mike was eight years old he was riding his bike around their elementary school with his buddies. One of the kids noticed some mounds of dirt and grass just beyond the school fence. So they decided to ride their bikes to the top of the mounds and play king of the hill. Just as Mike got to the top of one of the hills, it all caved in. He and his bike fell into a pit of molten lava.

We found out later that the man who owned the field where the boys were riding had a contract with Union Pacific Railroad to clean the grape pumice out of their trains. He piled the pumice around his field. Over the years grass grew to cover the material and it looked like innocent mounds. Little did anyone know that grape pumice will self-combust without oxygen.

Mike clawed his way out of the fiery pit, but the incident resulted in third degree burns on his hands and feet. Later we learned that we were lucky he didn't fall all the way to the bottom of the very deep pit. He crawled to a nearby neighbor's house who called the hospital. I was in the middle of some basic housework when I heard the ambulance siren. Moments later our phone rang. It was the hospital telling me my son had been hurt and I should come to the hospital immediately. Since we lived near the hospital, I arrived just before the ambulance did. I was stunned as they wheeled Mike's gurney out of the vehicle. His hands and feet were completely black. Right away he noticed how upset I was and he said, "Don't cry mom, I'll be okay."

He spent the following months in the hospital going through painful debriding of his burns and ultimately skin grafts. His pain was indescribable but he always had an upbeat spirit. I left his bedside only to take care of the other kids' basic needs. To this day, whenever I think of the burns Mike suffered I start to cry. This memory is often triggered by the sound of a fire truck or ambulance siren.

When Rick and Mike were in junior high school they started to smoke cigarettes. I tried everything I could think of to make them stop this filthy habit. Nothing seemed to work. Then I noticed some unusual odors and behavior from them. I suspected they were using marijuana with some of their friends. I decided to go visit the parents of their friends to suggest that we all join together to come up with a plan to stop them from using drugs. I was shocked and frustrated when the other parents declared that their sons would never do anything like that. I got the same reaction from Larry when I told him about it. I finally accepted the fact that I would not be able to change the situation, especially since I didn't have their father's support.

During our time in Kingsburg, Larry became more and more involved in his work. He had started his own company in Fresno, Larry Rocker & Associates, providing business property and casualty insurance as well as workers' compensation and healthcare insurance. Before long he began to travel a lot and stay out late, saying he had evening meetings with clients. He also began to spend more money than usual, buying new cars and expensive clothes. I never complained about this, but in retrospect I realized that I was losing interest in my husband. I enjoyed being busy with all the kids' school activities and expanding the scope of KCAPS but I occasionally missed the close relationship Larry and I used to have.

At some point Larry seemed to sense me withdrawing from him emotionally and said he wanted me to have another baby. I wasn't wild about the idea but I knew he would eventually win out, so I agreed. It felt like it was almost time to deliver and I was feeling some strong contractions. Pam, Rick and Mike were worried because they had never seen me in such pain and they didn't know what was going on. They kept gathering around my bed and hollering, "Dad come here, something's wrong with Mom!"

Finally I told Larry it was too stressful for them to see me like this and suggested he take me to the hospital. On March 26, 1976, after 24 hours of labor, the doctor performed an unplanned caesarian section and our youngest son, Matthew Clay Rocker, was born at Kingsburg Hospital. Pam was in her last year of high school at the time and loved doting on our sweet new baby boy.

Pam and I had a very close relationship. We talked all the time. As the women's liberation hit its stride in the 1970s, we frequently talked about how needed these changes in society were. When Pam left to go away to San Jose State University a year later, I missed her so much. She and I had such a close relationship for so many years—I sewed all of her clothes (until her junior high school began to allow girls to wear jeans to school) and taught her how to sew simple things like aprons. Now I was surrounded by teen-age sons and my only daughter was away at college.

Here we were, living in the middle of the beautiful San Joaquin Valley with grape vineyards as far as the eye could see. Larry had lots of friends in the agriculture business, many of whom farmed thousands of acres of Thompson Seedless grapes which they would transform into raisins. His friends often complained about the damage rain caused to the raisins, especially in early September. The only insurance available to raisin farmers at that time was through the government and it only covered complete crop loss. Larry was a really smart guy and he knew the insurance industry well. So, he decided to write an insurance policy for rain damage on raisins. After it was approved by the California Department of Insurance, farmers were clamoring for these insurance policies.

In 1978 President Jimmy Carter invited Larry to come to the White House to discuss his new rain damage on raisins insurance policy. Larry and I along with his partner, Joe Difilipo, and his wife Barbara, embarked upon a glorious, all-expense paid, trip to Washington D.C. We had our picture taken with Jimmy and Rosalind as well as other luminaries like Avrell Harriman and Alan Cranston. Larry reported that during his talk with President Carter and his insurance advisor, Carter invited Larry to work in his administration's insurance department. Larry declined saying, he was a small town kind of guy. I never understood that decision, but I knew better than to disagree with him.

The next year, 1979, Larry began to talk about wanting to move out to the country. Before long, he took me to see the ranch house we would soon move into. Even though it was very impressive, he got busy remodeling the house and renovating the yard. The 5,000 square foot four-bedroom house sat on 120 acres of Thompson Seedless table grapes (some managed for other growers and 20 acres that we owned). Larry hired a ranch manager and a group of workers to attend to the vines. The ranch manager and his wife and three children lived in a house toward the back of our property. The Haros became very good friends over the years. Thanks to them, both Baird and Matt became fluent in Spanish and have maintained that ability to this day.

The Haro family would frequently hold gatherings for their very large family using our enormous barn. We didn't keep animals in the barn; instead we used it for charity fundraisers (like our then famous *Hog Wild Hoedown*) and other gatherings. There was always lots of delicious food and lots of beer every time the Haros brought their extended family together. The beer was always cold and the homemade salsa was really spicy. They would never actually start eating until Sal, the father and our ranch manager, called me on the phone to ask me to come over. They didn't want to start eating until "La Senora" had eaten. I always felt this was a sweet, thoughtful way of showing their respect and gratitude.

One of their family members would prepare a plate of food for me as soon as I arrived, accompanied by lots of the homemade salsa and plenty of beer. Then they would watch me enjoy the food. When someone saw I was running low on salsa or beer they would yell, "Mas cerveza y mas salsa para la senora!" And then someone would hurry over with more. What a fun time that was!

One year I decided I wanted to learn how to prune our grapes. Our ranch manager, Sal, gave me a lesson along with the appropriate tools and turned me loose. The beautiful dark green shoots were sticking out in every direction. The goal is to choose two canes per vine and cut off the rest. Then the one on the right is tied to the connecting wire, as is the one on the left. So each vine has two arms, one in one direction and one in the other. This ensures that the grape clusters are well supported with space and nutrients.

The challenging part for me was actually cutting off some of the beautiful canes — they were so lush and vibrant looking. I would toss the severed shoots onto the ground after removing them from the trunk. I saw that the discarded shoots lay shriveled and lifeless on the ground when I went out to resume the project the next day. It was a sad sight. But it reminded me of the scripture verse in John 15:5: "I am the vine; you are the branches. If you remain in me and I in you, you will bear much fruit; apart from me you can do nothing."

I enjoyed learning how to prune the vines, but I especially enjoyed the real-life example of one of my favorite scripture verses. I shared my experience with a pastor friend of mine and he loved it so much that he used it in one of his sermons.

One year the Haro family went to visit their extended family in Mexico during December and January. We were glad they could get away for a while because they always worked so hard on our ranch. But their absence meant that I would need to play a key role in working on a grafting project for our Thompson Seedless grapevines.

I wasn't sure how to perform this task, but I asked some farming friends and they explained the steps involved in grafting rootstalk from another variety on to some of our Thompson vines to produce sweeter, larger grapes. Now I just needed to find some workers to help me.

I didn't know exactly how to locate these field hands since Sal Haro, our ranch manager, usually did things like this. I am embarrassed to say that my thought was, "I'll just ask a bunch of Mexican workers — they'll know how to graft the vines." Well, I located about a dozen guys, but when I got them out to the ranch and explained the project, I was surprised to discover that they didn't know how to graft vines.

Undaunted, I decided to teach them what I had learned from my friend. We all crouched down around the sample vines and the supplies — the rootstalks, the special knives, twine and the thick white growth enhancer. By now my Spanish vocabulary had expanded beyond everyday household words to include some ranching terminology.

I was trying to show them how to splice the vine and the rootstalk to their cambium and then use the white goop to hold them together as I wrapped the twine around the two. But all of a sudden I realized I didn't know the Spanish word for cambium. So I stopped and asked them in Spanish, "What is the name for this part?" (pointing to the cambium). One of them said, "El corazon." (which means the heart).

I will always remember that moment's powerful impact on me as I thought about joining my heart with God's heart and wrapping them tightly together for greater growth and strength. Eventually we finished the project – resulting in strong vines and sweet fruit.

Larry's remodel project included a 1,000 square foot master bedroom, renovated kitchen with the latest appliances, a cantilevered ceiling in the large family room, artistically designed, stunning stained glass windows and doors throughout, a beautiful dry creek in the front yard complete with 12 antique street lights, a pasture, horse runs, and various animal and poultry pens.

He was enjoying buying expensive new cars and pickup trucks, a large motor home and several stunning jet boats. It appeared that Larry's business was very successful, but he never bothered to discuss his business affairs with me.

While I was heavily occupied with adding our food bank to the KCAPS thrift store and developing the pre-school, Larry insisted that we needed a horse because we now had horse stables. So we went to the nearby horse sale even though neither of us knew anything about horses. That day we came home with a very large reddish-brown horse that we named Cinnamon. Larry said that since he had purchased the horse for me, the least I could do was ride it. I was petrified! Since I knew I would eventually have to ride the thing, I asked a friend to give me riding lessons. This helped a lot but I still didn't feel comfortable.

I signed up for a riding class at Reedley Junior College. I didn't know anything about the terminology used in the various class descriptions, so I just signed up for a class that met at a convenient day and time. The instructions said, "Show up the first night with a yearling." I happened to have a yearling because Cinnamon had a baby (which we named Nutmeg) soon after we got her. So on the appointed evening, I loaded Nutmeg onto my newly purchased single horse trailer and drove the 10 miles to class. For the first many weeks, we just learned how to teach the horse voice commands using a lunge rope and a whip. It was pretty easy getting Nutmeg to go around in circles and obey my commands.

Then one night, my instructor, Richard, said, "Ok Cynder, it's time for you to get on that beast." I was petrified. He put us in a round pen and he stood in the middle of the pen with a lead rope attached to Nutmeg's bridle while I sat nervously on top starring at her ears so I could see if she got upset. I couldn't look at Richard for fear I would miss a signal from the horse. Finally I looked over at Richard and noticed he was no longer holding the rope. He said, "I let go of the rope a long time ago. You're doing fine." I let out a big breath, just grateful to still be alive. So, little by little, I learned how to ride and actually began to enjoy it. Later we bought two more quarter horses, Disco Dawn, a well-trained four year-old mare, and Moose, a two year-old gelding.

Taking care of the horses was my responsibility which I gladly heaped on my plate along with my other responsibilities.

Every Wednesday afternoon I would load up Matt's horse, Black Beauty, in the trailer and drive us to Richard's ranch for his riding lesson. I had purchased Moose from Richard several months earlier and I was paying him to finish the training on this green broke gelding. One afternoon, Matt (who was about 11 at the time) asked me to ride with him in the riding arena. I said, "No Matt, this is your time to ride not mine." When he insisted that I ride with him, I asked Richard if I could ride Moose. He quickly agreed and I went to fetch Moose from the barn.

I attached a lead rope to his bridle and began to lunge him as Richard has taught me to do. Richard came by and said, "Just get on the beast and ride." I figured that meant that Richard had just ridden him earlier in the day. So I mounted Moose and rode into the riding arena to join Matt (I later found out that Richard had been gone for several days and had left Moose in the stall with no exercise). Moose felt very nervous under the saddle and when I passed by Richard I said, "Moose feels like he's ready to jump out of his skin."

I'll never forget Richard's words: "Ah go for it, Cynder!" I took this to mean "don't be such a baby" and I thought, "I can go for it as good as the next guy." So I kicked Moose and off we went. The next thing I knew he was bucking hard and high. I was determined to stay in the saddle but at some point my tail bone snapped, which made me unconscious. At that point, I fell off the saddle onto the decomposed granite of the arena floor without breaking my fall with my arms. I landed directly on my head and was unconscious. (This was before the days of wearing riding helmets.)

As I lay there on the ground on my back, I saw an angel. He was very tall, wearing a flowing white garment and speaking into the darkness over my head. I couldn't understand what he was saying but I had a feeling that whatever he was saying was keeping me safe from further harm. When I came to, a fellow riding student was kneeling next to me, praying with her hand on my leg. I had a feeling that there was some connection between her prayer and the angel's appearance. Someone whisked me off to the hospital and called Larry so he could pick up Matt.

It was discovered that I had a traumatic brain injury. While the rest of my body healed in a month or two, the brain injury lingered on. I couldn't function very well or think straight. Noise and commotion quickly sent me into sensory overload. I craved silence and calm surroundings. Elaine Olson, the most dedicated KCAPS volunteer, graciously agreed to keep things going with the various programs. She would drive the six miles out to the ranch every day or so to keep me posted about the assorted issues. I was so grateful for her faithful help.

One day about five months after the accident, I began to have flashes of memory of the accident. One morning I clearly saw the angel and the woman kneeling down praying for me. I knew immediately that I needed to find that woman to thank her. I asked a couple of fellow students the name of the woman with the paint horse. It took a while but I tracked her down by her horse.

I called the phone number they gave me. When she answered my call, I told her that I was the person who had the horse accident five months prior. I said I was calling to thank her for praying for me. She said immediately, "Oh gosh, I was so embarrassed about that. I have never prayed in public before but I found myself on my knees by you as if I had no choice in the matter." She went on to report that she had never been back to the class because of her humiliation. I told her I felt that her prayers saved my life and I really appreciated what she had done for me.

Just before I was ready to hang up the phone, I thought to myself, "I'll probably never see this woman again so maybe I can tell her about the angel." Up to this point I had told no one about the angel for fear they would think I was crazy or weird. I mustered my courage and said, "There was one more thing I remembered — I saw an angel when I was unconscious." She said very matter-of-factly, "Oh yes, I know you did. As soon as you came to, you said very excitedly three times that you had just seen an angel." I was dumbfounded to have this confirmation that my strange recollection was real and I wasn't crazy.

Little did I know that my ranch life experiences had just begun.

Best wishes to Cynder Rocker   *Rosalynn Carter*

With Rosalynn Carter at the White House in 1979;
With Hilary Clinton in Beverly Hills in 1996

October 30, 1996

Ms. Cynder Sinclair
Executive Director
Tres Condados Girl Scout
    Council, Inc.
Post Office Box 30187
Santa Barbara, California 93130

Dear Ms. Sinclair and Friends:

    Thank you for the Girl Scout cookies
and pin. They are a wonderful reminder of
my visit to California and the warm welcome
I received. I appreciate your
thoughtfulness.

    With best wishes, I am

                    Sincerely yours,

                    Hillary Rodham Clinton
                    Hillary Rodham Clinton

It was a thrill getting this letter from Hilary Clinton,
the first lady, following our meeting

With Matt and Baird at Kingsburg's Swedish Festival in 1979, then with my granddaughter and Peggy in 1984

We refurbished an old stagecoach to serve as
our official vehicle in the Swedish Festival.
Here we are with family and friends in 1981.
Our theme that year was
"Pioneers in Education"

The Swedish Festival remains a Kingsburg tradition

CHAPTER FIVE
A New Lease on Life

Sometimes it takes darkness and the sweet
confinement of your aloneness to learn
that anything or anyone that does not
bring you alive is too small for you.
– David Whyte

Eventually, our grounds were full of all sorts of animals—three quarter horses, a Welsh mare that Matt named "Black Beauty," a cow for the kids to ride, two black angus steers that Baird and Matt raised as 4-H projects, several sheep, a peacock, two pea hens, two ducks and lots of egg-laying hens with one rooster. We enjoyed taking care of all of these animals.

I especially enjoyed collecting the newly laid eggs every morning. I went out to the "chicken condo" (which I had built to protect them from coyotes) each morning wearing my oversized sweatshirt and carrying a stick. I would methodically go to each hen, use the stick to pry her off her nest (whereupon each one would protest with a loud squawk) and put the one or two eggs from each hen in my sweatshirt. Next I picked up any duck and peacock eggs from the ground. Whenever I was inside the chicken condo collecting eggs, the peacock would spread out his beautiful tail feathers and prance around the pen fluttering his tail, which made a noise like the wind. It was as if he was showing off for me. I always looked forward to this encounter.

The peacock eggs were very large, had hard shells and were a beautiful turquoise color. I learned quickly that I should crack the peacock and duck eggs and beat them up for scrambled eggs before the kids came into the kitchen for breakfast because the thought of eating anything except chicken eggs grossed them out. It worked like a charm.

We also raised several litters of pigs — Matt named the mother pig "Mama Snort" and she had 13 piglets with every litter. (A pig's gestation period is three months, three weeks and three days.) I would crouch down in the pen that I designed for her for a few hours every time she had a new brood so I could make sure she didn't roll over on the new piglets. Then I would clip their eye teeth with a special tool and cut their tails short with another instrument. For some reason this usually happened in the early morning hours.

When Mama Snort eventually weighed 900 pounds, we took her to the Fresno County Fair so the kids could see what a 900-pound sow looked like. One day, as I was trying to coax her into the horse trailer to take her to visit her boar friend to make more piglets, she tried to get away. I used all my might to get her in the trailer but she finally won leaving me lying in the dirt with a bloody leg while she ran gleefully through the grapevines. To this day I wonder why I thought I was stronger than a 900-pound sow!

Our golden retriever ranch dog, Coco, was as beautiful as you could imagine. She had long, thick reddish hair and was very sweet-natured. One day Matt and his friend Brandon Roach felt sorry for Coco because it was well over 100 degrees. They thought her thick coat of fur made her uncomfortable. Matt got the bright idea to use the shears we used on the sheep to cut off all of her hair so she could be cooler. I found them with Coco out by the sheep pen but it was too late — they had already shaved most of the poor dog's beautiful locks. She was so embarrassed that she hid under bushes for a long time until it began to grow back.

Our freezers were always full of the best cuts and grades of meat — beef, pork and lamb. I would call the butcher when it was time to slaughter a steer, a pig or a sheep and arrange for him to come to transport the animal at a time when I wasn't home. I didn't want to watch the process! He would routinely call me a few days later so I could join him at his butcher shop while he cut each section of meat to my specifications. It was an experience I really enjoyed — and, of course, the ultimate result was delicious and tender.

The drug habit that Mike acquired in junior high school started with marijuana, but it continued to increase. Mike was getting out of control and I had no idea how to deal with him. I was in a pickle because every time I suggested to Larry that we find some help for Mike's addiction, Larry would say I was imagining things. Yet Mike was becoming violent and I was getting really scared — for myself as well as for Baird and Matt.

One night while the boys and I were sleeping I received a scary phone call. The caller said in a gravelly voice, "If Mike doesn't pay me the money he owes me for the drugs I gave him, I'm going to come out there and kill all of you in your sleep." Of course Larry was gone on one of his many trips, so we were there alone.

I immediately had what I thought was a brilliant idea. I pulled one of the shotguns we used for duck hunting out of the gun cabinet and turned all the lights on in the front of the house which was filled with very large picture windows looking out onto the driveway. I began to pace back and forth in front of the windows, very methodically. I figured if someone really was going to come here to kill us they would see me in the window with the gun and be scared off. I marched back and forth like that for two hours and I finally put the gun away and went to bed when the sun began to rise.

The next day when I saw Mike, I told him about it and he angrily shrugged it off. After he went to his bedroom, I remember standing in the kitchen looking out onto the pool area. I was in a sort of trance. It was as if I was dreaming, even though I was wide awake. I was standing on the edge of a cliff looking down onto the huge abyss below, feeling like I could fall in at any moment. I carefully stepped back from the edge and said to myself, "This will never happen again. No one will ever get me that close to the edge again!" From that moment on, I have been vigilant about keeping myself safe from anyone using drugs, even when it's my own kids.

(Thankfully today Mike has a thriving business and two beautiful daughters, Koty and McKallah Rocker. Both of them successfully work in the field of audiology and really enjoy it. They are both very loving and have a close relationship with their dad. I always enjoy spending time with them when I can travel to their home in San Diego.)

When the kids were young and we were still living in Fresno, I started a Christmas stocking tradition. Back then I used lots of creativity since we didn't have much money. I read a particularly good idea from a Woman's Day magazine. The instructions said to sew a Christmas stocking out of red felt, add a little trim at the top, embroider the child's name in green and glue a green felt Christmas tree near the top to represent the child's first Christmas. Then each year thereafter you were to add something made out of a different color of felt to symbolize something important to each child that year. It was simple, inexpensive and the kids loved it. Little did I know that it would expand to encompass many people.

Over the years I made stockings for each of the children but also, as they got older, for their girlfriends and boyfriends. Each stocking told its own story. One funny aspect was that I have no artistic talent whatsoever so the little felt pieces looked somewhat strange sometimes. For example, I tried to cut a bike out of light blue felt to represent Mike's first bicycle on his sixth Christmas. I couldn't for the life of me figure out how to make the handlebars go the right way, so I just left them catawampus hoping people could figure out it was a bicycle.

One year at the ranch when the children were older, I had to call a repair man for my kitchen stove a few days before Christmas. We lived six miles from town and the stove was the latest fancy model. The repair man took one look at the situation and said, "I don't know if I can get this repaired in time for Christmas, ma'am." As he said this he happened to take a step back, glanced over his shoulder and was stunned to see 13 bright Christmas stockings all lined up along the mantel. He must have thought I had 13 kids, so he said, "I'll make sure I have this stove fixed in time, ma'am." And he did. I never told him that some of those stockings were for girlfriends of my sons or my daughter's boyfriend.

When Baird was in eighth grade, a young man named Maurice came to live with us. Maurice was 16 and part of John Perkin's Harambee (a Swahili word for "let's get together and push") Center located in an area in Pasadena that had the highest daytime crime rate in all of California. As a reward for memorizing scripture, the young members of Harambee would spend a week during Easter break at our ranch. Larry and I were impressed with Maurice and soon invited him to live with us. Larry took Maurice to his office every morning in the summer to learn filing and other office skills so Maurice would have a better chance for a productive life.

In September, Maurice started Selma High School as a junior. He was a tall, slender Black kid with natural basketball talent. I remember the day I took Maurice to high school to get him signed up for the basketball team. The coach was skeptical at first until I introduced him to Maurice. Then he fell all over himself getting Maurice signed up for the team. I never missed a game.

Whenever he would make a basket he would come over to the bleachers and give me a big sweaty hug saying, "Mom did you see that?" Since Maurice was the only Black kid in school (and parents at the school really didn't know me since my other children went to Kingsburg High), I always got some strange stares. But Maurice had a taste of success for the first time in his life.

One day he came home from school and told us about his new friend, Nicolas Sasse. Nicolas was a German foreign exchange student and his host family just moved, so he needed a place to stay. Maurice begged us to let Nicolas come live with us for the rest of the school year. We agreed and our family expanded even more.

Rick and his lovely wife, Peggy, were married in 1978 — right after they graduated from high school. Larry and I had been vacationing in Hawaii when their daughter Stephanie was born in 1979. She was our very first grandchild, so we hurried to fly home to welcome her.

Pam and her handsome husband, Jeff, were married in 1981 after meeting each other at San Jose State University. So Mike, Baird and Matt were our three remaining children still living at home. Plus, Maurice and Nicolas were still with us.

Stephanie (who was three years younger than Matt), often stayed with us, too, so her parents could go to work.

Needless to say, it was quite the active household.

Every weekday morning after I cleaned up the breakfast dishes, I made lunches for the children to take to school. I would line-up the five sandwiches so I could prepare them to each one's preference. They all liked regular mayonnaise except Maurice who insisted on Miracle Whip instead. Some wanted me to write their name on their lunch bag and others didn't. Lunch preparation was enjoyable but quite a production.

Nicolas was 16 — the same age as Maurice. But they were very different from each other. Maurice was very loosey-goosey and his bedroom was always a giant mess. Nicolas was very organized — everything in his bedroom was perfectly placed. When it was time for the school prom, Maurice decided he would have to teach Nicolas how to dance "the American way."

I was preparing dinner when I heard the two of them arguing out in the family room. When I went to see what was happening, Maurice was playing some rap music and Nicolas was saying, "I do not like this 'shake your booty' thing. I will dance with the French girl — she knows how to dance the proper way." Then Nicolas proceeded to bring out his boom box and insert a cassette tape. He was determined to teach Maurice how to waltz. So the two 6'2" 16 year-olds were waltzing around the kitchen, bumping into walls while I was trying to cook. Finally they both decided to forget the whole dance idea.

When I think back to our years at the ranch, I think of them as "the days of Camelot." Everything seemed so perfect and everyone's life seemed so ideal — at least most of the time. At some point, Larry decided that Matt and Baird and I should move to our vacation home in Murphys, a little town in Calaveras County in Mark Twain country. He said he felt Baird needed a fresh start since he was having a bit of trouble in school. I tried to talk him out of it, but he was determined. So, off we went to our little mountain hideaway.

The three-bedroom, two story house sat right on a beautiful golf course in the middle of an impressive new housing development called Forest Meadows. It was located about a two and a half hour drive from Fresno on Highway 4, at an altitude of about 4,000 feet. Up until this point, we had used this home for vacations only, although it was completely furnished — even with nice tableware, linens, and our clothes. We took our golden retriever, Coco, and my horse, Disco Dawn, with us. The complex was equipped with stables and a nice, covered riding arena.

I enrolled Matt in third grade at Michelson Elementary School and Baird in Brett Hart High School a few miles down the road in Angels Camp. Larry would come up to visit us on some weekends, but we quickly created a very nice life for ourselves in this sweet mountain community. We skied often at nearby Bear Valley ski resort and Matt enjoyed summer baseball. Every Wednesday night we went to Mountain Mike's for pizza with the other families, getting a discount if our sons wore their baseball uniforms. I also started an organization in Murphys similar to the one I started in Kingsburg. Even though many residents of this little town were fairly well off, there were many poor families who lived out of sight and went hungry, especially in the cold winters.

The idea first came to me just before Thanksgiving when I realized that many people living in this mountain town would not be sitting down to what I considered a normal Thanksgiving feast. I began to talk to my friend, Renee Weaver, about the possibility of hosting a festive meal at the Murphys Hotel. We didn't want the perception to be that it was only for poor families because we didn't want them to feel uncomfortable about attending. We decided to call it "Murphys Friends" and invite everyone who had nowhere special to go for Thanksgiving.

It was a big success. The townspeople donated all the necessary food and the hotel agreed to prepare and serve it. The first year about 50 people attended. It was so touching to see people of every kind — elderly, infirm, children, teenagers and adults — enjoying each other's company and a delicious meal. For two years I helped this fledgling program gain stability. Renee graciously agreed to take the reins when I had to leave to return to the ranch in Fresno. It continues to grow and bless the entire community even to this day, although Renee has now moved away.

A couple of years later, Larry informed us that we should move back to the ranch. Much later I discovered the reason he really wanted us to leave in the first place was so he could enjoy the ranch with his girlfriend, Pam Fields.

I guess I was pretty naive, always trusting his judgement and following his rules. I first began to suspect he had a girlfriend during our time at Murphys, soon after I received an invoice from Edmond's Jewelry store in Fresno. (I was in charge of the family checkbook.) The bill for $10,000 was for an engraved Rolex ladies watch. Right away I thought Larry had purchased the watch for me for our upcoming anniversary.

Since he usually forgot to get me anything for our anniversary, I hadn't planned to get him anything in particular. But I made a special trip to Columbia, the small mining town across the bridge from Calaveras County, where I found a beautiful, numbered duck print. He had always enjoyed duck prints and this was an especially handsome one.

I had planned to give Larry the gift when he came up that next weekend for our anniversary. I waited until it was almost time for him to drive back home thinking he was going to give me the watch any moment. When he didn't give me any gift, I gave him the duck print and told him goodbye. Puzzled, I decided to find out more about the Rolex watch. I called the jewelry store and pretended that I had forgotten who we bought the watch for and I wanted to keep our records straight.

The clerk knew me and quickly pulled the file and said it was engraved for Pam Fields. In that moment, it all fell together — Larry wanted me and the boys away from the ranch so he could entertain his employee, Pam. He had purchased the watch for her! Dumfounded, I didn't know how to approach him with this revelation. When I carefully asked him about it he said she wanted to buy a Rolex for herself but couldn't afford it so he bought it with the agreement that she would reimburse him over time. I knew that was a big lie but I also knew better than confront him about anything.

I left it alone but tucked the knowledge into the corner of my mind — and heart.

Back at the ranch, Larry was spending more time racing his jet boats and taking his big motorhome to the boat races. He was also getting more involved with a long-time friend of his, Paul Mosesian. As it turned out, Paul had purchased a racehorse a few years earlier for half a million dollars. Now, he wanted Larry to buy it from him for one million dollars, which he did (at least on paper).

Once they had established the value of the horse at one million dollars, Paul had Larry buy an insurance policy on the horse for one million dollars. A few months later, the horse mysteriously died. I didn't know it at the time, but evidently upon receiving the claim so soon after purchasing the policy, the insurance company hired an investigator to look into the transaction. Apparently the findings pointed to the probability that the horse had been killed for the million dollar insurance payoff.

Soon after that, Larry became very depressed and jumpy. He actually seemed paranoid, saying he had to do something quickly but never explaining his worries. He said we would have to sell the house in Murphys, so I went there to put the house up for sale and pack up any belongings I thought we wouldn't be able to sell. The house sold quickly and, thankfully, the new owners wanted to purchase most of the furniture, tableware and even many of the knickknacks. Packing up for the sale was a lot of work and very emotional. We had so many wonderful memories there and I had made some dear friends. The boys had made friends too and I felt bad when I had to pull them out of school.

Once we were all back at the ranch and involved in our new routines, Larry announced we would have to move. This news stunned all of us, especially since there seemed to be no logical explanation. Once again I began packing up. He said he needed to generate as much cash as possible, so he arranged with a company to sell many of our belongings. Our 6,000 square foot house was filled with beautiful old California oak furniture, much of which I had refinished myself over the years. A huge round oak table that accommodated 12 before adding the leaves, 12 chairs for that table with spindled backs, a very old highchair I purchased just before Stephanie was born (I wanted to use it for all of my grandchildren), two stunning hutches and many more impressive pieces.

Soon strangers were walking through our house putting a sticky note on whatever they wanted to purchase. I felt devastated inside but tried to show a composed demeanor on the outside in order to keep everyone calm. I also had to go through the heartbreaking process of selling our precious horses and other animals, my saddles and all of our tack as well as my horse trailers.

I'll never forget the final day. Larry had loaded the last of our belongings into a U-Haul truck and was driving it with

Baird and Matt in the front seat along the road in front of our house. The enormous house filled with treasured memories was now completely empty. I sat on the floor of what had been our lovely living room watching the U-Haul truck pass in front of the large picture window. I cried and cried, feeling emptier than I had ever felt before. I had no idea why we had to leave, where we would go or what would happen to us next.

Larry's friend Paul Mosesian had agreed to let us live in one of his Fresno apartments at no charge. Our new 1,000 square-foot residence felt odd but I was determined to make the best of it. I arranged our few remaining belongings and clothes in the respective rooms and tried to create a comfortable home environment. Months went by and Larry lay on the couch watching television in a depressed state. Finally after I offered to get a job, he found employment as a salesman at the local Earl Sheib auto painting facility. He didn't make much but it was enough for us to buy food and basic essentials.

But one day he came home happily relating stories about how he was able to help some of his co-workers by sharing some of his paycheck with them. It made him feel important and needed. I still didn't know why we had to abruptly leave the ranch or sell the Murphys house, but I began to feel like Matt and I were not safe. If Larry was going to give away the little bit of money he earned and he didn't want me to get a job how would we ever survive?

I arranged to have a part-time paid position at Highway City Ministries, the organization I had started years before through Northwest Church. Next I located an inexpensive apartment in town for Matt and me to live in. I knew I had to leave Larry. All I can say is that I didn't feel we were safe. I couldn't explain why I felt that way, but the sense of being unsafe was overwhelming. I knew if Larry found out what I was planning he would talk me out of it with his great salesmanship. So, I tried hard to act naturally while I put my plan together.

But I was pretty concerned when Larry and I woke up one morning and, before we got out of bed, he ran his fingernails down my face and said in a very flat tone, "If I can't have you, no one will. We will go to eternity together." I calmly changed the subject by saying I had to go to the bathroom and got out of bed.

The next morning, after Larry left for work I called my good friend, Helen Cummings, and told her about what he had said. She said, "You have to get out of there now!" I responded that I couldn't leave just yet because my new apartment wasn't ready. She called her husband, David Peck, for his input and he echoed her concern and instruction to leave.

I respected their opinions but I had nowhere to go until my apartment was ready, so I stayed for another week and tried hard to act like everything was normal. Larry didn't seem to notice anything out of the ordinary.

Finally the apartment was ready and after Larry left for work and I had dropped Matt off at school, my girlfriends, Mary Roach and Maryann Hunt, arrived with their pick-up trucks. We quickly packed up the essentials (I did not to take anything we didn't really need), drove to my new apartment and unloaded them.

I was nervous but felt so liberated and free. I knew I had done the right thing, I just didn't know why — yet. I left a note on the entry mirror telling Larry about my departure. It simply said, "Dear (that's what I always called him since I had simply not been able to call him by his name ever since he told me his name was Larry, not Rick), You will notice that Matt and I are gone. Please don't worry. We are safe. I will contact you soon and we can discuss things. Love, Cindy." I knew it was cowardly to leave with just a note, but I didn't know what else to do.

Thankfully Matt was still attending school at Northwest Church. I didn't know how I would be able to continue paying the tuition, but I wanted to do all I could to keep Matt's life as normal as possible...even though it was now anything but normal. Matt had attended this school since pre-school and now he was in the final months of sixth grade.

I asked the school principal, Helen (who was also my dear friend), if I could pay for the remaining tuition by giving her my diamond wedding ring which by now I had refashioned into a beautiful pendant. Helen agreed and wore that pendant around her neck every day for the rest of her life. She would often tell me that she wanted me to have the pendant back after she passed, but since she neglected to tell her family about this I never got it back. That was okay because I was just happy she let me use it to pay for Matt's tuition.

That year Matt's French teacher arranged for his sixth grade class to have an exchange program with a sixth grade class in Paris. My good friend, Mary Roach, and her son Brandon were part of the group. What a wonderful time we had for three glorious weeks staying in the homes of the French students. Within 24 hours of arriving, I noticed all the French classes I took in school paid off — I was completely fluent. We toured all the major tourist attractions as well as benefited from enjoying the everyday life of Parisian families. Later that year, the French families came to stay with our group's families for three weeks. Matt and I still have sweet memories from that experience.

A few days after I left Larry, he managed to track me down when I went to get some things from our rented storage facility in Kingsburg. He gave Matt some money to go buy a coke and sat me down for a chat. He tried his best to convince me to come back. But by then I knew I had made the right decision and I just politely listened to his pleading and then calmly said I would not be changing my mind. I have no idea where I got the courage to stand firm against his pitiful entreaties.

Since he wanted to spend time with Matt, I had to tell him where my apartment was. One night he knocked on my door and said, "I've decided to get right with man and God and I'm going to start with you." A bit dumbfounded, I invited him to come inside. That night we sat at my kitchen table for hours while he told me about all the affairs he had for so many years and how sorry he was. I was surprised to hear this but thankfully I didn't feel angry or hurt. I just felt this evidence justified my leaving him. It was becoming clear to me now why I had been having an overwhelming sense of not being safe.

The main feeling I had, though, was embarrassment. I was mortified to discover that several of the women were from his office. I had often visited his office and was friendly with all of his secretaries. Now I realized they had probably been laughing at me behind my back especially since my demeanor was always like "little miss sunshine."

I was glad for my part-time job at Highway City Ministries. I loved the opportunity to stay involved with the work I enjoyed so much. But Larry got in the habit of showing up at my office, unannounced, and demanding that I go with him to the Burger King next door to talk. I always acquiesced because I felt sorry for him. He was really quite miserable. Finally I knew I had to put a stop to his attentions. I was sure that the only way to do this was for me to have another man in my life. His ego would not allow that.

That winter I arranged to take Matt and his friend Brandon Roach skiing at Bear Valley. I thought it would take Matt's mind off of the disruptive events if he could do what he enjoyed with a good friend in a place he loved. We arranged to stay at the historic Murphys Hotel, right in the middle of Main Street. I thought Matt's fond memories of this town would help soothe his troubled spirit. After dinner one night, I left the boys in our room and went downstairs to the bar to have a nightcap. While there, I met the man who would become my second husband, Donald Baptista.

My prediction proved to be correct. As soon as Larry learned I had a new man in my life, he left me alone. After a year of dating, Donald and I were married in the chapel at Northwest Church. Matt, Donald and I moved into one of the homes he built as a contractor in Forest Meadows, the same subdivision located above Murphys that I lived in before. It was quite a bizarre coincidence.

One day while I was living in that home, I received a call from the FBI. They said Larry was going to stand trial for several charges including illegal business practices and killing a horse to collect the insurance payment. They wanted me to testify against him. I didn't know anything about any of this, but I knew better than to refuse because they could subpoena me. Still, I also knew I wanted to avoid testifying against Larry. I did not want our children to be able to say that mom was responsible for dad going to prison. I wondered how in the world I could make this happen.

Then a brilliant idea came to me as I was making the one-hour drive from Murphys to Stockton for the required FBI deposition. I would do my best to make sure the FBI did not want me to testify at all.

When I was a kid, one of my parents' favorite television shows was the George Burns and Gracie Allen Show. George played the straight guy and Gracie was his bubble-headed, ditsy wife. At the end of every episode, George would tell Gracie, "Say good-night, Gracie." And Gracie would say, "Good night, Gracie." They were really hilarious.

I decided I would channel Gracie Allen during the FBI interrogation. I would appear to be as dumb as a mud fence so they wouldn't want me at the trial.

When I arrived on the appointed day, I walked into the tiny, sterile room and six FBI men instantly came to attention and introduced themselves. They began asking questions about the horse. I deflected the questions, pretending not to know what they were after. At one point I realized they were getting a little frustrated so I said, "It seems that you guys really want to know about the horse. I remember the day the call came in about that." They all quickly sat up straight with pens poised on their yellow lined pads of paper.

"I was in our bedroom when the telephone rang. I answered it. Paul was calling for Larry," I began to explain. "You mean Paul Mosesian?!" they asked scribbling madly on their notepads. I calmly nodded in affirmation. I continued to explain that "I could tell that Larry was upset about something but I couldn't wait for the call to end, so I whispered, 'What's wrong?' He said, 'Doris died.' Oh my gosh, I felt so bad.

"You see, Doris was Paul's aunt. She and I were in the same aerobics class every Thursday morning. She seemed perfectly fine and, in fact, very healthy the last time I saw her. She couldn't work out as fast as I could but she did a fine job. I couldn't imagine what had happened. Finally Larry finished the call and I quickly asked him what happened to Doris. He said, 'Doris? I didn't say Doris, I said the horse.' I replied to him, 'What horse?' That's what I know about the horse."

My plan worked like a charm. Those FBI guys couldn't get me out of their room fast enough. They politely thanked me and off I drove, pretty sure I would never hear from them again.

Larry had his trial shortly after that. Just as I figured, they made their case against him without my help (especially since I didn't know anything anyway). The judge sentenced Larry to two years in the Federal Penitentiary in Pleasanton. Even though it was a minimum-security facility, I think he had a hard time there. To this day, I still don't know exactly what he did to warrant a prison sentence.

Mama Snort with her 13 piglets at the ranch;
(below) They're growing

Taking care of our three horses;
Part of our assortment of fowl

Baird with my handmade Christmas stockings; (below) visiting
with my good friends Helen Cummings and David Peck

Gearing up for dove hunting.

CHAPTER SIX
Befriending the Outcasts

*Bind up the brokenhearted and proclaim
liberty to the captives.*
– Isaiah 61:1

In January of 1989 I took Matt and his good friend, Brandon Roach, to go skiing at Bear Valley. That's where we all skied when we had our vacation home in Murphys. Matt loved it there and I thought a ski trip to his favorite mountain with his good friend would bring a bit of normalcy and enjoyment to his disrupted life. We stayed at the historic Murphys Hotel.

The first evening we ate at the beautiful hotel dining room and then the boys wanted to play games in our room. So I went downstairs for a nightcap and to listen to the live music. Before long a nice looking man, Donald Baptista, asked me to dance. We enjoyed each other's company and danced all evening. The boys and I stayed in Murphys and skied at Bear Valley for several days.

When we returned to Fresno, Donald and I began to date. He was a general contractor in a large subdivision outside of Murphys called Forest Meadows and had built many beautiful homes there. Coincidently, Forest Meadows is the same subdivision where Larry and I had the vacation home. Most of the time, Donald would drive the two hours from Murphys to Fresno and he would stay in a hotel for a few days at a time. Sometimes I would make the drive to Murphys to see him.

I relished spending time with Donald and I loved being back in Murphys. Our relationship developed quickly and in August of 1989 I married Donald. Following our wedding ceremony at the Northwest Church chapel in Fresno, we moved into a house Donald built in Forest Meadows. Matt, who was about 13 at the time, moved in with us. The house was two stories with the master bedroom, kitchen, and living room upstairs. Downstairs was the family room and Matt's bedroom. He enjoyed having such a nice large area all to himself.

Thinking back honestly, I probably married Donald as a way to get Larry to stop asking me to come back. But Donald actually gave me an unexpected gift. Right from the beginning he asked my opinion about things—the houses he was building, various aspects of his business dealings and the financing for his projects. He even invited me to come with him for a few client meetings. No one had ever asked my opinion about things like this, so I was quite flattered. Eventually I realized that he honestly wanted to know what I thought about things — he wasn't just being kind or polite.

Unfortunately, after some time I realized Donald had some addiction issues. He was also not as accepting of Matt as I would have liked, even though Matt was very easy going. Donald seemed to enjoy criticizing Matt about insignificant issues (like how much noise he made when he put the toilet seat down). I began to notice how critical he was of most other people including his ex-wife and his two grown daughters. I don't have much patience for negative thinkers and it seemed that, unfortunately, I had married one.

All in all, I realized Donald was not the right match for me and we divorced in June of 1993. About a year before the actual divorce, I realized it was not going to be a long-term relationship and I would have to find a job that could support Matt and me.

I decided to look for a job as executive director of a nonprofit in California. I had never written a resume before but figured I would list the organizations I founded in Kingsburg, Murphys and Fresno and say I was an executive director (since essentially that's what I was). I also decided that if anyone asked if I was paid for this work, I would truthfully say no, but if they didn't ask, I would not challenge their false assumption.

I began to scan the newspapers for potential opportunities. I quickly found an announcement for a position with CAPC. I didn't have any idea what the acronym stood for but I sent in my resume.

One day I received an exciting phone call. "Hello, this is Marianne with the Child Abuse Prevention Council in Stockton. We would like to schedule an interview with you for our executive director opening." I was thrilled and horrified at the same time. Thrilled because it was exactly the type of position I was looking for and it was only a little over an hour's drive from home. Horrified because of my personal history with child abuse.

"I can't work there! I'm sure as soon as they see me they will know I've been abused," I thought for a split second. Just around this time I was starting to remember what happened to me in my youth. But I told Marianne I would love to schedule an interview. I was hired within a few days in June of 1990 and began my next life adventure.

My friends in Murphys were horrified when they heard I would be working in Stockton because it had such a bad reputation for violence and poverty. And, as it turned out, my CAPC office was located in the middle of downtown right in the high crime area. In fact, the salesman for my first cell phone purchase pointed out that an added benefit was it could be used as a weapon since it was so large and heavy.

Undaunted, I thought, "There must be at least one good thing about Stockton. I will find it and focus on it." That's how I found the Catfish Café, which became my favorite restaurant and respite. Stockton is a 70-mile inland seaport with brackish water and the Catfish Café was a floating restaurant right on the delta. I would often sit on the deck and watch as huge ocean-going ships unloaded their cargo. Once empty, a tiny tugboat would push the ship's stern and little by little it would be turned around in the narrow channel and headed back out to sea. It was a remarkable sight.

At first I commuted by driving the hour and fifteen minutes from Murphys to Stockton and back every day. After a couple months of this grueling schedule, I made arrangements to rent an apartment in Stockton and spend a couple of nights a week there. Donald accepted this plan, but I felt a bit uncomfortable leaving Matt alone with Donald so much.

I knew there was a good chance I would be leaving Donald since I had increasingly strong instincts that I wouldn't be able to stay with him. I began to take a few more pieces of clothing and other personal items each time I went to Stockton. I did it gradually so Donald wouldn't notice. I knew he would not be happy with the idea of me leaving him for good. I bided my time until I felt I had as many things out of our house as I needed. Now I was ready, but I tried to act normally.

One night Donald had a little too much to drink, so I drove us home from dinner at our favorite restaurant, Sequoia Woods Resort in Arnold. Donald had never been violent with me in any way, but on the drive home he said, "A lot of guys, if they had a wife like you, would get a gun and shoot her." You can imagine how stunned I was after that comment. I kept a calm demeanor and put him to bed as soon as we got home.

I was pretty nervous since I realized I really didn't know him that well or know what he was capable of. But I didn't want to worry Matt. So as soon as Matt went to bed in his downstairs bedroom next to the family room, I tiptoed into his room and opened his bedroom door just a bit. Then I took my pillow and blanket and went to sleep on the family room couch downstairs. I figured if Donald decided to do something to me I could scream and Matt would wake up. But if nothing happened, at least I would be safe.

The next day I told Donald I would not be coming home anymore. He was shocked and pretty upset and refused to let me take the last of my possessions. I was relieved to be driving away from my life with Donald for the last time. He was determined that I would not receive anything of a financial nature from him. He gave me a quit claim deed on our house to sign, which I did willingly. I didn't want anything from him. I just wanted out and safe. Donald also tried to get the court to force me to pay him alimony. Since he was usually paid under the table, there was no official record of his earnings. Thankfully, the court declined and I was free.

Matt and I enjoyed our time in Stockton. He got his driver's license and a car and soon he had a job as a bus boy at the local pizza restaurant. He was even paying for his own gas and insurance. I was proud that Matt was becoming such a responsible adult. After about two years, though, that all changed. Matt came to me one day and said he wanted to go back to Fresno to live with his dad. I didn't think that was a good idea because I knew he wouldn't have the kind of individual support there that I was giving him. I also knew, though, that I would not be able to change his mind. To this day, I think this was Larry's way of getting back at me for leaving him. He knew how much Matt meant to me.

I was so sad the day Matt left me to go to Fresno because, at age 17, he was so close to creating a solid, productive life for himself. Now, I thought he was throwing it all away. This seemed out of the blue and I tried to encourage him to reconsider. I pointed out to Matt that he wouldn't have anyone to support him in Fresno, he would be just another brother. I felt abandoned and a bit betrayed because I had worked so hard to help him build a solid life for himself.

Years later I learned that instead of living with Larry, Matt was forced to live with his brother Baird because Larry's wife would not agree for Matt to live with them. Matt told me that that's when his drug use began. Baird was heavily involved with drugs and quickly Matt began using marijuana. For both boys the drug use escalated to methamphetamine. I suspect this initiated a deterioration that plagued the two boys for years.

I was really enjoying my work at CAPC. As the executive director, I provided moral and administrative support of all of our counselors who worked with the troubled families. I also served as spokesperson in the community, presenting our story at local Rotary clubs, building relationships with potential donors and soliciting support from local businesses.

It was quite a departure from my previous life, but I loved it all. Our 24-hour crisis nursery provided a safe haven for abused and neglected kids from 0-12 years old. Sometimes we had drug-exposed infants who were so tiny that it seemed their bottle was bigger than they were. We also provided in-home support and respite for families with an abusive history as well as classes for parents who were ordered by the court to learn how to be better parents.

On more than one occasion I was called in the middle of the night to rescue children and staff from an angry parent who was trying to remove a child from our nursery. As soon as I arrived, I would have everyone stand back from the windows, draw the blinds, lock the doors and remain calm. Once I assured everyone they would be safe, I would call law enforcement if the parent was out of control or, on a couple of occasions, actively trying to break down the door. It was quite a wild ride at times, but I found it very rewarding.

It was during my tenure at CAPC that I sought out counseling as a way to help me process the sexual abuse I endured from my stepfather as a child. Through the counseling sessions, I learned about the possibility of confronting my abuser. It was not recommended in all situations but it seemed to make sense for me.

In preparation for the confrontation with my dad, I wrote a one-page letter to him. I used the "sandwich approach" by beginning the letter with my thanks to him for all he had done for me and my family, then saying that the things he did to me as a child were very hurtful and ending with a reminder of how grateful I was for how he took care of me and my family. I also said I wanted him to pay for some therapy for me.

I made an appointment with my therapist to discuss my plan for confrontation. When she read my letter she cried saying, "This is the most beautiful and loving letter I've ever read." She cautioned me to be prepared for any eventuality. I wasn't sure exactly what she meant but I tried to be ready for any response he might have to the letter. I knew that most perpetrators deny the abuse, so I was prepared for that response.

I went to visit my parents on Labor Day weekend in 1991 when I was 45 years old. I told my mom that she should go take a walk or do an errand because I needed to speak with my dad alone. She was displeased when I told her the subject matter but I think she could tell I was determined, so she left in a huff. I walked down the long hallway to the family room where I found my dad sitting in his favorite recliner. After closing the heavy wooden door to the rest of the house and locking the latch I said, "Daddy I have a letter I'd like you to read. You can read it aloud or silently, but when you finish I'd like to discuss it."

I sat down on the chair next to his and tried not to look at him. He read the letter to himself and then took a big sigh saying, "I always felt bad about that. I guess I always felt like I owned you, like you were my property. Do you think the therapy will help?" I said it seemed to be helping and I'd like to stay with counseling. He agreed to pay for it. I got up from the chair, unlocked the door and walked back down the hallway.

Shortly after that my mother returned. As usual no one mentioned anything about the session. I felt like a huge burden had been lifted from my shoulders. I had successfully completed the confrontation. He had not denied it. And I was going to get more counseling.

Another powerful memory for me was when I spent time inside the state men's prison called Duel Vocational Institute (DVI) in Tracy, California. At the time all state prisons were required to do something to raise funds for victims of violence. CAPC qualified to receive these funds. I quickly became acquainted with the Arts in Corrections program where inmates would make paintings, woodwork and sculpture to sell to generate funds for us. I could see the potential for increased donations to CAPC so I decided to go to DVI to find out more and to encourage higher production.

The first time I went there they issued me a laminated photo ID pass and informed me that if there was ever a lockdown they would not bargain for my safety. For some reason, this warning didn't really bother me. I was focused on helping the inmates generate more funds for CAPC.

The prison housed 4,000 inmates but only 200 participated in the Arts in Corrections program. I went to this special area of the prison about once each month for nearly five years. I was impressed by the high quality of their artwork and they were inspired by my stories of the children they were helping through their efforts. Each year their art generated more funds.

One day a prison employee who they called "Coach" told me that some of the other inmates had heard about how the arts program was generating donations for abused children. In an effort to join in, they decided they wanted to do a run and lift-a-thon. The coach wanted me to come into their high-tech studio to make a video that he could use to encourage inmates to join the effort. I happily agreed and told them all about the children they would be helping and thanked them in advance for their caring and support. Just as I was about to leave, the coach asked, "Will you come out to help us count laps for the event?"

I stumbled a bit not knowing what that would entail, but I didn't want to say something like, "No just call me when the check is ready," so I said, "Sure."

The day arrived for the run and lift-a-thon and my lap counting duties. When I arrived at the prison, a guard met me and began to escort me to the appointed site. As we walked along this part of the facility that was unfamiliar to me, he asked, "Have you ever been to the yard?" When I said no, he patted his gun and said, "Well watch yourself out here. It's where all the action happens. But don't worry, I'm committed to protect you with my life."

As he said this, he opened a very large chain link fence and I gazed out onto a huge expanse of ground. All 4,000 inmates were out there and it felt like every eyeball was on me. I had to walk across the entire field for my lap counting duties. I had never been so scared in all my life! But I knew that I shouldn't show fear. So I walked without making eye contact with anyone, pretending I was taking a walk in the park. Thankfully it was a chilly day, so I was wearing a large coat.

When I was just getting the hang of my lap counting, the guard who had escorted me and vowed to protect me with his life told the coach he was going back. The coach reminded him he was supposed to stay and protect me. He replied, "Oh she'll be fine. I have things to do." And off he went across the field.

Shortly after that a group of six very large inmates came over to my area and asked if they could speak with me. I was pretty nervous but agreed. We walked a short distance away from the track and the spokesman for the group said, "We saw your video, Miss Cynder, and we want to thank you for letting us be part of raising money for the children." I was thrilled and near tears as I realized I was probably safer out there in the middle of the prison than I was on the streets by my office in downtown Stockton. When the event was over, I walked across the field with a very different mindset than I had earlier especially when many of the inmates greeted me with, "Thank you Miss Cynder."

After Matt left Stockton to move to Fresno, I decided to buy a home. My realtor, Floyd Bryan, did an excellent job for me and became a good friend — and later even a boyfriend for two years. My new home was a sweet little duplex located in the north of town in the middle of lots of water fountains and trees. It felt like my own little oasis and I was thrilled that I was able to buy it on my own. I planted lots of flowers, bushes and even a small Japanese maple tree with the help of my new friendly gardener, Joe. The back yard had lots of grass, flower beds and a covered patio with a cute table and chairs. I even bought a barbeque and taught myself how to use it (since only Larry and the boys did the barbequing when we lived at the ranch).

While at CAVC I worked closely with our program director, Dee Ptak, who became my very good friend. Dee and I took many fun-filled trips to Washington D.C. to fulfill the requirements of a large federal grant we had written and successfully received. Four years in a row we attended the National Council on Child Abuse and Family Violence (NCCAFV) meetings, interacting with hundreds of professionals from around the country. What an opportunity this was for learning, collaboration and relationship building! These experiences allowed me to really progress as a nonprofit executive.

My last and most touching moment at CAPC was when Katie, a 10-year-old girl being cared for at our crisis nursery, asked if she could walk with me to the "big house" (which is what they called my office area which was just across a short walkway). Katie and her younger sister were removed from her mother's custody because police found them living in their car and her drug-addicted mother was selling sex with her children for drugs. As Katie and I walked along the pathway she said trying to muster up a brave spirit, "I have a home, you know. And I'll go there someday. I just don't know where it is." I was speechless and, with a heavy heart, I gave her a big hug and assured her she was right.

After I had been at CAPC for five years, I began to yearn for a more positive working environment. I loved my work there, but it was beginning to take a toll on me. Most days I was able to juggle the two disparate functions of my job: 1) supporting and encouraging the staff as they worked with abused children and neglectful and/or incompetent parents and 2) communicating our message to the community to inform them and solicit financial support. One evening though, I was at home reviewing a video designed to train my staff on recognition and response to signs and symptoms of child abuse. I became overwhelmed with sadness and began to cry. I realized in that moment that I had reached the limit of my ability to be objective in this work. It hit too close to home for me. I don't know what tipped the scales for me because I had not struggled with the dichotomy in the past. But I knew I needed to work somewhere with a more positive mission.

So when I saw a job announcement for CEO for a regional Girl Scout council based in Santa Barbara in June of 1995, I decided to throw my hat in the ring. I liked the idea of working for Girl Scouts because I'd enjoyed my own time in Girl Scouts when I was a kid. I also liked the idea of living in Santa Barbara because it was closer to my parents' house in Manhattan Beach. But I didn't necessarily have a great impression of Santa Barbara. Perhaps I had driven through there once — and it was probably a foggy day. I thought to myself, "I think Santa Barbara is sort of a dreary place, but I'm sure I can find one thing to like about it and focus on that, like I did in Stockton." It wasn't too long before I discovered what a beautiful place it is.

Before leaving Stockton and CAPC, I wanted to bid farewell to several people, including the inmates at DVI. We had built a very trusting relationship with each other and I didn't want them to feel abandoned. I also wanted to make sure that they kept working hard to raise needed funds for CAPC. So one afternoon I drove the 20 miles to the prison. When I went inside, they said the same thing they said every time I went there, "Remember that if there is a lock down we won't bargain for your safety."

I acknowledged their comment and proceeded to walk inside with the heavy gate clinking solidly behind me. I went directly to the arts room but instead of the usual 200 guys, there were only about half that number. When I asked the reason, they said some of the people had been caught in a lockdown. I told the instructor, "After I say my farewell to the guys in the art room I will need to go to that lockdown place." He looked troubled but said he would check with Anna, the warden.

As I began to tell the guys that I would be moving away, several of them went to corners of the room to gather some of their creations from secret hiding places. One guy got a cardboard box with some newspapers. One by one the inmates gave me one of their treasures, sometimes writing their name on the bottom so I wouldn't forget them. They carefully wrapped each one and placed it inside the box.

One of these pieces sits on the mantle in my home today. It's a beautiful wooden bowl and on the bottom the inmate, whose nick name was Hippy, carved the message: "Always keep smiling and stay happy and don't forget me. Love, Hippy."

Then someone brought some folding chairs and placed them around in the center of the room, forming a circle. After we all were seated, they began telling me, one by one, what they appreciated about me and what they will miss after I'm gone. Some of them cried (which is never done in prison for fear of reprisal). Several of them said, "You are the only person in my life who saw me as just a regular person rather than a criminal." The messages were so powerful! I felt so honored to know them and humbled that they would share their feelings so deeply with me.

By now the warden gave permission for a guard to escort me to the areas of the prison that were locked down. I had never been in these spaces before and I was a little nervous but I dutifully followed along, knowing I couldn't leave without telling all of them goodbye. The first area was a double decker level of cells. "Taqua," a tall thin Black guy with a gold front tooth was the self-appointed town crier. He ran up and down the aisles exclaiming, "Miss Cynder is here, Miss Cynder is here. She wants to see you!"

When they want to show respect, they button their prison-issued blue shirts all the way to the top. When 22 of the inmates from this cell block came down the stairs to see me, they all had their shirts buttoned to the top and their hair slicked back with water. They looked like a bunch of little boys ready for mom to give them a treat.

I explained that I had to leave and I would miss them. I thanked them for all the work they did to raise funds for the children. I reminded them that, even though we were all close, they made and sold their art for the children, not for me. I encouraged them to do even more after I left. They all agreed and took turns telling me how much they would miss me.

Next it was time to go to another lockdown area. This time there was only one inmate. His name was Larry. His shirt was buttoned to the top too. He said, "Thank you for this very special moment in time." Later I thought how unusual it must have been for these guys to not only have a visitor when many of their friends and family had long forgotten them, but a visitor who asked for them by name. After one more lockdown area, it was time to go. As I walked outside into the cool night air, I felt thankful for the time I had spent with these guys and glad I could have been an encouragement to them in their time of distress.

A month after applying for the job with Girl Scouts, I was invited to have dinner with Janice Kroekel, the board president, after my interview. When I arrived at the Harbor Restaurant on Stern's Wharf, I pulled into the valet area and quickly noticed there was some sort of altercation taking place a few yards from the restaurant's front door. A man was standing next to his frightened wife who was holding their toddler's hand. The father was holding a stroller with a crying baby. I could tell the man was agitated and near a breaking point. As he yelled at his wife he picked up the stroller handles and smashed it down on the ground for emphasis, making the baby cry even louder.

I knew from my time at CAPC that agitated abusers sometimes think no one notices them. I felt helpless because I was there for a job interview and the man hadn't done anything wrong yet. So, I turned to the valet as I gave him my key and said, "If that man over there does something bad like hit his wife or one of the kids, you will call 911, right?" He looked up, noticed the little family and agreed. I knew that sometimes people just need for someone else to give them permission to act.

Then as I walked past him into the restaurant, I stared into the man's eyes for longer than was comfortable for him. I wanted him to know that someone saw him and knew fully well what he was doing. He seemed to almost shudder as if a trance had been broken. I gave the same message about calling 911 to the hostess who greeted me. She looked out the glass doors, saw the family and nodded in agreement. After an enjoyable dinner with Janice we walked outside to an empty sidewalk. I prayed for that sweet little family.

For the first several weeks I stayed in a nearby hotel and began to look for an apartment. Soon Janice said, "There's an empty apartment next to where my husband and I live. Come by today after work and see it." I loved it and moved in right away. At first I was a bit apprehensive about living next door to my board president, but I soon realized it was a perfect arrangement. We all had fun together — sharing wine on each other's deck and visiting back and forth. Her husband, Paul, even did some occasional repairs for me. I lived there for two delightful years.

My work at Girl Scouts of Tres Condados, which served the three counties of San Luis Obispo, Santa Barbara and Ventura, proved to be inspiring, fun and demanding. With over

10,000 girl members, 4,000 adult volunteers and a staff of 30 (that grew to 50 during summer camp), I was pretty busy. We had an office in each of the three counties, a 36-acre day camp property in Ventura County with several large buildings (Camp Arnaz Program Center) and an 18-acre summer camp in the mountains near Frazier Park, complete with lots of cabins and a swimming pool (Camp Tecuya).

I enjoyed spending time with the girls and their various activities, showing my appreciation to the volunteers and encouraging and training the staff. One memory that stands out for me at Camp Tecuya involves a very large mountain lion. The National Forest Service ranger said I was lucky to be here after that encounter.

I went to Tecuya toward the end of summer to help close up our summer camp where we typically served 200 girls. After spending the night in one of the cabins, I got up early the next morning — earlier than the rest of the staff. So I decided to go for a hike in the hills behind our camp which was at 5,000 feet elevation. I grabbed my plastic water bottle and off I went. After climbing about five miles I decided to sit on a large rock and enjoy some water from my bottle. Just as I was about to sit down, I spotted a very large mountain lion just a few yards in front of me. There was nothing between us except a very small bush.

I've been well-trained in outdoor survival so I knew what I should do — make noise, wave my arms over my head and act big. I couldn't do any of it — I was frozen with fear. I couldn't move as I watched him for signs indicating whether he saw me or not. His body was on a diagonal from me and he seemed to be gazing out over the hill. Next I did what you should never do — I turned around and ran, with my heart nearly pounding out of my chest. As I was running I decided I should keep an eye on the trail so I didn't fall and look over my shoulder frequently to make sure the lion wasn't chasing me. Soon I realized that if the lion wanted to get me he wouldn't follow the trail, he would go straight after me. So I just put my head down and continued running.

When I got to the bottom of the hill, the staff were awake and one of the National Forest Rangers was there to greet me. When I told him about seeing the mountain lion he said, "Boy are you lucky!" When I looked puzzled he explained, "We knew there was a lion up there because we've seen his footprints, but none of us has actually seen him, so you are lucky you saw him. Oh, and you are also lucky he didn't come after you." I felt relieved and then a bit ashamed as several of my staff chastised me for going on the hike alone rather than taking a buddy, which is the Girl Scout way. I agreed it probably wasn't a smart thing to do, but I secretly knew I would probably do it again.

The next year I drove the two hours up the mountain to help open camp for the summer season. Every year we hauled a trailer full of eight canoes down the mountain to Lake Ming so the girls could use them during camp. Camp counselors would make the hour drive with carloads of girls because there was no body of water at or near our camp. Since I was the only one who knew how to pull a trailer, I agreed to drive the trailer full of canoes to the lake.

The newly hired camp caretaker and his assistant loaded the canoes onto the trailer and hooked the trailer to our big diesel truck. My first mistake was not double checking the hitch hookup. I didn't do this for fear that the new caretaker might think I didn't trust him. So off I went along with my program director, Linda Reed, riding shotgun. My second mistake was leaving a little later than I should have to make the hour plus drive.

By the time we got to the top of the Grapevine it was already getting dark. All of a sudden I saw sparks from my rear-view mirror. I knew something was wrong and tried to assess

162

the situation while driving in the dark next to big rigs that seemed to pack several lanes. I saw the trailer swerve and knew it had come lose from the hitch. Linda was jumping up and down in her seat shouting for me to pull over immediately. I tried to tune her out because I knew I had to pull over very slowly to avoid a jackknife situation or a collision with one of the big trucks. I gradually pulled off to the side of the road and stopped only when I knew we were completely off of the freeway.

Now here we were in the dark, on the top of the Grapevine, with big rig trucks whizzing by and a heavy trailer hanging from the hitch by the chain. We dug around in the truck's side storage area and found the tire jack, carefully positioning it under the trailer's edge as close to the hitch as possible. We started to pump the jack, keeping an eye on the trailer to make sure it didn't topple over. Finally we got the trailer in place near the hitch and shoved it onto the hitch. Once we heard the loud clunk sound we knew it was in position. We locked it and reattached the chain, making sure it was all secure. I got in the driver's seat and ever so carefully drove back onto the highway. We pulled off the road as soon as we got to a service station, about five miles ahead. The bright station lights welcomed us and I breathed a little easier.

We explained the situation to the manager and he agreed we could leave the trailer with him overnight so he could check it out. Next we called camp and asked one of the staff to come pick us up. The next day someone drove us back to the truck so I could drive the canoes down to the lake. I learned a lesson that day — always double check the trailer hook-up — especially if I am driving.

Our beautiful property, Camp Arnaz Program Center, is located in Ventura's lush Ojai Valley nestled among tall oak trees. The girls and volunteers use it for day camping, training and events. Leaders take their troops there to work on various outdoor badges and prepare for larger outdoor gatherings during the year. I learned a lot about property management, water systems, easements and negotiations during my 12 years as CEO of Girl Scouts of Tres Condados.

Even though the camp property was fairly isolated, there were several families who lived in homes just behind our property. When it rained every year the creek by their homes flooded, sometimes making it hard to cross. Some of the neighbors asked if they could drive across our property when the creek flooded so they could avoid the flowing water. At first we agreed and, in fact, many of the neighbors had been driving across our property during the rainy season for several years. But over time, some families moved away and others moved in, so some of the individual homeowners changed.

One day a group of volunteers asked to meet with me. They explained that they had been camping at Arnaz and teaching their girls how to camp in the rain. They said several cars belonging to the neighbors were speeding across our property, putting the girls in danger. They demanded that I do something about it. I could tell it was potentially a dangerous situation, so I contacted our attorney, Greg Faulkner at Mullen & Henzel Law Firm. At his recommendation, we circulated a letter to all the neighbors informing them they would no longer be allowed to drive across our property, citing the danger to our girls and volunteers. Next we posted signs at the entrance and exit and installed a large chain and padlock on our back gate which leads to their area.

Needless to say, the neighbors were not happy with this new development. After they filed a million-dollar lawsuit against our Girl Scout council, the court ordered we all enter into mediation. What a fascinating process. I learned so much as I watched the mediator take turns listening to each group, make suggestions and then sometimes reach agreement.

Eventually the county built a bridge spanning the creek so the neighbors could safely reach their homes during the rainy season — but this happened after I left the organization.

One day I became aware that our very old well was becoming problematic. The engineer we hired said the best solution was for us to connect our property to the city water system. Since I was CEO it was my role to lead this fascinating process, which at one point became a bit contentious. Once again, Greg Faulkner came to our aid. After lots of paperwork and many inspections, the Casitas Municipal Water District agreed to let us connect to their system. But as we were preparing to move forward with the project, the engineer informed me that in order to install the proper lines we would have to cross private property. Now I was on the other side of the private property issue.

A man named Buzz Bonsall owned the few feet of land we needed to cross to install the water line and he was known to be difficult to deal with. Undaunted, I arranged a meeting with Bonsall, Greg and the engineer. In preparation for the meeting Greg and I crawled all over rocks, across creek beds and under very low culverts to identify the exact location of the easement we would be requesting from Bonsall. He was pretty stubborn at first, but I kept reminding him about the girls who depended upon the water connection. Finally after many meetings he agreed to give us the tiny easement for our water connection. The project was a success and dependable water is guaranteed for the property for many years to come, but it sure was an excellent learning opportunity.

In 1998, three years after I started working at Girl Scouts, my dad passed away from a massive coronary. When my brother, Rick, called to tell me about it I was devastated. Even though my dad had done some pretty bad things to me as a youngster, he was also my rock. He believed in me and valued my intellectual curiosity and determination to succeed. Now he was gone.

I began grief counseling sessions through Hospice of Santa Barbara with Joann Talbot. She helped me process my sorrow as well as the dual role he had played in my life. I will be forever grateful to her for helping me navigate this turbulent time in my life.

I wanted to make sure he had a proper funeral service because I have always felt bad when a funeral officiate makes it obvious he didn't know the deceased. I was determined that wouldn't happen for my dad — so I decided to do it myself.

I found his personal Bible with several scriptures underlined and chose some of them to include in the service. I tried to invite my brother, Rick, to be part of the service by reading some scripture, but he declined. I told the pastor what I would like his sermon to focus on and I played the role of family spokesperson. As I looked out into the audience I saw people from his many years of working for Rockwell and Hughes Helicopter, a few neighbors and some friends and co-workers of mine who had come from Santa Barbara to support me. My mother and grandmother sat in the front row in constant tears.

Leading this service was one of the most difficult things I had ever done. I wanted to make my comments about my dad personal, but I didn't want to cry. It was a tricky task. In fact, the night before the service I called my good friend, David Peck. I told David about what I planned to do and that I was really nervous about it. David asked, "What are you the most concerned about?" I replied that I didn't want to break down and cry uncontrollably and make everyone uncomfortable.

David said, "I want you to get a picture of you standing in the pulpit and completing the service. Can you picture this?" I said yes. Then David said, "Now I want you to picture yourself standing at the pulpit and breaking down in tears, crying beyond control." I said, "I can't see that." David said, "I thought so. You'll be fine." And I was — but it was hard.

I began driving back home after the funeral service, and just as I came around the bend of the 101 freeway at the Rincon area, I came upon a blazing sunset. The sun was slowly sinking down into the ocean right in front of me. I became transfixed, unable to take my eyes off of the sun. I thought that if I drove fast enough and got home before it actually set, my dad wouldn't really be dead. This crazy idea held me tightly in its grip until, finally, the sun ducked behind the horizon. I was overcome with tears. But then I looked up and saw that the setting sun had transferred its brilliant color to the nearby clouds, lighting them up in a wash of color. I thought this could be seen as a sign of how my dad's life had touched so many people in so many ways.

A year later, in 1999, my grandmother (my dad's mother) passed away where she lived in Ambridge, Pennsylvania. During the five-hour plane ride to attend her funeral, I got a little bored and decided to memorize a poem. I happened to have John O'Donahue's book *Anam Cara* with me, so I memorized the poem on the first page, *Benacht* (which means blessing in Gaelic). It's a beautiful poem and very long, but I had plenty of time, so I committed the entire poem to memory.

When I arrived at the funeral, I was greeted by many cousins, aunts and uncles. It was a dark room with folding chairs lined up in classroom style. Even though the funeral was being held at the church she attended for years, I found out that they had a new pastor who had never even met my grandmother. I asked my relatives who was going to stand up to share stories and memories of my grandmother and was told that only the pastor would be speaking.

I knew right then that I would have to be the family spokesperson once again. I couldn't let my grandmother's funeral be impersonal — someone had to speak about her life and how she had blessed so many with her sweet spirit. I asked the pastor if he would be inviting people up to speak about my grandmother. He said he planned on it but that everyone he spoke with had declined. I told him I wanted to do it.

When he asked for people to share memories, I walked up to the pulpit. I had not prepared any remarks but I had plenty of lovely memories of my grandmother; which I shared. As I gazed out into the audience I realized that every one of these people had known my whole life that she wasn't really my grandmother but no one had ever said anything. That I would be the only one to stand up for her struck me as incredibly ironic. I ended my remarks by reciting the poem I had memorized on the plane ride. It gave everyone a gentle, encouraging message to ponder. (The reader can find this poem in a special section of this book.)

An assortment of the artwork made by inmates of the Duel Vocational Institute for our Arts in Corrections program; (below) I accept a check from inmates and staff

Inmates making art projects for our program

Some of the concepts were wild, but they were good sellers

A thank you speech; A light moment with inmate Michael Grant

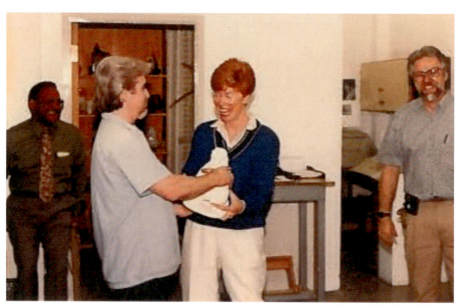

CHAPTER SEVEN
Adventures Galore

Courage is not the absence of fear or despair;
it is the capacity to continue on despite them,
no matter how great or overwhelming
they become.
— Mark Twain

I began working as CEO of Girl Scouts of Tres Condados, serving the tri-county area, in June of 1995. A representative from the local United Way met with me shortly after I began working there. She said that United Way had decided to add the nonprofit sector to their annual campaign cabinet, their workplace giving program. She wanted to know if I would be willing to be in charge of it. I hesitated because I didn't know many people in town yet, but I figured this might be a good way to meet people, so I agreed.

The idea was that each business conducted a campaign in their workplace to raise funds for United Way. Now nonprofits were going to be invited to conduct similar drives. I looked through our financial records to see how much Girl Scouts had raised for the United Way campaign in past years, since I thought it would be important for my organization to set a good example for the others. I discovered that we had contributed very little.

I decided to create an incentive for my staff to contribute to that year's campaign. I asked several staff members and even some of the girls for their suggestions. It was decided that if 100 percent of staff contributed to the campaign, I would kiss a pig. I quickly agreed because I figured there was no way they could reach that level of giving.

I was wrong. All of the staff enthusiastically gave to the workplace giving drive and they were thrilled that their new CEO would now have to kiss a pig. United Way dressed someone up in a large pig costume for their big celebration, and I had to kiss it while everyone clapped loudly. But the girls had another idea. One of them was a member of the 4-H Club and she was raising pigs. She decided she would bring one of her animals to our headquarters for me to kiss in front of staff, volunteers and other girls. That made for some pretty exciting theater, but I didn't tell them that it wasn't nearly as crazy and gross as they thought it was going to be for me — because I used to raise pigs when I was rearing my children.

Next, it was time for me to organize a meeting of all the leaders of the nonprofits in the region to let them know about United Way's plan to include nonprofits as their own category for the year's fundraising. I hadn't met most of the executives yet, but I used the opportunity to introduce myself. I cheerily announced that the nonprofits would have their own special place in the campaign this year. Silence filled the room and I noticed many squirming nervously in their seats.

I discovered that most of the organizational leadership was angry at United Way because of a funding shortfall the previous year that had a devastating impact on them. So they weren't eager to help United Way raise money.

I invited them to meet me at my office to discuss it further. We had many meetings over the next several months where they vented their anger at Paul Didier, United Way's CEO, blaming him for the shortfall. They demanded a meeting with him. I figured that he had enough on his plate since the campaign had begun and I didn't think anything positive would come from such a meeting. So I invited them to my office for yet another meeting. I said, "Let's think of a project we could all do together for the community with or without the help of United Way."

The mood changed as they voiced many exciting ideas. The most popular one was to have a summer camp program in the park for low-income children. Each nonprofit would contribute its own expertise. We decided to call it *Fun in the Sun*. I met with Paul to tell him about the plan after we completed our program design. I told him that United Way would be invited to participate and contribute if they liked, but it wasn't necessary. He was mildly in favor of trying the idea. He still didn't know that the plan had grown out of such anger and distrust and that I had shielded him from the consequences.

Five nonprofits worked together for three years to create a beautiful day camp experience for many local low-income children. United Way was impressed with the growth of the program and offered to take over the leadership and an increased amount of funding. They also enlisted the help of several other nonprofits and opened it up for businesses to participate, as well. Today *Fun in the Sun* has grown into one of the largest and most popular programs of United Way, involving hundreds of volunteers and many nonprofits and businesses.

I remember when I initially came to Santa Barbara and attended my first United Way fundraising event. It was a fancy affair held at the elegant Coral Casino with over 200 guests in attendance. I stood just inside the entrance, gazing around at all of the lavish décor and impressive crowd — none of whom I knew. It was my job to meet people and mingle with these attendees, but I felt self-conscious and somewhat embarrassed. I didn't know what to do first.

In a flash I said to myself, "Pretend all of these people have come to your home and it is your job to make them feel welcome." Before long I was meeting people and enjoying lively conversations. I've used that lesson on many occasions over the years and also taught others this secret trick of feeling comfortable in new situations.

I benefited from many leadership development opportunities while serving at Girl Scouts. There were 400 Girl Scout councils in the country and the national organization conducted many conferences, bringing in top-notch presenters such as Jim Collins, Frances Hesselbein, Stephen Covey and Peter Drucker. I eagerly attended all of these meetings and devoured the various books and materials. One of my favorites was Frances Hesselbein's admonishment that leaders should focus on their "being" rather than their "doing." She said a leader should first know who they are and what values they hold dear. Their actions should always flow from their belief system. That advice has served me well for many years.

One of my favorite approaches to leadership has always been as a servant leader. The premise of this style is that the most effective leaders are those who see themselves as a servant first and a leader second. The servant leader focuses primarily on the growth and well-being of each of their staff members. Sharing power and putting the needs of others first helps co-workers develop and perform at higher levels. This, in turn, creates a stronger team and organization. It has always given me great pleasure to pass these ideas on to my staff to help them develop in their career. Of course, this approach requires that co-workers are competent and committed. I've noticed that those employees who don't respond well to this method of leadership usually self-select to work somewhere else. I have consistently had the good fortune to work with top notch co-workers.

One of the first organizations I joined when I relocated to Santa Barbara was the Downtown Rotary Club. I made so many friends there, found board members for Girl Scouts, and developed relationships with donors. I loved sitting in the Reagan Room at the Doubletree Hotel on Fridays, eating lunch while gazing out at the beautiful beach walk area. One day they had a raffle with the main prize being an all-expense paid trip anywhere in the world. I bought a few tickets and gave them to the member in charge, but I wasn't able to attend the meeting on the day they pulled out the winning ticket.

I received a phone call from my friend and fellow Rotarian, Robert Dibley, announcing that they pulled my ticket out as the winner. I was stunned. I don't think I had ever won anything before, and certainly not such a big prize. I tried to think of all my options but kept coming back to a trip to Ireland. I had always wanted to go there and since my mother told me I had Irish heritage, it made this choice even more attractive. I always preferred active vacations, so I began looking for available bike rides on the Internet. Before long, I chose one, made my plane reservations and was off on my grand adventure.

My plane left from Los Angeles, then on to Heathrow and then landed in Galway City for my seven-day biking vacation with Irish Cycling Safaris. Once checked into my hotel, I met the group — which consisted of 17 women from all over the world and John McDermott, our trip leader, who was actually a schoolteacher. My friend, Lisa Lundquist, with whom I had worked at CAPC in Stockton, accompanied me on the trip.

Every day we gathered to hear about the route we would take and where we would meet up at the end of the day. There was always a hard way with hills and an easier, flatter route. I always chose the more difficult path and Lisa would choose the less challenging route. Everything was so green with lots of fluffy sheep everywhere I looked. Thankfully there were hardly any cars, so the riding was without a lot of hazards. On the fifth day, we rode to Croagh Patrick and a few of us climbed the steep 2,500-foot mountain. The word Croagh means cone-shaped mountain in Gaelic and the story is told that St. Patrick climbed to the top to throw all the snakes into the sea — which is why there are no snakes in Ireland. At least that is the story.

Climbing that mountain was an incredible experience. Locals consider it a pilgrimage to honor St. Patrick, so as people walk up or down the mountain they greet each other with one word — "Pilgrim." When I got about two-thirds of the way up, it got even steeper with round, slick rocks sliding over each other making it hard to get a foothold. I had to squat down low to be able to continue climbing and coming down the mountain was even more challenging. When I got home, I read a travel book on Ireland that I had neglected to read beforehand. It said, "We don't recommend climbing the final third of the mountain because it is very steep and many people are injured coming down." Most of our group didn't go all the way to the top, but I'm glad I did.

Later that afternoon we were preparing to ride the remainder of the 30-mile journey through the beautiful Delphi Valley into the quiet village of Leenane. As we rode down the hill into Leenane, I intentionally positioned myself at the end of the line of cyclists because I always carried a first-aid kit and wanted to be in a good position in case anyone needed help. We were riding in a line at a pretty quick pace when the metal water bottle belonging to Helen, the cyclist directly in front of me, fell off and landed right in line with my front tire. I hit it and went flying over the handlebars right into a stone bridge. I don't remember many details, but I recall seeing my blood all over the road.

John called the ambulance and, as we waited, one of the riders fashioned a sling out of scarves for my injured right arm. The ambulance finally arrived and drove me over a very rough road for an hour to the hospital in Galway. I was glad when Lisa insisted on coming with me in the ambulance. I felt every bump because my injuries were so extensive. Thankfully I was wearing a helmet because it was destroyed instead of my head. In fact, John asked me if he could keep the helmet to demonstrate to his students the importance of wearing a helmet.

I barely remember being x-rayed but soon after a doctor came out and said in a very harsh voice, "There is nothing broken." I replied, "Oh gosh, why am I in so much pain and can hardly breathe?" He barked, "I do not know. I am not in your body. But there is nothing broken. You are free to go." Despite the fact that I explained how my head hurt and that my thinking was very muddled, he never brought up any concerns over a head injury.

I thanked him and off I went to figure out how to get back to the hotel. I had indeed banged my head pretty hard and I just couldn't think straight. Plus, the doctor basically said I was okay. So I thought to myself, "Just buck up, the doctor said you're fine."

I still don't remember how I got back to the hotel but as soon as I lay down on the bed I felt so much pain that I knew I wouldn't be riding the next day. I called John and told him. Early the next morning I was in such agony that I knew I had to go home. We were just a little over halfway through our seven-day trip and I'm not a quitter, but all I could think of was getting home. So about 5:00 a.m. I called a taxi to take me to the airport. When he arrived, I hauled my heavy suitcases down the steep stairs and put them in the cab (I was still remembering that the doctor said I was fine).

When I arrived at the airport with my luggage, I went to the ticket counter and asked if I could get on the next plane from Galway to Heathrow. The woman said, "It's Labor Day weekend so you'll have to be on stand-by. Go sit over there and I'll let you know if there's a seat left." I wasn't thinking straight because of my obvious head injury, so it never occurred to me to explain that I had been injured and needed help. I just went over to the bank of chairs and sat down. After what seemed like a long time, I went back to the counter to inquire about a seat. She said there was one seat left and I could have it. I gratefully shuffled down the walkway onto the plane and took the only remaining seat. My brain was foggy and my body hurt all over.

When the plane arrived at the Heathrow Airport, a short impish looking porter arrived at my seat with a wheelchair and motioned for me to sit in it. I thought there was a mistake. No one knew I was hurt. I asked if he was sure the wheelchair was for me. He never spoke but just gestured for me to sit in the chair. I gingerly got up and sat down as instructed.

Then I was off for a wild ride. Heathrow is enormous and this porter, who never said one word, whisked me up one corridor and down another, up multiple elevators and through large crowds of travelers. I closed my eyes when I became dizzy.

We finally arrived at the gate for the plane to Los Angeles. I asked the gate attendant if I could get on the plane. I had no idea how the porter knew where I needed to go. He seemed almost like a real-life angel. The attendant quickly replied, "This is a busy weekend and the plane is full. Sit over there and I'll call you if there's a seat left." The porter deposited me in a seat as instructed and off he went without a word.

Right at the moment when I was thinking I should go check in with the gate attendant to see if there is a seat left, the diminutive porter reappeared with his wheelchair and motioned for me to sit in it. As soon as I sat down he rolled me onto the plane and motioned me to sit in the only seat left on the plane, in the front row. Once again he vanished without a word. I felt relieved to have a seat but I was in so much discomfort. All I could do was sit there in pain without moving or even speaking with my handsome, male seatmate.

When we were five or six hours into the 11-hour flight I said to myself, "Hey I think I am in sitting in business class. I think this is where they give you champagne." I asked the flight attendant for some champagne. When she brought the glass I drank it right down and said to her, "I need a lot of champagne and I need it now, please." After a couple more glasses of bubbles the pain subsided. I sighed and thought, "Alright, I think I'll be okay."

At that point, I could actually have a conversation with my seatmate. I learned his name was Hank and told him about the bike accident and that I was on my way home to Santa Barbara. Hank said he was a professor at UCSB and was on his way to Santa Barbara as well. When we arrived at the Los Angeles airport, Hank helped me to the ticket counter where the attendant reiterated that I would have to wait as stand-by. At the last moment, she said there was one seat left (it happened to be right next to Hank). I boarded the plane and was off to Santa Barbara.

While on the short flight home, Hank said his girlfriend was picking him up at the Santa Barbara airport and offered to drop me off at home. I gratefully accepted his kind offer.

When we arrived at my charming mother-in-law type cottage in the middle of the Hope Ranch estates, he carried my luggage inside and bid me farewell. Of course, I thanked them both profusely. The first thing I wanted to do was lay down on my bed but as soon as I stretched out I felt such pain that I immediately struggled to get off the bed and onto my feet.

Now I was standing in the dark in the middle of my living room, not knowing what to do. My brain was rattled and every part of my body ached. I couldn't think of a solution — all I wanted to do was go to sleep. I picked up my portable phone and dialed my neighbor Kathy's number. She lived just across the walkway in a similar cottage. Kathy immediately came over. After assessing the situation, she brought me an old crusty blue pain pill she found in her medicine chest and arranged pillows on my living room futon so I could recline a bit. After Kathy covered me with a blanket, she returned home. Thankfully I was able to sleep.

I woke up at 5:00 the next morning thinking I had plenty of time to get ready to go to the 9:00 mass at the Old Mission (which is where I went every Sunday). I knew better than to try driving myself there, so I asked Kathy. She said she wanted to take me to Cottage Hospital's Emergency Room for x-rays but I explained that I already had x-rays at the hospital in Ireland and the doctor said I was fine. She reluctantly drove me to the Mission.

I found a seat in the second row from the front, which was exactly where I usually sat. Part way through the mass I began to feel nauseated. I carefully let myself out the side door and into the bathroom just down the hall, where I vomited. After rinsing my mouth out I quietly returned to my seat. When it was time for communion, I rose with the others and took my place in line. I took the host from the priest and walked over to take the cup from the deacon, George. He looked at me and motioned for his wife, Clare, who was sitting in the front row, to come over. When she did he said, "Something is wrong with Cynder, I hardly recognize her. You need to take her home right away."

Clare drove me home and helped me lay down on my futon. After she left, I had the feeling I should let someone know there was something wrong with me. The only person I could think of was my friend, Sister Helen Heher, I had visited at the Benedictine Monastery in Erie, Pennsylvania. I don't know why it never occurred to me to call my mother, or my co-workers, or local friends or any of my kids. I did know that Helen and her fellow sisters would actively pray for me. I guess I still figured I was fine.

As it turned out, Sister Helen thought I sounded very strange on the phone and was worried about me. She was good friends with Kristin Frascella and Linda Reed, both of whom I worked with at Girl Scouts. Helen called Kristin to tell her to check on me and then Kristin called Linda. Kristin and Linda were both busy so Linda called her sister, Jo Little. By now my neighbor Kathy had come over to check on me and insisted on taking me to Cottage Hospital. When Jo called to check on me, I explained I was on my way to Cottage. Jo said she would meet me there.

As soon as I arrived at the hospital a nurse gave me a shot of morphine because I was in such pain. What we didn't know at the time was that among other injuries soon to be discovered, my lung had collapsed. So the morphine further depressed my system. As I lay on the gurney, I thought to myself, "Well I guess it's time for me to go." As I thought this, I seemed to drift out of my body and hover near the ceiling looking down on myself. Later Jo told me that at that moment the nurse ran down the hallway yelling, "Help, this woman is having a cardiac arrest!" Of course, I don't remember any of this. I just recall that I woke up in a hospital bed upstairs.

Dr. Naomi Parry examined me and determined that I had broken ribs, a collapsed lung, a bleeding liver and a traumatic brain injury. I also had multiple contusions, several hematomas and my bike pedal had gone into my leg to the bone. Dr. Parry couldn't believe that I had survived the plane ride home alone with such severe injuries. I was in the hospital for 10 days while they evaluated and treated my wounds. I was released to the care of Dr. Parry and a neurologist, Dr. Harbaugh. My physical injuries healed after a month or so but Dr. Harbaugh continued treating my head injury for a year.

When I expressed frustration at how long the healing was taking, he said, "You have the worst head injury a person can have and still be alive, so be patient with yourself."

Dr. Parry also referred me to Michael Luan who was a chiropractor and acupuncturist specializing in cranial-sacral work. He was very intuitive and immediately recognized that I had serious injuries the moment I walked into his office. His work was very instrumental in my healing process.

Most days I just lay on my futon with the sliding door open so I could hear the birds through the screen door. My friends, Kate Silsbury and Dodie Little, brought over food and meals and kept me company. My landlady, Kate Bird, wanted to comfort me and often brought me a little dish of ice cream.

My buddies, Andy and Annie Clark, came over one day and asked what they could do for me. When I couldn't think of anything, they got busy and swept my patio and cleaned up my yard. I asked them to drink the beer in my refrigerator because

I wasn't much of a beer drinker. They gladly complied. Father Vince from the Mission came by several times to pray for me. All in all, I was well taken care of. I just didn't have much energy, my thinking was fuzzy and I slept a lot. Of course, my neighbor Kathy kept a close eye on me.

After a month or so, I was strong enough to go back to work at Girl Scouts. I couldn't drive myself, so each day one of my staff would pick me up and drive me home. One staff member, Jena Jenkins, decided to take matters into her own hands by organizing a team of caretakers for me. She created an itinerary of duties and then invited everyone to sign up for a shift. She arranged for people to drive me to work, bring me lunch, take me to the various doctor appointments and drive me home. Jena declared, "When you drive Cynder to the doctor you have to go in with her and write down what the doctor says because she can't remember anything. And then you have to make sure she follows instructions."

I healed gradually during the year following the accident. Everything seemed in slow motion — my mental and physical functioning was at a pretty low level. It was so contrary to my usual abundance of energy and curious mind. I couldn't even manage to be frustrated because everything was so foggy. But thanks to great friends and staff watching after me I pronounced myself "healed" after a year. I did (and still do) however, have a few remaining issues: a little short-term memory loss from time to time, sensory overload when the environment is too chaotic and an inability to cope with noise or commotion. All in all, I know I am very lucky to be alive and grateful to have healed so completely.

When I returned from Ireland I had to ask for a leave of absence from my Master's program at University of Phoenix because I couldn't focus on the computer screen or complete any of the assignments. Thankfully they granted my request, and I was able to resume my studies after a couple of months. Sometime later, when it was nearing time for graduation, I received a request from the university asking if I would consider speaking at the graduation ceremony. I was honored and thrilled to be asked but I was nervous about the idea because I still had some short-term memory loss and crowds and loud noise bothered me a lot. But I agreed to do it because I didn't want to pass up this unique opportunity.

When I arrived at the graduation, I learned there were 6,000 people in the audience. I was deeply afraid that I would forget my speech or get flummoxed by the crowds. But thankfully my speech went smoothly and was very well received. I was pretty proud of myself — and I still am.

Two years later, in September of 2002, I decided I wanted to go on an extended backpacking trip. I already had a lot of the equipment because of all the camping I did with Girl Scouts, but I made a list of what I needed and went to REI for the lightest gear they had. I identified an outfitter that led 10-day backpacking trips throughout Southern Utah. I signed up and carefully followed all of their instructions on packing, preparation, and driving directions. I was pretty excited because I had never been on such a long and arduous journey like this, especially all by myself. As it turned out, there were six couples on the trip and me. This meant the couples could share the weight burden between themselves, but I had to carry the 50-pound pack by myself. Thankfully I was strong and it worked out fine.

I met them all in St. George, Utah and we proceeded to drive the 40-mile washboard road to the trailhead in Escalante National Park. I drove my relatively new copper-colored, stick-shift Saturn and provided transportation to two other hikers. I had never been on such a bumpy road before — the jarring route seemed unending. Finally we arrived at the site, parked our cars, loaded up all of our gear and headed to the trailhead.

The Grand Staircase rock formations we walked through were incredibly beautiful, towering over the red rock landscape. I had never seen anything so beautiful! We hiked several miles to our first campsite. Even though my pack was heavy, it was fairly comfortable and I was glad that my hiking boots were serving me well. I was surprised to notice that we were the only people out there—it was like our own little world.

After setting up our tents and organizing our campsite, each of us put together a day pack and hiked a mile or so to the Escalante River. We actually walked through the river, with the chilly water advancing to our waist in some areas. It was pretty hot, so the cool water felt good. Just as we rounded the bend of the river I looked up to the top of a massive rock formation with a hole in the top and saw an eagle fly right through the hole. I was in awe!

We took many day hikes during the 10-day period and made camp at three different locations. We traversed the Grand Staircase rock formations, swam in freezing cold pools of water and explored the Anastazi cave drawings. After this incredibly exhilarating and tiring trip it was time to head back. We piled all of our gear into our respective cars and began the long drive down the 40-mile washboard road.

But now there was a big problem — it had been raining while we were gone and the narrow road was covered in a sort of mud soup. I had to keep my eyes on the road and feel the car's movement every second so we wouldn't slip over the edge of the road down into the deep ravine below — as many 4-wheel drive trucks had already done. I was glad for the stick shift because it gave me good control, especially at the slow speed we had to drive.

It was important to me to get back to our hotel at the appointed date and time because I had to log onto my school site to get credit for a class I was taking for my Master's program with University of Phoenix, which I had started just before the trip. This was before modern-day Wi-Fi and I knew that the dial-up modem could present a challenge. Everyone was talking about how they wanted to take a shower and eat dinner when we got back, but I was focused on getting connected to my class, regardless of how dirty or hungry I was.

Just then I saw a big problem. The heavy rain that fell while we were gone had created a flash flood that was blocking the road back to town. At that point I didn't really know what a flash flood was. I had heard the term but didn't know what it meant. I just saw it as a bunch of water obstructing my path to my goal of logging into my class. I was determined to get through.

I quickly devised a plan. I positioned my car about 25 yards from the water, put it in park and started walking toward the flooded area. I wanted to walk in the water to see where the highest side was so I could aim for that to get across. Once I determined it was higher on the left side I walked back to the car. My two hiker passengers were very nervous about my plan. I calmly explained my plan to them and said they could wait on this side of the flood and I would send someone to get them later or they could stay in my car. They decided to stay in the car.

My plan worked perfectly! I got up speed and then downshifted and punched the accelerator just as I got to the water. The car shot through the water like a rocket and we made it safely to the other side. It was only after I got home and told someone the story that I found out what a flash flood is and how dangerous it can be.

After many false starts (including moving a couch away from the wall so I could access the modem) I was able to log onto my class and write a short paper to get credit. Of course, the dinner and shower felt divine when I finally got to them!

In June of 1995, shortly after I started my new position at Girl Scouts, our HR manager walked into my office and asked for my vacation dates. Vacation was not even on my radar, especially since up to that point I had never taken one alone. I told her I didn't have any dates but she insisted that collecting every staff member's vacation dates was part of her job. I gave her some dates and began to wonder where I would go.

My parents had owned a nice condo on the Big Island of Hawaii in Kona for many years and we had gone there often together. I decided this would be a good place for my vacation. After purchasing my plane ticket, making arrangements to use the condo and packing my suitcase, I left for my 10-day Hawaii trip. I felt like Alice in Wonderland because everything was so new. I wasn't used to going on such an adventure by myself and didn't know what to expect. When I arrived at the Kailua-Kona Airport, I gathered a big selection of trip brochures describing all sorts of outdoor activities. I got settled into the condo and spread the pamphlets on the dining room table so I could begin to make plans.

Every day after breakfast I would go on an adventure, return home to shower, plan the next day's adventure, put on a sundress and go to a fancy hotel on the water to order a Mai Tai and watch the sunset.

The first day I made reservations for a kayaking trip. I had never been kayaking, so the idea was pretty thrilling. When I arrived I discovered that the rain had driven away the others with reservations and I was there alone with the tour guide. After teaching me the basics of maneuvering and paddling a kayak, we launched out into the ocean.

I was glad to have all of his attention since I didn't really know what I was doing, but I caught on pretty quickly. We paddled out past the waves and then dropped anchors to keep the kayaks from drifting. Then we dove down several feet beneath the surface and the guide pointed to an octopus. He raised it up and it squirted out a black inky substance. After admiring the octopus for a while, we returned it to its home.

Visiting Hawaii and creating impromptu adventures became my preferred way of vacationing over the next several years. I visited Kauai, Maui, Oahu and the Hilo and Kona sides of the Big Island. Each time I had new and exciting escapades.

I drove to the top of Haleakala on Maui just before dawn; where it was so elevated that the temperature was below freezing. I then rode a bicycle the 26 miles to the bottom of the steep hill. Thrilling! I hiked the Iao Needle in Maui's Iao Valley years before it became a tourist attraction. Just as the character in one of my favorite books — *The Lion, The Witch and The Wardrobe* — I walked through the thick bushes into a wonderland stretching for miles along a meandering stream. I never saw a soul that day and didn't worry about getting lost because I could follow the stream back to the entrance.

I sat under a lush Koa tree and proceeded to eat the lunch I carried in my backpack and then meandered through this magical forest. Many hours later I emerged from the secret glade and headed back to my condo.

While on Maui I also rented a car and drove the long, windy road to Hana. I'm glad I had this experience but I probably don't feel the need to do it again because I got so sleepy on this long drive. I remember driving faster the sleepier I got, thinking it would help keep me awake; looking back I realize that probably wasn't the best strategy. Thankfully I made it back intact.

I hiked the famous 11-mile Kalalau Trail on Kauai, moving along the stunning Na Pali Coast to the Hanakapiai Falls and then on to Kalalau Valley. There weren't many people on the trail that day because the recent rain created a muddy, treacherous path. The sheer drop-off to the rocks and waves below required sure footing. I couldn't resist hiking that trail that day — I was just really careful and kept my eyes focused ahead. When I returned to my hotel, I was absolutely filthy and covered in mud. I felt bad for the chambermaid because no matter how hard I tried I couldn't get all the mud out of the bathtub.

One year several of my fellow Girl Scout CEOs asked if I wanted to go scuba diving with them on the Big Island. I said, "Sure that sounds like fun." I didn't tell them that I had never been scuba diving. I was hoping I could learn and get certified before the trip — which was three months away. I quickly signed up for scuba lessons at Anacapa Dive Center in Santa Barbara. The first few sessions were in their large swimming pool.

As soon as I climbed into the wetsuit and put on the big tank, regulator and fins, I realized that my long history with claustrophobia would be a problem. Still I was determined to go diving with my friends, which meant I had to complete my scuba certification. The first of the required three dives was from Butterfly Beach. As I walked across the warm sand on that hot day I felt claustrophobic before I even got in the water. I told my assigned diving partner that if I had to go back to shore early he should just keep going.

As I swam further out into the ocean the panic grew. What if I couldn't get out fast enough and couldn't breathe? Once again I remembered my resolve to complete the dive. I calmly said to myself, "Okay you have two choices. You can go back up to the top and stop the dive or you can go a little further and take a closer look at that fish and the reef over there." The more I looked at the underwater mystery unfolding before me, the less panicky I felt. Whenever I felt anxious I made myself find something interesting to investigate on the ocean floor.

After successfully finishing the beach dive, it was time for the two required boat dives. We all boarded the Truth dive boat and set out for the three-hour ride to the Channel Islands to begin our dive. I used much of this travel time to remind myself about my newly acquired skill at ignoring the fear and focusing on the beauty below. Jumping into the cold Pacific waves off of Anacapa Island was pretty scary, but once I was in the water I began to feel confident. I hurried beneath the surface to find something beautiful to keep my mind off of the dread. Before long I was feeling comfortable and completely enjoying the ethereal beauty of the coral reef and fascinating types of marine life.

I felt so proud of myself when I completed the certification. I had a wonderful time in Hawaii with my friends and never told them about my newly acquired certification. I even got a tattoo of a dolphin on my shoulder by a local tattoo artist while my friends cheered me on from the sidelines.

While serving as CEO of Girl Scouts I developed close friendships with many of my board members, including Cathy Steinke, who was the HR Director for Santa Barbara Bank & Trust. One day Cathy invited me to go with her to church at the Old Mission. I said, "Oh Cathy, I can't go to the Mission." When she asked why I replied, "Because I think it's Catholic."

She said, "Of course it is." I responded, "I can't go to a Catholic church because they have all these rules about when to sit and stand and what to say. I won't know what to do and I'll embarrass you." She assured me it would be fine and said, "Besides we're all going to brunch afterward."

That next Sunday I took a seat with Cathy near the front by the aisle. As I turned to watch the processional, I was transfixed by the beauty and symbolism. Each gesture of the priest and others in the procession brought to mind a scripture — my mind was like a computer on steroids connecting each movement and symbol with a different scripture. It was as though all of the Bible reading and study I had done over the years was coming to life as a carefully orchestrated play right before my eyes.

It wasn't long before I was deeply immersed in life at the Mission and went through the process of becoming a Catholic. I served as a lector, a finance committee member, a Eucharistic minister and I even taught RCIA class for the adults who wanted to become Catholic. Every Sunday, for many years, I enjoyed a rich spiritual experience at the Mission.

One day Cathy told me she wanted me to meet Michael McGrath, a friend of hers. She introduced us during brunch at Harry's Restaurant following mass at the Mission. At first, Michael and I accompanied Cathy and her partner, Mark Gross, to dinner and various events. Michael and I quickly hit it off and began to date frequently.

Michael was a great dancer and we often went to SoHo to dance after dinner at The Chase or one of his other favorite restaurants. He had a great sense of humor and was very charming. Michael had served as a public defender for Santa Barbara County for 35 years. He was also a staunch Catholic and beloved member of the Mission, attending mass every day of the week. The worst thing he could ever say about someone (usually a judge) was, "Oh he's hard to love."

One evening, after about six months of dating, he took me to El Encanto Restaurant for a romantic dinner. After our nightcap we walked out to the balcony where he asked me to marry him. When I said yes, he put a beautiful diamond ring on my finger. Six months after that we were married at the Old Mission.

Father Vince who conducted our pre-marital counseling and officiated our wedding ceremony, along with Father Virgil, told Pat, their assistant, "Hurry, bring the cameras, this will be the best wedding ceremony ever!" Because of my deep knowledge of scripture and my love of the Catholic rituals I wanted to be sure that every part of the ceremony reflected Michael and my beliefs.

As we planned the ceremony Father Vince would often say, "Oh we don't usually include that in a wedding ceremony." For example, I wanted the priest to be the first to walk down the aisle holding the cross up high but this is usually only part of a regular Sunday mass. I wanted the initial focus to be on the cross and all it represents rather on the bride and groom. And I wanted a deacon to follow with an incense urn to represent our prayers as sweet fragrance to God. This, too, was normally reserved for Sunday mass.

The stunning Old Mission was packed to capacity on our wedding day, February 28, 1997. Jane Mauer's angelic voice resounded from atop the nave throughout the church, blessing every ear with sweet melodies. Madeline and Nicole, Michael's two daughters, gave the Epistle and Old Testament readings, Father Virgil read the Gospel, and Father Vince gave a touching homily.

When we were planning the wedding reception I told Michael that I learned that Catholics like pot-lucks and red wine. I suggested that we invite our guests to bring their favorite dish for the reception rather than a wedding gift. We hired two people to dress in formal attire and receive the food as wedding attendees drove into the Mission parking lot. They put the dishes in the refrigerator or oven, as appropriate.

Once the reception started, these same people kept the food coming out at optimum temperature. Of course there was plenty of red wine. Later people raved about the food (mainly because attendees made their favorite recipes since it was our "gift"). We hired the popular local band Raw Silk to perform the dance music. Our guests said it was the best reception they had ever attended. In fact, many years later people were still referring to our wedding and reception as "the party at the Mission."

I moved into Michael's sweet house on a hill overlooking Santa Barbara and we began to establish our routine, which included daily mass attendance at the Mission. It wasn't long before I began to notice something in Michael I had not seen before. He was controlling and had a temper. Since I don't respond well to someone trying to control me or angry outbursts, I began to question the wisdom of this marriage. I tried to calmly discuss things with him and asked him to simply tell me when I did something that angered him so we could discuss it. He would say, "No! When you're angry you have to yell." He was pretty stubborn and set in his ways so I knew his behavior would never change.

I was so surprised by his change in conduct that I jokingly told him he had a drop-down menu called "wife" but it can't be accessed until one becomes the wife. At any rate, after six months I was convinced the marriage would not last and after ten months we separated. Our amicable divorce was final on August 13, 1999. We were both very social and recognizable people in the Santa Barbara community, so many people knew about the situation pretty quickly. One of the most embarrassing tasks I had was to ask the various boards and groups I served on to change my name plate from McGrath back to Sinclair.

One unexpected positive outcome happened when I went to the Santa Barbara Courthouse to sign the final divorce papers. I had created the last name Sinclair when I first moved to Santa Barbara because I didn't want to carry any of my ex-husbands' names and I didn't really have a real maiden name. I had changed my last name with credit cards, social security, and driver's license but I had never made it "legal" through the court.

When I arrived at the courthouse to sign the divorce papers, the clerk asked, "Will you be taking back your maiden name?" I said to myself, "I wonder what she thinks my maiden name is since I don't even know myself." I hesitated a couple of seconds because I know that when there is a void the other person will usually fill it in. Sure enough she said, "Sinclair?" I replied, "Yes." Once I signed the papers my new name was official.

Thankfully Michael and I remained friends and I never saw any more anger or attempts to control me because I was no longer "the wife." Sadly Michael passed away on August 29, 2016 at age 75. Unfortunately I was unable to attend his funeral because I was out of the country.

Our group pauses during a hike in Ireland one day
before my bike wreck and brain injury

Getting ready to put on a show at Girl Scouts

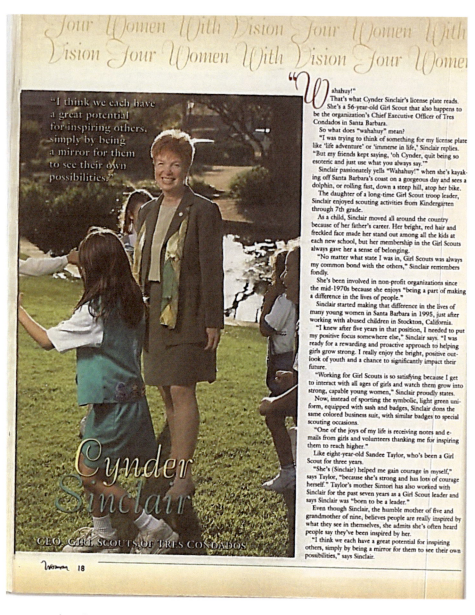

"I think we each have a great potential for inspiring others, simply by being a mirror for them to see their own possibilities."

Cynder Sinclair

CEO, GIRL SCOUTS OF TRES CONDADOS

"Wahahuy!"

That's what Cynder Sinclair's license plate reads. She's a 56-year-old Girl Scout that also happens to be the organization's Chief Executive Officer of Tres Condados in Santa Barbara.

So what does "wahahuy" mean?

"I was trying to think of something for my license plate like 'life adventure' or 'immerse in life,' Sinclair replies. "But my friends kept saying, 'oh Cynder, quit being so esoteric and just use what you always say.'"

Sinclair passionately yells "Wahahuy!" when she's kayaking off Santa Barbara's coast on a gorgeous day and sees a dolphin, or rolling fast, down a steep hill, atop her bike.

The daughter of a long-time Girl Scout troop leader, Sinclair enjoyed scouting activities from Kindergarten through 7th grade.

As a child, Sinclair moved all around the country because of her father's career. Her bright, red hair and freckled face made her stand out among all the kids at each new school, but her membership in the Girl Scouts always gave her a sense of belonging.

"No matter what state I was in, Girl Scouts was always my common bond with the others," Sinclair remembers fondly.

She's been involved in non-profit organizations since the mid-1970s because she enjoys "being a part of making a difference in the lives of people."

Sinclair started making that difference in the lives of many young women in Santa Barbara in 1995, just after working with abused children in Stockton, California.

"I knew after five years in that position, I needed to put my positive focus somewhere else," Sinclair says. "I was ready for a rewarding and proactive approach to helping girls grow strong. I really enjoy the bright, positive outlook of youth and a chance to significantly impact their future.

"Working for Girl Scouts is so satisfying because I get to interact with all ages of girls and watch them grow into strong, capable young women," Sinclair proudly states.

Now, instead of sporting the symbolic, light green uniform, equipped with sash and badges, Sinclair dons the same colored business suit, with similar badges to special scouting occasions.

"One of the joys of my life is receiving notes and e-mails from girls and volunteers thanking me for inspiring them to reach higher."

Like eight-year-old Sandee Taylor, who's been a Girl Scout for three years.

"She's (Sinclair) helped me gain courage in myself," says Taylor, "because she's strong and has lots of courage herself." Taylor's mother Sintori has also worked with Sinclair for the past seven years as a Girl Scout leader and says Sinclair was "born to be a leader."

Even though Sinclair, the humble mother of five and grandmother of nine, believes people are really inspired by what they see in themselves, she admits she's often heard people say they've been inspired by her.

"I think we each have a great potential for inspiring others, simply by being a mirror for them to see their own possibilities," says Sinclair.

Article about my service in Girl Scouts in the Santa Barbara News Press' 'Woman Magazine,' 1998

198

With my co-worker Linda Reed at our Girl Scout Camp Tecuya, 1998; (below) Lose the bet, kiss the pig

CHAPTER EIGHT
Courage is the Key

Until one is committed, there is hesitancy . . .
the moment one definitely commits oneself,
then Providence moves too. All sorts of things
occur to help one that would never otherwise
have occurred . . .whatever you do,
or dream you can do, begin it. Boldness has
genius, power and magic in it. Begin it now.
– W.H. Murray

I never thought I would be able to buy my own home in Santa Barbara. It was 2004 and I had rented various apartments and condos in town for nine years. My good friend, Stanley Weinstein, who was a colleague at Santa Barbara Bank & Trust, told me he was sure I could find a place I could afford. He set up an appointment for me with one of the mortgage bankers and, to my astonishment, the numbers showed that I could indeed afford to purchase a home.

Another friend recommended Penny Collins as a realtor. Penny asked about my preferences and parameters and she got busy researching potential sites. One day she picked me up after my Rotary meeting to look at property.

From 1:30 to 5:00 she showed me 17 homes between Goleta and Carpinteria. I could see why she came so highly recommended. As soon as I saw the sweet condo in Carpinteria, flooded with natural light and just the right size for me, I knew I would live there. Penny said that in her many years in real estate she had never shown so many properties in such a short time and had the buyer decide so quickly. Penny walked me through every step of the complex purchasing process and in November of 2004 I was the proud owner of my condo.

The single-story end unit had two bedrooms, two bathrooms, a connected two-car garage, a really nice kitchen, a dining area, a good-sized living room and a cute patio off of the breakfast nook area. It was one of 33 condos built in 1990 and part of a nicely landscaped complex, located less than a mile from the beach.

Penny arranged for a painter to repaint the walls with lush shades of rust, sage, peach and cream. By the time I moved in everything was all ready for me. My next project was the garage. I've always been pretty organized and never one to keep unpacked boxes laying around after a move. Penny arranged for a professional garage organizer to tackle the project. We built floor-to-ceiling shelving units and a unique rack for storing my water toys. On the garage's back wall were a tandem kayak, a single kayak, a prone board and a stand-up paddle board. There was a special area for my ski equipment, bicycles, scuba gear and backpacking paraphernalia.

I had always been a faithful member of a gym wherever I lived and I kept a pretty rigorous workout schedule. I wanted to make sure my body was always ready to perform my various outdoor activities. In fact, I quickly adopted the routine of riding my bike through the dark to the gym in Carpinteria at 4:30 in the morning so I could work out and have plenty of time to get ready for work. But when the gym closed I decided to create my own gym in the garage. There was plenty of space left after I parked my car in there, so I created a small gym in the extra space. It worked out great although I did miss my early morning bike rides a bit.

One of my first challenges was how to transport my single kayak to the beach. It was such a hassle to put it on top of my car to drive the short distance to the ocean. So I bought a special trailer designed to pull a kayak behind a bicycle. It was so cool! I could easily strap the kayak to the trailer, hook the trailer to my bike and pedal to the beach. I was quite a sight, but it worked just fine.

When I was still living in Santa Barbara, I learned to surf my kayak in the ocean — out of necessity. Whenever I would finish a school project for my intensive online Master's degree, I would grab my kayak and go directly to the beach. But I wanted to ride the waves into shore to release some of my pent-up energy, not just paddle peacefully in the ocean. The problem was that I didn't know how to surf a kayak. Sometimes I would catch the waves and easily ride them to shore, but other times I would about kill myself as I lost control of the kayak. So I decided to take a lesson. After that I was able to enjoy my water sport without as much danger.

Over the years I've had lots of fun and hair-raising adventures with kayaks. One time my friend, Linda Reed, and I decided to rent kayaks from Paddle Sports on the Santa Barbara harbor — and row from Stearn's Wharf to Hendry's Beach and back. We launched our kayaks from the harbor, loaded our water and lunch into the boats and began paddling the four miles to our destination. We were surprised by the size and force of the waves as we began to ride into shore. But we made it in without much trouble.

We sat on the warm sand enjoying our sack lunch and began to notice the waves were getting bigger. Some surfers were walking by with injuries from trying to get out. Linda began to express worry about whether we would be able to get through the big surf but I assured her the waves would be smaller by the time we were ready to go. I was wrong. But since we had paddled there, we had only one way to get back to the harbor and that was to paddle. So I told her we were just going to go for it with gusto and blast through the waves. She was somewhat unconvinced but agreed to try. (Linda was quite a bit younger than me and very fit, so I was sure she could do it.)

We each took our place by the shore, positioning our kayaks perpendicular to the waves. At just the right moment I jumped into my kayak and began paddling furiously out toward the monster waves. I was making good progress when all of a sudden a huge wave was about to crash onto my head. I had no choice but to put my head down and paddle with all my might through the wave. I was shocked and relieved when I came up on the other side of it into relatively calm water. I was pretty proud of myself.

I expected to see Linda come up beside me but she was nowhere to be found. The wave had washed out my contacts so I couldn't see very well, but I searched the distant shore to try to see her. I couldn't imagine she would still be there. But as it turned out, she was not able to get through the powerful waves. So I reluctantly decided I had no choice but to paddle back in. I had quite a wild ride to the shore but I made it successfully. Now we were stuck. How were we going to get our kayaks back to the boat rental place?

I used the nearby pay phone (that tells you how long ago this was) and called Paddle Sports. I explained our predicament and someone there agreed to come pick us up with a truck. I was quick to help him load the boats when he arrived. I felt bad that he had to interrupt his business just to come retrieve us and our kayaks. The first kayak went into the bed of the truck with ease, but I could tell there wasn't much room left for the other one.

So I placed the bow on the truck gate and then came around to the stern and pushed with all my might to make sure it went in all the way. I pushed too hard! The bow went right through the back window smashing it into a million little pieces. I was horrified. Now I really felt bad. We fished some flat pieces of cardboard out of the dumpster and laid them on the front seat so we wouldn't be sitting on the broken glass and rode back to the shop. The owner had a good sense of humor about it but he never let me forget that crazy event.

I also enjoyed hiking in the Santa Barbara front country. Every Friday evening my friend, Mary Jean, and I would gather around the fountain at the Old Mission with other Sierra Club hikers to listen to the guide tell us which trail we were going to hike that day. Everyone was required to bring water and a flashlight. About 15 hikers would then pile in their cars once the announcements were finished and drive to the appointed site. The hikes usually lasted a little over two hours and we would return to the Mission dirty and tired.

Mary Jean and I had a little game we played with each other as we walked along the trails. One of us would relate a recent dream to the other one. Then the other one would say, "I'm a Martian and I don't understand these words. Please explain." The idea was that embedded in each dream were symbols of things going on in our life. Each word held special meaning for the dreamer and the only way to discover the significance was to carefully describe the main words.

It was a sweet, enjoyable addition to our hikes. When we got back to the Mission it was always time for dinner. So we would go to Carlito's to enjoy a delicious Mexican meal complete with strong Margaritas. We always hoped no one would notice how grubby we were.

I have enjoyed skiing since high school and, thanks to my good friend Kate Silsbury, I had many opportunities for thrilling ski trips over the years. Kate was on the board of directors at Girl Scouts when I first arrived in Santa Barbara and she had a time-share condo in Whistler, British Columbia. Kate took me as her guest for many years to magnificent ski resorts like Whistler, Mount Tremblant and Panorama. I liked both alpine and Nordic (cross country) skiing and Kate preferred Nordic, so I would trade off skiing downhill one day alone and cross-country with her the next day. We always had a glorious time and ended each day with a delicious dinner at one of the delightful local restaurants. One time we even participated in a wine and fondue event at the mid-mountain lodge at Whistler. Afterward I skied down the lighted run through the dark while Kate took the gondola down. We could always count on having a good time together.

One of my most treasured memories is the time I spent in a year-long program called Courage to Lead, based on the distinctive work of Parker Palmer. It is a unique opportunity for nonprofit leaders to slow down and reflect as we renew our heart, mind and spirit. We learned practices to help sustain our vocational vitality and build a safe and trustworthy community of peers.

This unique program consists of five quarterly multi-day retreats held in a peaceful rural setting, providing a perfect setting to help participants begin to hear our inner voice. Each group includes 20-30 nonprofit executive leaders. To date nearly 200 nonprofit execs have completed this distinctive program. Monthly small group circles of five to six members provide an intimate setting to continue the work.

The practice of reflection through carefully chosen poetry, journaling and deep listening are part of the fabric of their approach. Our wonderful retreat leaders, Ken Saxon and Kim Stokely, have dedicated their lives to ensuring a deep, meaningful experience for every participant. The people in this program gave me valuable insights into my life and character that I had not noticed. They gave me the powerful message that I am enough and that I have unique and valuable gifts to bring to the world. I am grateful for this rare opportunity.

Sometime in 2007 I began to receive letters from my youngest son, Matt. He was in the Fresno County jail. It wasn't the first time he had been in jail, but it was the first time he sent me letters while incarcerated. His letters said he wanted to find a sobriety program so he could get clean and sober. At first I thought it was just a pipe dream. But I realized he might be serious about this goal as the letters continued with the same message. I talked to him a couple of times on the jail phone and each time he seemed sincere about his desire to get clean.

I began to research rehabilitation sites around the Fresno area and beyond. Every place was very expensive and completely out of my price range. One day I heard about the Rescue Mission in Santa Barbara. No fee was required and it sounded like an excellent program. I told Matt about it and he seemed to like the idea. I didn't know if the program would have room for him. It sounded too good to be true.

Coincidently the Rescue Mission had just hired a new executive director, Rolf Geyling. I had a practice of always inviting new executive directors to have lunch with me at the University Club, so I invited Rolf. I had decided that I wanted to make sure Rolf knew I genuinely wanted to welcome him to the community. I didn't want him to think I had a hidden agenda so I didn't plan to discuss the situation with Matt during lunch. But toward the end of lunch it seemed appropriate to mention Matt's predicament. Rolf enthusiastically said he would have room for Matt and that he was welcome to join the program. This was an answered prayer — more than I had ever imagined possible.

There was one main rule: new participants had to test clean and sober when they checked in for the first time and they had to stay that way throughout the year-long residential program. I knew the only way I could make sure Matt met this requirement is if I picked him up from jail and took him directly to the Rescue Mission. He was sure to be sober since he had been incarcerated for five months.

About a month before his release date, I reluctantly agreed to pick him up from jail and take him to the program. I was terrified at the thought of being alone with him in the car for so long. I hadn't seen Matt for a few years and I had read a lot about how methamphetamine can make users extremely violent. Matt is a big guy (6'4" and 200 pounds) and it was a four-hour ride from Fresno to Santa Barbara. I had never known him to be violent, but I didn't know what he was capable of these days.

The more I thought about this during the 30 days prior to his release, the more agitated I became. On more than one occasion I broke into tears as I was using the elliptical machine at the gym. The fear consumed me every day. Several of my friends advised against the plan saying it was a risky idea to bring him to Santa Barbara, the place I now called home.

Finally the date arrived. I was in the habit of participating in four century bike rides (100 miles) each year. One of my favorite rides was the day before I was scheduled to pick him up. I was also in the middle of an online class I was taking for my Doctorate degree. I was determined to complete the ride as well as complete my class requirement. So I loaded up my bike in the back of my SUV, tucked my laptop into the front seat and drove to Creston (near Paso Robles) to get ready for the ride. I was so hot and tired when I finished the ride, but I started up the car and headed to Fresno.

I checked into a hotel, brought my bike up the stairs into my room and unloaded my laptop. I logged into my school site and completed the required paper just under the deadline. Then I took a shower, set my alarm for 1:00 a.m. and climbed into bed, drifting into a fitful sleep. The jail released inmates at 2:30 in the morning in the most dangerous part of downtown Fresno. I knew I had to be there when he was released so he wouldn't have a chance to take any drugs. I also knew he wanted to see Jamie, his partner, and their two children. I knew I would have to carefully orchestrate this maneuver in order to ensure he couldn't get any drugs. If he showed up at the Rescue Mission high they wouldn't accept him and I would be stuck with him in Santa Barbara.

I picked up Jamie and the two girls about 1:30 in the morning and drove to the jail explaining to Jamie that Matt and the girls could visit with Matt on the car ride to her house but he would not be coming inside the house. I explained the reason, but since she was a meth addict too, I figured it didn't really sink in. I pulled in front of the jail at a little after 2:00. It was dark and about a dozen menacing-looking guys were hanging out on the front steps leading to the jail. Now I was really scared! But I knew I would have to walk through the group to get to the front door. I told Jamie I was locking all the doors and that she should not open the door no matter what. I told her that her life and that of the girls may depend on it.

I mustered my courage, put on a mean-looking face, locked the car doors and marched through the group of thugs into the entrance. I kept my eyes fixed on the front door, not making eye

208

contact with anyone. No one bothered me other than making a few unpleasant comments.

I was shocked and disappointed to see Sarah, Matt's latest girlfriend, standing in the foyer. She was a serious meth addict and I knew she would try to talk him out of coming with me if she got to him first. And I also knew that Matt would likely go to her first as soon as he saw her. I went over to her and said as sternly as I could, "Sarah, I want you to know that Matt will be coming with me. You may have 30 seconds to greet him and say goodbye and then you will need to leave."

It came time for Matt's release. I could see his face behind the tall, wire-laced window. He went directly to Sarah the minute they let him out. He had his back to me, hugging Sarah, and she was facing my direction. I walked calmly over to them and stood behind Matt, in front of Sarah's direct line of sight. I held up my left wrist and pointed to my watch while keeping my eyes focused on hers. I told Matt it was time to go to see his family in the car once the 30 seconds were up.

Thankfully Sarah walked out the door and Matt came with me to the car, climbing into the passenger seat. I explained to him that he had only a few minutes to visit with his family because I was dropping them off at their house and he would not be going inside. Jamie and the girls got out of the car, gave Matt hugs and went inside their house. Matt and I started the long drive to Santa Barbara. Thankfully it was uneventful.

He asked if we could stop at a drug store so he could pick up some basic supplies. I agreed but stayed with him the entire time, never leaving him alone. He was clearly uncomfortable being in such a large space. He acted like a caged animal, constantly looking over his shoulder as though expecting someone to come up behind him. We made our purchase and drove the short distance to the Rescue Mission. Thankfully I had timed it perfectly so that we arrived at 6 a.m. just after they opened. When we walked into the Mission office, Matt acted the same way he did in the drug store. He was clearly afraid and desperate to escape. The clerk seemed to recognize Matt's behavior as usual for new residents and told me I should leave.

He explained that Matt and I could have no contact for the first 30 days and that we could have short visits after that. I left there feeling extreme relief and the rush of pent-up adrenaline. Matt stayed in the year-long program and made good progress. I visited him several times each week over that year and we went to Delgado's often, which was his favorite restaurant.

In March of 2008, Matt had another month before he was scheduled to complete the program, but the Rescue Mission decided to let him be part of the regularly scheduled graduation ceremony anyway because he was making such good progress. It looked like Matt would be residing in the sober living area of the Rescue Mission when he finished the program. They also had a job lined up for him upon completion.

On March 8, 2008, 10 family members and friends joined us at the Montecito Covenant Church to witness Matt's graduation. What a moving ceremony it was! We were all so proud of him. After the event we all went to Moby Dick Restaurant on Stearn's Wharf for a celebration dinner. I enjoyed watching the sweet interaction and conversation among my friends and family.

The next morning we all gathered for breakfast at the Summerland Beach Café to celebrate my 62nd birthday (March 9). There was certainly a lot to celebrate with these dear people.

On April 6, 2008, Matt completed his year-long program. As he and I were driving to Delgado's to celebrate his accomplishment, I received a phone call from my Doctoral advisor, Dr. Hall. He said, "Congratulations Dr. Sinclair! The committee has officially approved your dissertation." I was bowled over! I had submitted my final dissertation to the IRB at the beginning of March but had no idea when, or if, it would be approved. I was trying to focus my attention on Matt's accomplishments rather than my own. But we both enjoyed celebrating our achievements over a delicious Mexican dinner. The future looked bright for both of us.

A couple of days later it all changed. Matt told me he didn't want to continue living in Santa Barbara; he wanted to return to Fresno. This news puzzled and devastated me. I tried to get him to change his mind by pointing out how far he had come in the last year and how positive his life had become. I also reminded him about what a good support team he had in Santa Barbara and how destructive his time in Fresno had been. I was pretty sure he would be throwing away all his progress if he returned to Fresno.

After he left Santa Barbara I learned that, sadly, he had started using meth again just days after completing the program. I was crushed but it all made sense now. This is why he wanted to go back to Fresno — he was hooked again and all his drug connections were there. I was heartbroken at the news but I also felt betrayed and foolish — betrayed because Matt told me he wanted to change and foolish because I had believed him even though I knew he was a drug addict. For my own mental health, I just let it all go, even though I still felt an overwhelming sadness. I had learned long ago from a doctor when my son Michael was in drug rehab that, "You didn't cause it and you can't fix it." Thankfully I took that to heart.

I decided to go to Fresno for a visit while Matt was still in rehab at the Rescue Mission. I wanted to see some of my other kids and some of my grandchildren. I also wanted to check in on Jamie and see how my granddaughters, Sarah and Ashley, were doing. I told Matt about my impending visit and he said he was worried about the girls because Jamie was probably cooking meth in her new apartment. I asked him to explain to me how I would recognize meth preparation. He carefully told me what to look for.

I had the address of Jamie's new apartment but had never been there. I called to let her know I would be coming by for a visit and she agreed.

I arrived to see Sarah, age three, and Ashley, age two, walking around the apartment with nothing on but a diaper. Jamie was clearly high and there were three sinister-looking guys hanging around inside the apartment smoking. I knew immediately that I was in a potentially dangerous situation. I didn't want Jamie or these guys to know I suspected anything out of the ordinary. So I acted very chipper, greeting everyone and appearing to ignore the obvious signs of danger. I casually walked into the kitchen and saw all the signs Matt had described to me. I quickly told everyone goodbye saying how nice it was to see them.

I walked out of the apartment, down the steps and climbed into my car which was parked across the street. I immediately called the Fresno Child Protective Services and the Fresno Police and reported what I had seen. I knew from my work at the Child Abuse Prevention Council that one of these agencies would be required to remove the girls from this actively dangerous environment. I also gave them the name, phone number and address of Jamie's parents, who were trustworthy and lived a couple of miles away.

Sure enough the authorities came right over to Jamie's apartment and removed the girls, taking them to their grandparent's house. Jamie's parents always thought Matt was the one who got Jamie started on drugs, so they were never very friendly toward me. Still I was glad I was able to arrange for the girls to be in a safe environment, even though no one knew that I was the one who called the authorities. The grandparents did an excellent job of raising the girls for the next 10 years, for which I will always be grateful.

In 2006 I decided to journey back to my birthplace, Selma, Alabama. I thought that was an appropriate way to celebrate my 60th birthday. I had not been there since we moved to Florida when I was a year old.

My mother gave me the addresses of the two places we had lived there when I was a baby. I printed out maps from Mapquest for these houses as well as the location of Selma General Hospital, where I was born. I had no preconceived ideas of what I would accomplish, I just wanted to see this famous city with my grown-up eyes. I hoped to get a feeling of this place that had played such a pivotal role in my life and our country's history by just observing its people and places.

I rented a car when I arrived at the Selma airport and began just driving around a bit. After I checked into my hotel, I drove to the famous Edmund Pettus Bridge and walked across, trying to imagine the tragic Bloody Sunday events in 1965. I was impressed with the lush vegetation lining the Alabama River. It was very warm and humid, but the sky was blue and the scenery beautiful.

On Sunday, March 7, 1965, in Selma, some 600 marchers lining up behind the Student Nonviolent Coordinating Committee's John Lewis and Southern Christian Leadership Council's Hosea Williams did not seem to expect much violence. This was despite the city's notoriety for violence against the Civil Rights Movement. The group planned to march to the state capitol in Montgomery, 54 miles away, to protest the February 26 murder of Jimmy Lee Jackson by police in nearby Marion, Alabama during a protest and the persistent denial of voting rights to blacks.

Earlier, SNCC had decided not to participate because it felt that such marches gained little and spilled too much blood. But it had also decided that those in SNCC who wished to participate could do so on a personal basis. Thus the presence of John Lewis, Bob Mants and others from SNCC.

On the bridge that day, state troopers in gas masks and Dallas County Sheriff Jim Clark's mounted posse were also gathered. State police confronted the marchers as they started across the bridge and ordered the marchers to halt. Instead they knelt. The troopers then fired tear gas as the posse charged into the ranks of the marchers swinging billy clubs and letting loose with rebel yells. Beaten marchers like Lewis crumpled; many fled as best they could. All of it was televised across the nation and became known as "Bloody Sunday."

As I drove through the downtown area I noticed how old everything looked compared to California. The brick buildings and narrow sidewalks seemed to be from a different era — and I suppose they were. But people were walking into their offices, eating at local lunch counters and seemingly going about their everyday lives.

The next day I drove to the house where my mother, my grandmother and I lived when I was a baby. I found the address quickly and parked my car on the street in front of the modest wooden house which was located several yards from the sidewalk. It looked like no one was home so I began to take some photos. I noticed four large Black males out of the corner of my eye just as I had taken the first picture. They were on the front porch of the house next-door and were all looking my way. I thought, "This probably isn't a real good idea. You could really be in danger here." I felt fear creeping up the back of my spine as they all started walking across the grass to where I was standing.

I mustered my courage and hollered to them, "Hey y'all! Will you please do me a big favor?" They looked surprised and curious but kept getting closer. "This is the house I was born in back in 1946 and I would love for one of you to take my picture standing in front of it," I continued (trying to sound friendly and hoping no one noticed I was out of place in this obviously all-Black neighborhood).

Right away they seemed excited. They began to argue over who would be the one to take my picture. I suggested they take turns with the camera so I could have several shots. They eagerly complied, I thanked them profusely and headed quickly back to my rental car.

I found the next house we had lived in a few blocks away in a quiet neighborhood. It was a large two-story white house with a veranda on the top floor and an expansive porch in front. Like the other houses, it was set back several yards from the sidewalk. I couldn't tell if anyone was home, but I thought I saw someone standing in the upstairs window.

I stood on the sidewalk across the street from the house. A Black couple pushing a baby carriage walked by me right after I had taken a couple of photos. They stopped and said, "I wouldn't be taking pictures of that house if I were you. Some very mean people who use drugs live there. You could be in danger if you stay out here." I thanked them and quickly got back into my rental car, glad that I had a couple of pictures.

Back at the hotel I logged onto my computer to check my email. There was an interesting message from Tom Thomas who was President and CEO of Santa Barbara Bank & Trust. His email said that I should expect an email with a job offer from his HR director soon.

Just before I left for this trip I had been feeling like it was time for me to leave my position at Girl Scouts and find another job. The national Girl Scout organization was going through an extensive reorganization which would dramatically affect our tri-county council. It looked as if I would need to move to San Jose if I wanted to retain my position.

I began to let various community members know that I might be looking for a job soon, since I wasn't wild about the idea of a move. When I mentioned my potential job search to Tom, he said, "Oh Cynder, we want you here!" I was surprised because I had never worked at a for-profit and knew nothing about the banking industry. I didn't know whether to take his comment seriously or not.

So I was surprised when I, indeed, received an email with a job offer from the HR manager the next day. I reminded myself that I could learn to do any job I wanted to and decided to at least consider the offer. I responded to the email asking for a meeting when I returned from my trip.

The next day I pulled out my map and drove to Selma General Hospital. I wanted to see this place for myself but I also thought it would be cool to have an official birth certificate from the hospital. I walked through the empty halls and found a woman sitting at a desk behind a half door. When she asked if she could help me I explained that I was born here and am hoping to have a copy of my birth certificate. She was happy to oblige my request and went scurrying to look through her filing cabinet.

She had a strange look on her face when she returned about a half hour later. She exclaimed, "You and I were born in the same hospital on the same day!" She handed me a manila envelope containing my birth certificate, we chatted a bit, I thanked her and drove back to my hotel. I packed up my suitcase and prepared to leave for the airport to come home the next day.

I met with the HR director from the bank a few days after returning home. I signed the paperwork and agreed to begin work after I had given notice at Girl Scouts. Tom greeted me warmly when I arrived at my new office and said enthusiastically, "Cynder you can just create your own job

216

here!" I was astounded. I knew nothing about banking so how was I supposed to know what needed to be done?

My office was located in the exclusive area known as upper village Montecito. I was part of the wealth management team with the title of vice president. I began to listen and pay close attention to what my colleagues discussed so I could figure out what kind of job I should create for myself. I began to notice that whenever something was new and important they called it an *Initiative*. I decided I would create the *Nonprofit Initiative*.

I had noticed that bank employees responsible for acquiring new customers did not realize the opportunity that nonprofits presented to them. These charities routinely held large fundraising dinners at the local high-end hotels. Banks would typically purchase tickets for a table of 10. However, just days before the event everyone would scramble to find bank employees to fill the seats.

Part of the Nonprofit Initiative was training for employees, known as relationship managers, so they could develop a strategic plan based on which charity events typically attracted the greatest number of high net worth individuals. My long involvement with the nonprofit community helped me inform their planning.

I showed the relationship managers how to "work a room," how to fill their table with potential clients and how to follow up with them after the event.

I also helped them realize that many charity boards and finance committees were filled with the type of customers they wanted to attract. I began to lend myself out to the bank's nonprofit clients in the name of the bank to perform board training, to offer coaching to organization executives and to arrange for banking presentations to their boards of directors.

In addition, I offered my services to wealthy, philanthropically inclined bank customers who were new to the community and looking for nonprofits for their charitable donations. These people were quite grateful to the bank for my help in choosing just the right organizations for them to invest in and for introducing them to nonprofit leaders and board members.

While at the bank I brought together a cross section of businesses and nonprofits to learn from each other about how their work could be mutually beneficial. Large and small businesses explored how their charitable financial contributions could benefit their business reputation as well as the community in general. Nonprofits learned how to more effectively relate to and partner with those in the business sector.

The Nonprofit Initiative became popular throughout the bank even as it attracted new nonprofit clients to the bank. But in early 2008 when the financial markets took a severe downturn, the bank let me know that they wanted me to start a training program to be a "real banker."

I had started taking my extensive Doctoral classes in 2005 while I was still working at Girl Scouts. I had planned for my dissertation to address the process of merging nonprofit organizations since I had been working closely with the Girl Scout reorganization project. But I changed my topic when I left Girl Scouts and started working for the bank, because I would no longer have access to the necessary resources.

I decided that my Doctoral dissertation would focus on the cross-industry relationship between banks and nonprofits. It was a perfect match for me because I had access to both the nonprofit and banking industries.

When the bank asked me to register for banking training, I told them that I appreciated the opportunity but that I wanted to get back into the nonprofit sector. My supervisor said, "Okay we understand. Just keep looking for the right job, continue working on your dissertation, come into the office when it is convenient and let us know when you find a new job." I was astounded by and grateful for this amazing gift!

In February of 2008 I accepted the job of CEO for Santa Barbara Neighborhood Clinics (SBNC), which provides healthcare for the low-income population. Their three medical clinics and one dental clinic provide much needed care for vulnerable patients who cannot afford to pay for services.

I did not have a background in the healthcare field, but I knew I could bring organizational leadership, efficient systems, staff development, fundraising expertise and community engagement to SBNC. They had a history of being led by medical doctors so — their healthcare services were excellent — but they wanted improvements in their organizational systems and their relationship with the community at large.

I got busy doing what I'm best at and what I enjoy most — bringing SBNC's message to the community and to potential donors and board members. I established SBNC as a thought leader in healthcare by writing articles for Noozhawk, the local online newspaper, and by actively engaging print journalists with our message. This was during the early stages of President Obama's Affordable Care Act. I learned all I could about it and discovered that each of our major local healthcare providers understood only part of the plan.

I didn't comprehend all of it, but I knew that we could learn from each other. So I began to convene representatives from the hospital, the major medical clinic, the county health department and other key providers. I even brought in our U.S. Representative, Lois Capps, to make a presentation to the group and answer questions. Everyone agreed this cross-section group brought value to all participants.

I expanded SBNC's board of directors to include a wide variety of community leaders, brought in more donors who were inspired by our mission and worked with the staff to increase their job performance and sense of camaraderie. When it was time to hire a medical director, I invited a representative from each of the major healthcare providers to join the interview panel. I compiled an interview process, plus a list of questions and a scoring system to be utilized after the initial job announcement and preliminary screening of candidates. It all worked like a charm and we chose an excellent candidate while also deepening our relationship with the other healthcare institutions.

I learned a valuable lesson while at SBNC: don't expect medical doctors to have a high value for efficiency or financial stability. Their main focus is patient care and providing the best medical care possible — which, of course, is great for the patient. Most doctors are not trained to work together as a team or to pay attention to internal systems. Eventually I learned I was wasting my breath to discuss financial or system improvements with the doctors. I discovered that if I wanted their attention I had to start by saying I had a suggestion that would help them provide better patient care.

I enjoyed my work there, I learned a lot and I feel good about my accomplishments, but after four years there I knew it was time to leave and make way for a different type of leader. They needed what is known in the healthcare industry as a "white coat connection." The next leader would need to be a medical doctor, but one with the rare interest in administration.

2010 was a big year for our family because my beautiful granddaughter, Taryn Hoffman, was married to her handsome husband, David Gluckman, in a stunning wedding. She was my first grandchild to be married and it was a joyous occasion. 2010 was also the year my darling granddaughter, Mellissa Rocker, was born to my son Matt. Mellissa's grandfather, Larry, and Matt share the duties of raising her as she is developing into a beautiful and smart young woman.

With my mentor at the University of Phoenix for my doctorate ceremony, 2008; (below) My daily gym routine

Jackson Hole, Wyoming, 2016

Stand-up paddle boarding, Santa Barbara Harbor, 2016

A 100-mile bike ride, the Lighthouse Century, 2010

Skiing with my amazing partner, Dennis Forster,
at Snowbird Utah, 2015

Skiing with my good friend Kate Silsbury at Whistler Mountain
Ski Resort in British Columbia

Three of my delightful granddaughters
Sarah, Melissa and Ashley

CHAPTER NINE
Focusing on my Purpose

*Obstacles are those frightful things you see
when you take your eyes off your goal.*
– Henry Ford

In 2012 I left Santa Barbara Neighborhood Clinics and decided that rather than trying to find another leadership position, I would start a consulting business. I had a lot to give back to the nonprofit sector — to staff leadership, to boards of directors and to the community — and I wanted to contribute what I could.

I started the process by reading William Bridges' seminal book *Transitions*. He explains that most people want to start at the beginning when they are starting something new. But he says that first we must start at the ending. Describe what has ended, what we learned about ourselves from the ending and what we have realized from other endings. Next, he says there comes a neutral zone — a time that feels flat but is a time for evaluation. Not much happens during this time, but it is the perfect opportunity to prepare for the new beginning. We are ready to begin a new venture only after we have processed the ending and experienced the neutral zone.

I started to make lists of all the endings I have had in my life and the lessons I learned from them. I prepared for a new beginning by researching nonprofit consulting, interviewing various nonprofit leaders about their needs, and informally letting people in my network know that I will be starting a consulting business. I began by meeting with Michael Kramer from Ameravant, a website design firm.

Michael has a gift not only for excellent web design but also for helping his clients clarify their intentions regarding the scope of their new business. He asked astute questions and gave me lots of homework. I followed every piece of his wise advice. He began to design my website, he helped me create the name, Nonprofit Kinect — and my new venture began to take shape.

Next, I needed a logo. I knew I couldn't afford to hire a marketing artist, so I visited a website called 99 Designs. For $99 they sent my logo parameters out to designers all over the world. I received over 30 different submissions. After choosing the one I liked best, I paid the company and gave my new logo to Michael to use on my website, business cards and stationery. Next I started a new Facebook page for my business.

I invited a dozen of our local nonprofit executives to meet at the University Club so I could ask their opinions about the services I planned to offer. They enjoyed getting together as a group to discuss topics of mutual interest, so I widened the circle by starting the Executive Director Roundtable. Every month I would ask them for suggestions about topics and we would discuss one the next month. Sometimes I invited special community leaders to make a presentation and other times I would simply facilitate a group discussion focused on a particular topic of mutual concern. Over the years this ED Roundtable grew in numbers and scope.

When I worked at SBNC I learned that whenever I wrote articles on a particular topic (in this case, healthcare), the public began to see me and my agency as thought leaders in the field. I decided to use that lesson with Nonprofit Kinect. I began to write articles about a wide variety of issues affecting nonprofits for the online newspaper, *Noozhawk*. Soon they gave me my own column called *Kinecting Dots*. Since 2012 I have been writing two articles each month focusing on a variety of nonprofit topics. I have been told that many local people and nonprofit leaders think of me as the nonprofit guru. I enjoy being able to use my wealth of experience to benefit these fine organizations.

Board members and executive directors began contacting me to enlist my services for facilitating their board retreats, planning their fundraising approach, conducting board governance training, creating their strategic plan and providing executive coaching. I've worked with a wide variety of nonprofits and it feels really good to be able to add such value to their important work.

At one point, Fielding Graduate Institute and Antioch University asked if I would teach classes for their MBA programs. I was eager to try this, even though I hadn't done anything like it before. I enjoyed working with all the students, but one thing I learned about myself is that I prefer interacting with individuals rather than groups. I liked being a coach more than I enjoyed teaching. I think I did an acceptable job, but I wasn't eager to re-enlist when the classes were over.

One of my Antioch students was Matt Schuster who was the executive director of TVSB, the public access television station. He asked me if I would be interested in hosting a TV show for them called *805 Focus*, interviewing nonprofit leaders about their mission. Inside my head I thought, "Oh my gosh, Cynder, you can't do that! Don't you remember you were on TV once and you were really scared?" But I quickly responded, "Sure Matt that sounds like fun."

I was a little nervous the first time I interviewed someone on the show, but by the second episode I felt calm and began to enjoy every minute. Since I started with TVSB in 2016, I have conducted well over 150 interviews. I am inspired by every guest on the show — their passion is contagious. I was determined from the beginning that the dialogue would be interesting and lively; I did not want audiences to be bored by them. I got worried when, sometimes, a guest would seem low on energy; but once I asked them about their mission they would light up with enthusiasm.

Interviews are only 15 minutes long and the time goes by quickly. I ask general questions about their mission and invite them to build a bridge between whatever I ask and the message they want the audience to hear. It works like a charm every time. Sometimes it can be tricky closing off the conversation at just the right point, especially when a guest is in the middle of an interesting story. But television production requires that we stay within a certain time frame.

In 2015 I received a phone call from Girl Scouts of the USA asking if I would consider accepting a six-month assignment as interim CEO for a Girl Scout council in South Dakota. This council's territory was all of South and North Dakota and part of Minnesota. They had lost their CEO and needed my help keeping things running, holding the organization together and helping to find their next CEO.

I had a lot of questions and concerns, especially since I had never been to that part of the country and I had never served as an interim. But ultimately I agreed and, before I knew it, I was notifying clients of my plans, locking up my condo with my cute blue Prius in the garage and packing my suitcases for the trip.

I arrived in the spring when the weather was quite pleasant. The council headquarters was in Sioux Falls, South Dakota, and they arranged for me to have an apartment less than a mile from their office. Some mornings I would actually walk to work and back home, although they also gave me a rental car to use during my stay. I had my beloved Colnago bicycle dismantled, shipped to Sioux Falls and reassembled so I could use it during my stay. The town has miles and miles of excellent bike trails along the river and through the countryside.

I quickly discovered that the CEO and COO had been terminated. Understandably, the staff members were somewhat rattled and unsure of what to expect, especially when they found out that their interim CEO was from California (known as the land of the fruits and the nuts). The organizational culture expected each person to stay in their own area and not speak with others who were not in their department. Staff and board members were not allowed to speak to one another. Many people were afraid of voicing their opinion.

The 150,000 square mile service area presented another challenge for meaningful communication. Thankfully they had a robust technology system that allowed them to conduct remote meetings for board and staff.

I began by meeting one on one with each staff member to get to know them, to find out about their areas of responsibility and to help them get better acquainted with me. That process seemed enjoyable and beneficial for most everyone. Next I conducted cross-departmental meetings, combining in-person gatherings with remote sessions simultaneously. I encouraged every individual to contribute to the conversation, especially those who were uncomfortable doing so. They found this approach to be very different from their usual manner of interaction. Some people liked it and others preferred to stay in their own silo.

Decision making was another area that needed improving. They expected me, as CEO, to make all the decisions — because that's what they were used to. I assured them that I would make some choices, but I told them my favorite approach is participatory decision-making, where all those concerned with the outcome contribute their best thinking on the topic.

I would often invite cross-sections of groups to meet with me to consider a specific outcome. I would stand by the flip chart and just ask questions and record their answers and ideas on the paper. Most of these discussions would result in a group decision. It took them a while to get used to this method of working together, but eventually they enjoyed it and were glad to be able to voice their opinions, especially about issues affecting them.

I believe it made all of us more effective as a team. Thankfully most staff members were committed, competent and willing to embrace new ideas.

I wanted to explore as many parts of North and South Dakota as possible during my stay, especially since I had never been there before. I began asking various staff members about their favorite spots for camping, hiking, kayaking and biking. I quickly realized that I could access the 28-mile bike path along the Big Sioux River from my apartment. It took two hours for this bike ride, taking me through green rolling meadows, little waterfalls, corn fields and bison pastures. Sometimes a 30-mile an hour wind would come up seemingly out of nowhere and I had a hard time keeping my bike upright; but I never turned back. Other times I would get lost on the trail and it would end up being 36 miles instead of 28. (I have a reputation for getting lost easily.)

I kept hearing people talk about a famous dam, so I wanted to go check it out for myself. I made arrangements to rent a cabin at Lewis & Clark Lake Resort which was located on Lake Yankton in South Dakota. The lake is part of the Missouri River and includes the famous Gavins Point Dam. Coincidently, Stacey, my administrative assistant, and her family were camping at Cottonwood Campground just about two miles away. I arranged for a kayak to be delivered to my cabin so I could explore the lake and see the renowned dam for myself.

Big storms are common in this part of the country and on the day I planned to paddle out to the dam there was lots of rain, wind, thunder and lightning. I waited until the storm abated a bit and then I headed out in my rented kayak, bringing my iPhone in a dry bag so I could take some photos of my adventure. The dam was three miles across the lake from my cabin, but I was confident I would be able to navigate the short distance.

I paddled through the choppy water toward the dam, enjoying the beautiful scenery without another soul on the lake. Soon I reached the dam. I gently paddled around the area trying to get a good view of this place everyone seemed to marvel at. I was taking a couple of photos, being careful not to let my phone get wet, when out of nowhere I heard a loud voice over a megaphone say, "Get out now!" I couldn't figure out who was speaking or who they were talking to.

I looked around to see what was happening and saw no one. And then I glanced up at the hill overlooking the lake and saw several men waving their arms, yelling and looking my way. I heard them say something about a lady in a kayak and I pointed to myself as if to say, "Who me?" They hollered over the megaphone again, "Get that boat over on the shore and get over here, now!"

The wind had picked up a bit and I paddled through the choppy waves, around the bend and landed on the sandy shore. I pulled my kayak up further onto the beach and looked around to see who had been yelling. I couldn't imagine what someone would want with me, especially since I was so far from home and no one knew I was here. All of a sudden two very angry men appeared and escorted me up a hill to a wide flat area covered in grass. I looked around and noticed that there were five men and each one had a very large pickup truck. I learned that two were federal agents, two were state officials and one was a local water ranger.

They demanded to know where I was from and what I was doing there. I explained that I worked for the Girl Scouts, was visiting from California and came to check out the lake and dam. They demanded to see my identification, which thankfully I had with me in my dry bag in a little pocket attached to my phone cover. They took it from me and all gathered around to look at it.

Then one of them said, "Well, you don't look like a terrorist." I chuckled politely because it sounded like he was making a joke. He immediately barked, "This is not a laughing matter, ma'am! This is a Homeland Security issue." I had absolutely no idea what they were talking about or why they were so mad.

Later someone told me that they were upset because just beyond the dam, on the Missouri River, is a secret bunker from which the government can operate the country in case of a disaster. Supposedly officials took President Bush to this facility after the 9/11 attack. Water and electricity would be cut off to the area if the dam were to be destroyed by a terrorist. I don't know if this is true or not, but if so it would explain why they were so intensely angry at me.

One of them explained that this was private government property and off limits to the public. They were seriously considering arresting me for trespassing and for possibly being a terrorist. I tried to act somber and assure them I was only a tourist visiting the area. They kept going over several yards away from me to have private conversations and glancing back at me from time to time.

By now I was getting pretty nervous. Finally, one of the men walked over, returned my identification and told me that they had decided to let me go with a warning. They demanded that I get in my kayak and return to my cabin. I was relieved until the water ranger noticed I didn't have a life jacket on or in the boat. He said I wouldn't be allowed back on the lake without proper safety equipment. One of the others saw my dilemma (how could I get back to my cabin without kayaking on the lake) and offered to lend me one. I gratefully accepted it, put it on and got in my kayak to paddle back.

The wind was really picking up and I could hardly make my way through the waves that were now crashing over the bow. The borrowed life jacket was one of those old puffy orange ones and it was hard to sit up straight with it on, making paddling even harder. I was afraid to take it off, though, for fear the men would see me and change their minds about letting me go. So I put my head down and paddled and paddled and paddled. I thought I would never get to shore but finally after a very long time I did. I was so tired and agitated that I could hardly pull my boat up and secure it.

I went inside my cabin and lay down on the bed to rest. Stacey and her family had invited me to have dinner with them at their campsite, so I took a shower, put on dry clothes and drove over to their campsite. Soon after I arrived they began talking about the scene they witnessed earlier in the day as they drove over the bridge, returning from their grocery shopping trip.

They reported having seen a woman surrounded by pick-up trucks and officers by the side of the lake and wondered what had happened. They were shocked when I told them that the woman was me. And then I explained the whole situation and that I felt lucky to have escaped arrest. Of course, Monday morning Stacey made sure all the staff knew about their CEO's latest adventure.

I decided I wanted to take a road trip to meet in-person with the staff in each of our offices throughout North and South Dakota. It took nine days. With Stacey's help, we were able to see a lot of this expansive, beautiful area. I remember being impressed with the constantly changing, beautiful cloud formations. When we visited our office in Spearfish, South Dakota, we decided to hike to a place called Devil's Bathtub in the Black Hills area. The hike was only about a mile long, but there was so much to see and the terrain made it pretty tricky to maneuver. We enjoyed trekking through the lush green thickets, climbing over spectacular rock formations and wading through the river.

We met three young men from nearby Ellsworth Air Force base on our walk. They were quite familiar with the area and urged us to experience plunging into the "bathtub." I was eager to participate in this fun activity, but some staff from our office declined. It turned out to be pretty hair-raising. I began to climb the large rock and finally made it to the top with the encouragement of our three new friends. Once I got to the top it was really scary. Fast moving, freezing cold water with great force was cascading from the top over a slick slide-like rock into the pool below.

I had second thoughts, but our three Air Force friends kept egging me on. I had to crouch over the cold water in a precarious position with one foot on a rock on one side of the water and the other foot on the opposite side in order to get into position to slide down. Now I was really nervous but it was too late to go back. I lowered myself into a sitting position with the freezing water pounding on my back. The three young men, a couple of my staff and a few other hikers were gathered around the pool shouting encouragement to me.

I finally let go and the water propelled me down the slick rock face and I plunged down deep into the pool. Everyone was cheering when I came to the surface. I felt lucky to be in one piece.

My t-shirt and shorts were dripping wet as we continued on our hike. Thankfully it was a hot day so it felt good to be cooled off. We saw another pool at the bottom of a pretty tall cliff as we rounded a bend. Our three new friends jumped off the cliff into the cold water and urged me to do the same. The height above the water was a little too much for my comfort but it did look like fun. I took several false starts out of fear but I finally jumped in, went all the way to the bottom and bobbed up to the top, glad to be unharmed. It was really thrilling and I'm glad I took a chance. Stacey told me later that when I was at the top of the rockslide one of the young men asked her, "Just how old is she anyway?"

Our next stop took us to the impressive Mount Rushmore National Park in the Black Hills of South Dakota where we met up with a hundred Girl Scouts on an excursion with their troops and parents. We hiked all over the park and listened to fascinating presentations by the park rangers.

A couple of troop leaders asked me to visit their camping event and make a presentation when we returned to our Sioux Falls office. I happily agreed to drive there on a Saturday morning. One of the volunteers sketched a map for me on a small white piece of notepaper. The directions looked pretty straight forward so I wasn't worried, even though (do I have to say this again?) I tend to have a bad sense of direction and get lost often. Also the camp was several miles out of town in the countryside.

Off I went in my rental car trying to follow the little map. After an hour of driving I found myself at a dead-end road and none of the street names matched the map. I was smack in the middle of miles and miles of corn fields with no clue where I was.

I looked across the deserted road and saw about a dozen burly guys standing near their Harley motorcycles. I got out of my car, crossed the road (pretending I didn't know I looked strange in my Girl Scout t-shirt and shorts) and walked toward the group. They all turned to stare at this unusual sight. I knew I was taking a chance, but I didn't know what else to do since I was completely lost.

I walked up to the guy closest to the road and said, "Hi fellas, I'm lost. Do you think you can help me please?" Several of the men gathered around to listen to my story and look at my little hand-drawn map. They had several ideas of which way I should go and where to turn. Finally they all agreed and I wrote it down, thanking them profusely. As I walked back to my car one of them shouted, "Hey we're here every Saturday. You can stop by and have lunch with us any Saturday." As I turned to thank them for their kind invitation I saw they were all standing together, smiling and waving good-bye. Thankfully, the new directions worked just fine and I found my way to the campsite where I enjoyed a delightful afternoon with scores of girls of all ages and their troop leaders.

My staff members were flummoxed when, on Monday morning, I told them about how my new Harley friends came to my aid in the middle of a cornfield.

They call it simply "weather" in South Dakota — when the rain is coming down hard together with high winds and thunder and lightning. It happens often. I experienced it several times during my six months there. One time I was at the fairgrounds with 10,000 folks attending an outdoor concert by Boz Skags. We were all sitting around on folding chairs positioned on multi-colored blankets, eating our boxed dinners and sipping our wine as we enjoyed the music under the stars.

I noticed it was getting really windy and I overheard some people nearby talking about a radio announcement describing a tornado in a nearby county. Then someone stepped up to the microphone interrupting the concert and announcing, "We have weather. I am asking everyone to calmly pick up your things and walk back to your cars. Don't dilly dally but don't panic either." I could tell this was fairly routine for many of the attendees. I picked up my things and joined the 10,000 people moving like a slow but deliberate river toward our cars. It was quite an evening!

I unpacked my things, reorganized my house and got my bicycle reassembled when I returned to California from South Dakota. I felt like I made a significant contribution to the organization as well as the individual staff members. I was glad I had accepted the opportunity and proud of what I accomplished. It was particularly gratifying when a number of employees and board members made it a point to thank me for the contributions I had made. I was also delighted that I had experienced such a variety of fun activities there and had seen so much of the country.

I quickly got back in the groove of consulting with local nonprofits, but something was missing. I knew my contributions helped organizations improve their systems and training — and I knew they were grateful for my help. But my work in South Dakota showed me how much I prefer being part of a team, proclaiming one mission to the community and helping individual staff members become better versions of themselves. So I decided to find a job as CEO of another nonprofit. I was 72, but I had lots of energy and a strong desire to make a difference.

I saw a job announcement for CEO of Community Action of Ventura County (CAVC) in 2016, an organization helping the disenfranchised raise themselves out of poverty. This organization was part of President Johnson's War on Poverty program in the 1960s and is still making great strides today. The funding sources and strict regulations still support 1,000 sites in the U.S. and 50 in California. Each Community Action group provides different programs, but all of them focus on helping the poor.

The organization sounded terrific and I'm glad to report that I was hired as the new CEO. CAVC has four main programs including a homeless day center serving 100 individuals daily, a weatherization team to go to homes of low-income families to reduce their utility bills by making their homes more energy efficient, an energy assistance program to help pay utility bills for low-income families and a food distribution program serving over 150 families weekly.

When I interviewed for the job, I was struck by the similarity of the mission of CAVC and that of the organizations I founded in the San Joaquin Valley in the 1970s and 1980s. It was obvious to me that board members and most staff members were very committed to their work. Thankfully most were also very competent. There were a few exceptions, though.

Every month all 40 employees came together for an all-staff meeting. I knew they were probably wondering what this new leader was like and how my style would affect them. So when I got up to speak, I tried to keep the mood light. I told them that my overriding expectation of every staff member was to always treat each other with mutual trust and respect. I said, "I know I can't force anyone to respect someone else, but I expect you to behave in a respectful manner to your co-workers.

And I will follow the same rule." There seemed to be a collective sigh of relief — and later I found out why.

I began my tenure by meeting with each staff member, one-on-one. The first ones to meet with me were a little nervous, not knowing what to expect. But soon the word got out that I just wanted to get to know them, find out about their particular job duties, ask about ways CAVC could improve and solicit their comments for how I could help them be more successful in their career. I took lots of notes and wrote up summaries for myself after each interview. Then I made sure I followed up on each suggestion anyone made. They were surprised at this.

I soon became aware that several of the people seemed to be afraid of something — I just couldn't figure out what it was. So I just kept watching and listening, not only to what was said but also to what was not said. I continued to ask how I could make the work environment and our services better. Finally after about two months, people began to trust me and I found out they were afraid of the HR director — who had also applied for the CEO position and had been there for six years.

This woman had created an atmosphere of fear and intimidation. Workers were not allowed to speak to each other unless necessary, staff and board were not to talk to one another, opinions and ideas were routinely shot down and she exercised complete decision-making authority. She was interim CEO and reported to the board before I was hired — and she knew how to charm them. So the board had no idea how she was treating staff. People just kept their head down and did their work, hoping they didn't get in trouble for anything.

I knew I had to terminate her but I was concerned that, since the board wasn't aware of her behavior, they might not support me dismissing her. I met with our attorney to lay out a plan of action; I wanted to make sure I was completely prepared. I invited her into my office one morning — ostensibly to meet a guest. I didn't tell her that the visitor was from the attorney's office (I needed to have a witness and didn't think it appropriate to have a staff or board member perform that role). I told her she was being terminated and began to go through the paperwork I had prepared for her. She flew into a rage as soon as she realized what was happening and stomped out of my office and into her own office, slamming her door and refusing to come out.

She called the board chair while she was in her office, hoping he would come to her rescue. I didn't know him that well since I hadn't been employed that long and I realized that he could easily take her side and tell me to reinstate her. Thankfully he said, "The board has one employee and it's Cynder. The board and I will support any decision she makes."

I gave her three warnings and then called the police to escort her out. She left abruptly when she realized I had actually called law enforcement. I predicted her exit would not be easy and that staff would be worried and upset. So I had arranged for an all-staff meeting in advance. When they all gathered downstairs I explained what happened and everyone cheered. Two additional employees self-selected to work somewhere else over the next few weeks. Now we could begin building a strong cohesive team.

I arranged for each department to conduct regular meetings to share ideas and challenges and made it clear that each department head was in charge of their team's work. I encouraged participatory decision making while acknowledging the authority of the group leader. Next, I built a strong leadership team comprised of the head of each department. I worked with them individually, as well as in a group, to help them develop their abilities and achieve their goals. Together we streamlined internal systems, achieved more efficient use of our resources and encouraged camaraderie through employee recognition programs.

I began to meet community leaders, create relationships with the media, reach out to potential donors, arrange introductions to local politicians and join a few carefully selected groups. Before long people were talking about the good work of CAVC and donations began to flow in.

I always believe in having a strong succession plan, so I began training the person who I thought had the greatest promise of taking my place when I departed. Not only does this prepare the organization for eventualities, but it encourages the individual being trained and sends a message to staff that leadership is dispersed and inclusive. Whenever I would travel – sometimes for two weeks or more — this individual would be in charge. Thankfully extensive time off for travel was a pre-arranged agreement of my hire.

I had been in the position for almost three years and I felt this individual, whom I had been training for nearly that whole time, was ready to become CEO. I was also getting a little weary of the commute. Originally the drive was only 30 minutes from my home in Carpinteria to my office in Oxnard. The drive along the coastline was quite beautiful and I was going against traffic. But the commute became over an hour and a half round-trip when I decided to move to Santa Barbara. I was finding it challenging to make the drive, especially after late night board meetings.

I decided to retire, even though I was about three months short of my contract agreement. I gave the board six months' notice and accelerated the training for my replacement. I notified our partners, community leaders and donors, hoping they would take comfort knowing my exit was conducted with attention to detail. I wanted to leave behind a carefully planned hiring process so that the staff and board would feel that we had used an objective approach to choosing the next CEO.

I enlisted three board members to serve on the search committee and administered a questionnaire for staff and board to identify desired qualities and competencies in the candidates. I compiled a list of interview questions for them to ask, along with evaluation criteria. I also sent out an announcement to staff inviting interested candidates to apply so they would feel the process was inclusive. To my surprise, one of the staff applied. Now we had two candidates — the one I had trained for over two years and another one who was younger and rather inexperienced.

I left on a previously scheduled trip overseas and arranged for the search committee to interview the candidates while I was gone. I felt comfortable leaving since I had thoroughly prepared the committee members to execute the process. They spent considerable time conducting multiple interviews with each of the two candidates. I was astonished and a bit saddened when, upon my return, I discovered the committee had chosen the young, inexperienced candidate rather than the one I had trained.

I tried to make the best of the situation by attempting to schedule training and orientation sessions with my replacement over the remaining weeks. I was a bit frustrated when the candidate always seemed to have excuses for not participating in the sessions. I was also confused as to why this inexperienced new CEO would not want to take advantage of my expertise, especially since we had worked together so well in the past. It became clear that my offers were falling on deaf ears and I was being ignored. Finally it was time for the holiday break and, coincidently, my last day of work.

Ironically I was taken to the hospital for an emergency appendectomy on the night of my planned retirement party, with nearly 100 attendees registered to attend. It seemed, indeed, to be time for me to go. Even though I felt proud of all I had accomplished at CAVC, I also felt bad that I wasn't able to leave in the organized manner I had planned.

As I look back at my carefully laid exit strategies at the various organizations I served, I realize that just because I do my best to establish a healthy work culture and lay the groundwork for smooth succession, the environment I created may not endure after I'm gone. At first I thought it was poor planning on my part or failure to consider certain aspects of the transition. But now I recognize that the best a leader can hope to do is create a solid environment for the organization while she is there. It may or may not continue after she departs.

Even Bill Gates saw evidence of this when he stepped away from day-to-day involvement with Microsoft to focus on philanthropy. Similarly, Jack Welch was frustrated by the poor performance of General Electric after his departure. Both leaders had spent years building strong systems and creating solid cultures.

I noticed another example of this conundrum when I look back at the ranch where we raised our children in the Fresno area. We built a beautiful environment there with horse stables, a riding rink, lush green pastures and emerald grass gracing the carefully constructed dry creek in the front yard. It was a real showplace and we enjoyed every minute there.

However, the property was sold to a family with a trucking business who had no appreciation for the beauty we had created — they just liked the open spaces for their trucks and the large barn for storage. Before long the grass was brown and the pastures overgrown with weeds. I realized it was beautiful because we created the beauty — there is no guarantee it will endure when you are gone. So the message I take away is to always bring beauty to the present regardless of what the future may hold.

Girl Scouts - Dakota Horizons Staff Retreat

Photos from my days with the Girl Scouts in South Dakota

Girl Scouts - Dakota Horizons
Rapid City, SD

Meeting with the staff in South Dakota

I took my bike and did plenty of riding
in and around Sioux Falls

Showing nerves of steel, I slide down into Devil's Bathtub
in Spearfish, South Dakota

Interviewing Geoff Green, CEO of the Santa Barbara City
College Foundation, on my television show, 805 Focus

CHAPTER TEN
Overwhelming Grief

Grief is the reminder of the depth of our love.
Without love, there is no grief.
So when we feel our grief, uncomfortable and aching
as it may be, it is actually a reminder
of the beauty of that love, now lost.
—Dalai Lama

My son, Rick Rocker, was a charming, smart and fun-loving guy. Even though he didn't spend a lot of time studying, he always earned top grades in school. He loved going with me to pick strawberries from the local patch when we lived in Kingsburg and then he would help me make the most delicious strawberry freezer jam. We had a very special connection.

Rick made it a point to take over as "man of the house" whenever Larry would be gone on his many trips. One time, as

I stood at the kitchen sink washing our dinner dishes, Rick came up and stood behind me and put his arms around my waist because he had often seen Larry do that. This is a very sweet memory.

Rick always said his only goal in life was to follow in his father's footsteps. So Rick went to work for Larry at his insurance office as soon as he graduated from high school rather than attend college. He was so happy to be working so closely with his dad and Larry was proud to have him as a junior partner.

The next thing Rick wanted was to marry his high school sweetheart, Peggy Roberson. They had dated for most of their high school years and were very much in love. Larry and I put together an elaborate wedding ceremony and reception for them, with over 300 guests attending. It was a joyous event shared by friends, family members and Larry's co-workers.

Rick moved out of our home and he and Peggy moved into their own apartment nearby to start their new life together. I was sad to lose him from my daily life, but very glad that he and Peggy were so happy. I remember trying very hard to be a good mother-in-law by not bothering them too much or offering a lot of suggestions.

Rick and Peggy's first child, Stephanie Ann, was born a little over a year after they were married. I began to take care of Stephanie on weekdays and often overnight since they were both working full-time. Matt was only three years older than Stephanie and they eventually became good play mates. I remember holding Stephanie in my lap many times as I sat on our antique oak rocking chair, trying to comfort her as she sobbed, crying, "I want my mommy and daddy." She eventually began to enjoy all of the animals and fun activities on the ranch. Over the next several years three more children were born to Rick and Peggy — Ashleigh, Richard and Jarod.

I have enjoyed these darling grandchildren very much over the years. Each one continues to impress me with their intelligence, strong work ethic, empathy and joyful spirit. As I write this in 2020, they have given me four beautiful great-grandchildren to cherish. They have all graduated from college and have excellent jobs, contributing to the well-being of their communities. I am so proud of them all.

Unfortunately, at some point Rick and Peggy began to use drugs. Years later I discovered that they eventually squandered everything, became homeless and started to take advantage of the good nature of their children. I was consumed with the duties of my new job at Girl Scouts and didn't visit Fresno often during this time. They always made an effort to cover up evidence of their deteriorating lifestyle whenever I would come for a visit. Rick was a smooth talker, just like his father, so he was able to easily explain away any concerns I had from time to time.

Thankfully as I write this, Peggy has pulled her life together beautifully. She married a really nice man, is a wonderful mother to her children and a doting grandmother to her grandchildren. I am thrilled to see the whole family so healthy and happy.

All of my children, grandchildren and great children share bloodlines with the Peoria Indian tribe, which is part of the Cherokee Nation, through their father's genetics. They have enjoyed many benefits over the years such as funding for higher education, healthcare and other living expenses. Rick and Peggy had moved to Oklahoma, living on the Peoria Indian reservation, when he became very sick just after he turned 50 years old. They decided to move back to Kingsburg to be near friends and family. I soon realized that Rick was much sicker than anyone had expected.

I was at a board meeting for Santa Barbara Neighborhood Clinics when Rick's doctor called me. I excused myself and walked out into the hallway to take the call. The doctor said Rick had an advanced case of liver cancer. I asked about the process and the prognosis and he said Rick would receive regular treatments of chemotherapy but that he probably wouldn't live longer than six months. I asked if Rick's long-term use of methamphetamine likely contributed to his cancer and the doctor said he wasn't sure but that meth damages all of a person's organs.

The news hit me hard but I walked back into the board meeting and took my seat until it was over.

I made a visit to Hospice of Santa Barbara the next day. I remembered how helpful their grief counseling had been after my dad died, and I knew they could give me some guidance about how to support my family through this crisis. Jim Hill, a Hospice counselor, met me at the door and invited me inside. I explained the situation and asked if I could have some of their booklets to distribute to my family members. He asked, "What about you?" I said I would deal with my own grief after the fact because I needed to give my energy to my children and grandchildren. He responded, "I'll give you plenty of booklets if you agree to come meet with me every Wednesday at 4:00." I quickly agreed and gratefully took several of his pamphlets. I read through them and decided which one to give to which person.

Rick and Peggy eventually moved into a small studio behind Baird's house and I began to make regular visits to Kingsburg to check on Rick's progress. Thankfully I kept a journal to record many of these visits. Of course all of Rick's siblings, children and his wife were devastated by the news. I knew right away that I would play a key support role throughout his journey over the coming months. I felt honored to be able to provide this encouragement.

I tried hard to be completely present to each person during my visits. I felt so privileged to have been able to walk beside these dear ones in their journey through grief, confusion, and sadness — especially since I was a fellow traveler along that road. The next few pages are taken from the journal I kept during my visits.

I arrived in Kingsburg at Baird's house on a Friday evening in mid-May, 2012 to find Rick and Baird sitting on the couch located on the patio beside the house. I sat with them while they bantered about where to eat and what to wear. Peggy came in wearing a pretty blue blouse and got caught up on the where-to-eat banter.

Finally, at about 7:30, the big dinner decision was made and we all loaded into my car and off we went on the long, but beautiful drive to Reedley where we planned to eat at the Schoolhouse Restaurant (previously Sherwood Inn).

It was a little unnerving driving at my usual fast pace on the country roads where you never know when a fruit-laden truck or slow-moving car might appear out of nowhere. I used to drive these roads with ease when I was raising the kids — even in dense fog. But now I was used to driving on city roads and freeways, not country roads, so I felt very vulnerable.

We arrived at the restaurant around 8:00. It was a place that held years of memories for each of us. The hostess seated us at a booth and we settled in to read the menu and discuss favorite dishes and engage in long-forgotten reminiscing of how the place used to look years ago. Finally our dinners arrived; we were all hungry and dove in with gusto. I looked at Rick, who had taken three bites of his dinner, and his hands were covering his face and he looked like he was going to get sick or cry. Immediately Baird got up to take him outside to the car.

While they were outside, Peggy and I had a rare few minutes to talk. This time could not have been orchestrated if we tried. I expressed my sorrow for her pain and acknowledged her rough journey. She cried and seemed to appreciate my concern for her. I urged her to take advantage of Ashleigh's offer to take her on a tour of the local Hospice facility so she could become familiar with their services. I explained a bit of the difference between the goals of a medical professional vs. that of a hospice worker — the former tries to heal the patient, while the latter works to make the last weeks and months as comfortable and rewarding as possible.

Soon Baird was back and we asked the waitress to box up all our dinners, and then we left the restaurant. Rick lay down in the back seat, feeling sick. Evidently he was supposed to eat frequently to keep from feeling nauseated, but because he knew we were going out to eat, he had not eaten for too long a period of time. So, after taking just a few bites of his dinner he felt nauseated. I arrived back at my hotel around 9:30 after taking everyone home and fell into an exhausted sleep.

The next morning I did a few exercises in the Kingsburg Hotel gym, had a bit of coffee, answered a few emails and then packed up and drove to Fresno to visit with my son, Matt, and his youngest daughter, Mellissa. After that I left to drive to Ashleigh's apartment where I met up with all of Rick's children — Stephanie, Ashleigh, Richard, and Jarod — who were just finishing up helping with a summer church day camp for low-income kids in the neighborhood. All sizes and shapes of kids filled the large park-like setting, playing games, eating hot dogs, and just hanging out. After cleaning everything up and putting away all the tables, chairs and equipment, we loaded up and drove to the Chinese restaurant in Kingsburg to meet Baird for lunch.

Once we were seated, I gave each of them a booklet from Hospice about how to have meaningful conversations with someone who is dying. I talked a bit about what I had learned from my Hospice grief counselor and urged them to go to Hospice counseling themselves. I told them I learned about how we all die in the same way we have lived and, therefore, they should not expect their dad to change his ways just because he is dying.

I also reminded them to be gentle with their mother because she was in the process of losing her husband of 34 years. I suggested to Ashleigh that she take Peggy for a tour of the local Hospice so she could get more comfortable with the idea of their eventual help.

After lunch I headed south to Baird's house in Kingsburg for a final farewell. I sat next to Rick who was sitting on the couch on the side patio. He admired my horseshoe ring that I'd had for so many years, and then touched my hand and teared up saying what a big part of his life I had played for so many years. He asked, "Mommy can you take this away?" We just sat there for a long while and I hugged him as we rocked back and forth.

After a while I left and Baird walked me out to my car. He said he was able to get Rick to sign the advanced health care directive, which was a big deal. I brought one on my last visit, but Rick was too overwhelmed to sign it or even consider it. I was glad this important detail was taken care of. I asked Baird who was appointed as Rick's health care agent. He said it was him and started crying. We stood out on the driveway, Baird and I, while I held him close and he sobbed and sobbed. He said how hard it was for him to see the life leaving Rick's body each day. I told him how brave and courageous he was to take on this role for Rick and the family. And I acknowledged how hard it must be. We parted with another hug and I drove home.

My next visit to see Rick was mid-June. He looked much worse than the previous month. I guess I shouldn't have been surprised about that, but it was so hard to watch him deteriorate like this. He was skinnier, sadder and more tired. He was declining more rapidly and his distended stomach made him look like he was seven months pregnant. He was scheduled to get his stomach pumped the next week and then go to the oncologist to have the reading of his CT scan. At that time he would decide, once again, whether he would continue with the chemo treatment or not.

We went to the Kingsburg Chinese restaurant, at his request, only to have him get sick after two bites. We boxed it all up and drove home. He and I just sat quietly on the couch outside. He told me that I had provided him with a wonderful childhood and he really appreciated it. He said it was important for me to know this. I thanked him and told him it meant a lot to me that he felt that way.

I took Stephanie, Ashleigh, Matt and his three daughters to a very nice lunch at Red Robin. Stephanie and Ashleigh cried as we talked about Rick in the parking lot. Afterwards I took Matt and his three daughters to the zoo, trying to maintain a certain degree of normalcy for the young ones.

In July I drove to Fresno to visit Rick and to make plans for his funeral. Rick looked worse than ever. He was skinnier, couldn't talk very much, and couldn't focus his eyes. He had not eaten for several days. I reminded Baird and Peggy that a loss of appetite was normal for the end stages of the dying process. I reminded them of the booklet I had given them called *Journey's End* and encouraged them to read it to prepare themselves for the physical stages of dying.

During this visit I had dinner with my long-time good friends, Helen Cummings and her son, Bill. It was a warm time of connecting with old friends who care about me — just what I needed. After dinner I went to spend the night with my close friends, Mary Roach and her husband, David Burchard, who gave me loving support, like angels ministering to me.

Ashleigh called me the next day to say they put Rick in the hospital because he was bleeding internally. I went to Fresno Community Hospital and stayed with him, along with Peggy, all day for the next two days. I could tell I was getting sick but tried to keep it to myself. I had intended to stay two more days, but I had to leave because I had a terrible sore throat and could hardly talk.

While I was sitting by Rick's bed patting his arm, he reminded me that this was the third time I had sat at his hospital bed patting his arm. I was curious which three times he was referring to. He said the first was when he had his appendix out in eighth grade; the second was when he was badly burned when trying to incinerate his trash with gasoline; and this was the third. He said, "You've always been there for me, Mom, no matter what." What a precious moment that was.

About a week later, I was having a glass of wine with a friend at a local Santa Barbara winery when my phone rang. It was Peggy in tears. I could hardly understand her through her sobs, but she seemed to be saying something about having read the booklet I gave her and that she just realized Rick was displaying all the signs of dying. I comforted her the best I could and guaranteed I would be there for her.

Ashleigh called me after I got home to say that Rick was near death. He was still in the hospital but the doctors were meeting at 11:00 the next morning to determine when to send him home to die. She said they had already removed all the IVs and monitors.

I packed my things and left early the next morning so I could be there for the meeting with the doctors. I'm so glad I was there. Peggy and Ashleigh were present, but they clearly deferred to me to ask questions, remember answers and talk with the clinicians. After that, we all sat vigil at Rick's bedside every day until they sent him home on Saturday, July 14. Peggy and I drove in my car and they transported Rick in an ambulance to the little studio behind Baird's house in Kingsburg. Peggy and I stopped by CVS to drop off a prescription for Rick and by the time we got to Baird's house, Rick was already there. He was sitting on the outside couch — for the last time.

I stayed with Rick and the others for most of the day Saturday and then I drove back to Mary and David's house for a little personal respite. I had planned to drive home once I was sure Rick was settled into his studio. But something told me to stay. Hospice was coming on Sunday to officially sign him up as a patient, so I decided to stay for that to make sure everything went smoothly and everyone felt good about it. By the end of Sunday, though, I could tell Rick didn't have long to live, so I decided to just stay. I visited with Rick and the others the next day and did a few funeral errands. I had touching talks with Baird, Matt, Peggy and all of Rick's children.

The next day, Tuesday, people began to arrive to tell Rick goodbye — Pam, Margaret (Rick, Pam and Mike's birth mother) and Jeff (their brother). Mike called me to say he would arrive the next day.

I felt an overwhelming need to say just the right thing to everyone and to Rick to ease his transition, but I couldn't think of what to say. I walked across the other side of the street for privacy and frantically called Hospice in Santa Barbara, hoping to talk to Jim Hill or to get someone to read parts of the booklet, *Compassionate Conversations*, to me since I had not brought my copy. The lady who answered talked to me, but mostly reiterated the key points I already remembered — except she reminded me that hearing is always the last sense to go.

So, that gave me an idea. I called Mike and told him Rick would probably be dead by the end of the day and if he wanted to, I would hold my cell phone to Rick's ear and he could say his goodbyes. He liked the idea and it worked perfectly. I held the cell phone to Rick's ear and, even though Rick was non-responsive, I could tell he knew what was going on and was glad to hear from Mike.

Ashleigh called Pastor Chris, their family minister, who arrived that afternoon. He invited everyone to join him around Rick's bed for prayer. There were about 15 people there. Pastor Chris stood at the head of the bed, read scripture, prayed for Rick's perfect healing and then anointed his forehead with oil. A few people said some parting words to Rick and then we all filed out of the room. People went back to mingling and talking in small groups and wandering into Rick's room from time to time.

Everyone was feeling so bad about the suffering Rick was enduring. He was breathing only because of the oxygen machine, hadn't eaten for a very long time, couldn't swallow and couldn't speak or focus his eyes. About 15 minutes after the prayer, Rick passed. It was so sad but also beautiful!

I had a tough talk with Peggy the day before. I said that her kids and I had all told Rick that it was okay for him to leave, and I had promised Rick I would make sure Peggy and the kids were always okay. But I told Peggy that I thought Rick might be holding on because he knew she wasn't ready for him to go yet. I urged her to find a time soon to tell him she was ready. She cried and said she wasn't ready. I told her that she would never feel ready, even 10 years from now. She agreed to tell him so he could be relieved of his suffering. I believe that was part of the reason he was able to finally let go.

About an hour after Rick died, Hospice arrived and then called Creighton's Funeral Home, which sent two transporters to bring his body to the funeral home. They were very kind people. My whole being was riveted on watching Rick's body as they covered him with a sheet and transferred him to the gurney. I couldn't take my eyes off of him as they wheeled him toward the waiting hearse — I reasoned that if I could still see him maybe he wouldn't really be gone.

There were only about three or four of us involved in this process. The others were sitting around talking, clearly relieved that Rick was finished suffering. As I stood by the car and they were putting him inside, I cried and cried. My eyes searched for the last sight of his fuzzy beard sticking up from the sheet. Then the door was closed and off they went. Love went riding in the hearse that day.

I decided to stay the next day so I could take Peggy to the funeral home and wrap up the final funeral details. Ashleigh and I spent the day together doing funeral errands — headstone design, florist, supplies for the reception and caterer. We picked up Peggy and went to the cemetery to pick out the plot and then to Creighton's for her to sign the papers and make final arrangements. Finally, I left Kingsburg at 5 p.m. to drive home. I was so tired already and I had almost four hours to drive. But I used the time to call a few people to let them know about Rick's passing — my mother and brother, some of Larry's long-time friends and a few of my friends.

I arrived in Carpinteria just before 9 p.m. and all I could think of was going to Corktree Cellars (my favorite restaurant) to get a hug from Annie (the manager), get a glass of wine and some of their homemade macaroons. I went there but Ann had already gone home, so I ordered macaroons to go. As I stood at the bar waiting for them, I saw my friend, Jordan, sitting with his parents at one of the tables. I tried to ignore him because I was too tired to talk, but thought better of it. I went over to say hi and he gave me a hug.

His father said I looked tired and I explained that I had just driven four hours from Fresno. His father said he hoped I had had a good trip to Fresno. With that, I started crying and told them my son had just died. I felt foolish but couldn't help myself. I picked up the macaroons and went home to eat them with a glass of wine and watch an Ally McBeal television show, which turned out to be about a guy dying of cancer!

Now it was time to prepare for the funeral. I took a bunch of old photos to Samy's Camera store to make copies, so I could make a collage of Rick's life. The sales lady tried to show me how to use the scanner, but it was too complicated and overwhelming and I just started crying, saying I would pay the extra amount for her to do the scanning for me. She was very kind and understanding. I picked up the scanned photos from Samy's the next day and took them to Aaron Brothers where the people there were very kind, put the collage together and finished it by the next day. It was beautiful and they were very proud of the result.

My friend and co-worker, Bonnie Campbell, took the program I had designed to Boone Graphics where they printed it on fancy card stock. They delivered it to me in just a few hours and didn't charge me anything. It seemed I had angels ministering to me everywhere.

Thursday, July 19, two days after Rick's death would have been his 52nd birthday. His kids and I agreed that we would all eat chocolate cake with chocolate frosting drenched with milk in his honor because it was his favorite birthday dessert.

Rick's funeral was on Thursday, July 26, 2012 at 10 am. It was everything I had hoped it would be — beautiful guitar and keyboard music by Ashleigh's friend, a lovely solo by another of her friends, great bagpipe music by Richard's friend, Tim Greene, and lots of touching stories shared by friends and family. About 150 people crowded into the little chapel with standing room only. Many Kingsburg people came who saw the obituary I had written in the newspaper just the day before — Wayne Larson (our long-time family friend), several members of the Workman family, people from KCAPS and many other folks we knew when we lived in Kingsburg.

All of our children except Matt attended. Larry did not attend. Both absences were a source of additional sadness to many people there. Wayne wept as he asked me why Larry wasn't there. I will probably never understand why Larry and Matt were not willing to set aside their own discomfort to pay their respects to Rick. It seemed selfish and disrespectful; disrespectful to Rick and also to the family and all the other people who showed up.

I served as the emcee, welcoming everyone in the beginning and then inviting people to share stories. I was delighted that so many people shared such tender stories — even Penny Workman who talked a bit about the night her brother, Scott, was killed as he, Rick and Dave Wells were celebrating Rick's 21st birthday. I was afraid that people wouldn't share, but I was glad that they did. Pam wasn't sure if she was going to share, but she excitedly called me the day before to say she had thought of some stories to tell. Her stories were particularly moving.

At the end of the service, Richard's friend, Tim, played the first verse of Amazing Grace on the bagpipes standing at the front of the chapel. Then he walked down the center aisle playing the next verses while Richard carried the box containing Rick's cremains, walking behind Tim. A framed drawing of Rick, drawn by Jarod, sat at the front of the church surrounded by flowers. Jarod also etched an image of Rick on the cremains box — and it was absolutely beautiful.

After the service, we hung out a bit outside the chapel and then we got in our cars and followed the hearse to the cemetery. My friend, Dee Ptak, rode with me. The interment service at Kingsburg Cemetery was short but very nice. Family members placed a white rose on the cremains box area (Peggy's rose was red) and I handed out six small red boxes of cremains to those who had requested them.

Afterward we gathered at Rick's good friend Tony George's house for the reception. Lots of people were there and we had a nice time visiting, eating together and sharing stories about Rick. I was so glad to see my nieces, Karin and Laurie Rocker, and I was touched that my good friend, Mary Roach, attended and stayed a long time. I left to drive home around 4 p.m., tired but satisfied that Rick had a good send-off.

Rick visited me in my dreams often for the next three months. This was both comforting and disconcerting — comforting because I loved having him so close and disconcerting because each of the dreams was so real. One time we were lying on the living room floor on our backs, touching fingertips, and he said, "You are receiving and I am transforming." Another time he interlaced his fingers with mine and said, "When I hold your hand I am transformed by your energy." In another one he said, "Mom, it was so important to me that you were there for me and my family."

There were some funny dreams, too, and I am grateful that I wrote so many of them down at the time. Looking back to when Rick was starting his family, I treasure the times he would call me out of the blue and thank me for being such a good mother to him. He always wanted me to know how much he appreciated me.

I learned several lessons through Rick's dying journey. I realized that Jim Hill at Hospice had given me a valuable gift when he insisted that I meet with him weekly. I actually had a counseling session with Jim at 4 p.m. every Wednesday for nine months — giving me the support I needed for my family during the months leading up to Rick's death, helping me through the dying journey itself and working with me for several months after Rick's passing to process my own grief.

I also learned that we die the way we lived. We shouldn't expect the one who is dying to behave in any particular way, especially not in a way that is different from the way that person had lived. If that person had been quiet and emotionally unavailable in their life, the same behavior should be expected during the dying process and vice versa. We must be careful not to expect someone to die the way we would die because the way we would die is the way we live.

Our natural tendency as humans is to turn away from any type of pain — physical or emotional. But with the pain of grief (and perhaps other types of pain as well), it's better if we try to turn into the pain and face it, in fact, embrace it. Only if we do this will we be able to fully experience the blessing of a loved one's final moments. We must diligently work at being present with the one who is dying and with our own pain and grief simultaneously. If we do this, we will open places deep within ourselves that can't be opened any other way and may otherwise remain hidden from us.

On the second anniversary of Rick's passing, his children asked if I would create a ceremony for us to commemorate his life. They all came over to Carpinteria for the weekend and we had a precious time together. I designed a ceremony using the four elements: Fire, Water, Air and Earth. We all gathered under an oak tree around a wooden picnic bench on a little sand hill by the ocean for this observance of his life.

Fire: *As fire cleanses dross; May the flame of passion for life burn away all sorrow.*

We passed a lighted candle around while each one shared a memory or a dream.

Water: *As water comes to us as the voice of grief, the cry of love, the flowing tear; May all our inner voyaging keep us attuned to God's love.*

We dipped a sprig of fresh rosemary into a bowl of water and I asked each person to anoint the person next to them with the water.

Earth: *Let us thank the Earth that offers ground for home and holds our feet firm to walk in space open to infinite galaxies.*

Each person read a stanza or two of the poem, *Trespasses*, by David Whyte and then took a red ceramic heart as a souvenir.

Air: *Kingdom of spirit where our departed dwells, nearer to us than ever, where God presides.*

We lit a sprig of fresh sage and each person passed it over the head of the person next to them saying, "May this spirit of the air bless you and wrap you in a warm cloak of love."

Some of my favorite poems and quotes about death and grief

Unconditional by Jennifer Wellwood

"Willing to experience aloneness, I discover connection
   everywhere;
Turning to face my fear, I meet the warrior who lives within;
Opening to my loss, I gain the embrace of the universe;
Surrendering into emptiness, I find fullness without end.
Each condition I flee from pursues me;
Each condition I welcome transforms me, and becomes
   transformed
Into its radiant jewel-like essence.
I bow to the one who has made it so, who has crafted this
   Master Game;
To play it is pure delight;
To honor its form—true devotion."

Prayer by Mary Oliver

"May I never not be frisky,
   may I never not be risqué.
May my ashes, when you have them, friend,
   and give them to the ocean,
   leap in the froth of the waves,
   still loving movement,
   still ready, beyond all else,
   to dance for the world."

Fluent by John O'Donohue

"I would love to live
Like a river flows,
Carried by the surprise
Of its own unfolding."

When Death Comes (last three stanzas) by Mary Oliver

"When it's over, I want to say: all my life
I was a bride married to amazement.
I was the bridegroom, taking the world into my arms.

When it's over, I don't want to wonder
   if I have made of my life something particular, and real.
I don't want to find myself sighing and frightened,
   or full of argument.

I don't want to end up simply having visited this world."

In Blackwater Woods (last two stanzas) by Mary Oliver

"To live in this world
you must be able to do three things:
   to love what is mortal;
   to hold it
against your bones knowing
   your own life depends on it;
   and, when the times comes to let it go,
   to let it go."

The Well of Grief by David Whyte

"Those who will not slip beneath
   the still surface on the well of grief

turning downward through its black water
   to the place we cannot breathe

will never know the source from which we drink,
   the secret water, cold and clear,

nor find in the darkness glimmering
   the small round coins
   thrown by those who wished for something else."

From *The Lost Hotels of Paris* by Jack Gilbert

"But it's the having not the keeping that is the treasure."

"Don't turn your head away; keep looking at that bandaged
place. That's where the light comes in." – Rumi

My beautiful son Rick, whose passing saddened so many

273

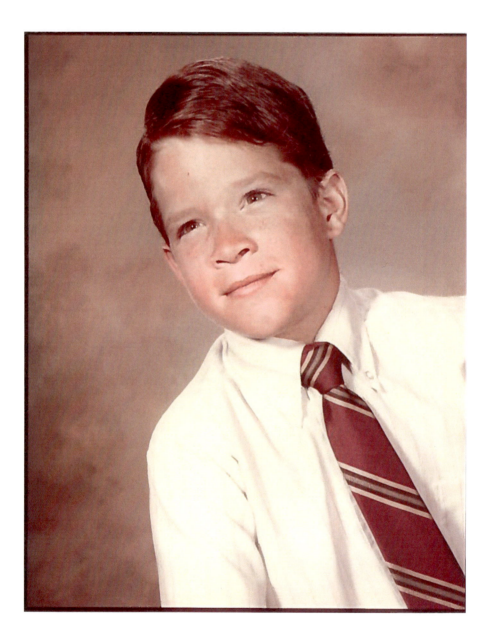

Rick in junior high

Rick holding his brother Matt

Rick and I making strawberry jam

Rick married his lovely high school sweetheart Peggy

CHAPTER ELEVEN
Finding My Soul Mate

Hope sends us dancing around dark corners
embracing a tomorrow we cannot see.
– Joan Chittister

I had participated in the mid-June annual bike ride to benefit the American Lung Association for eight years. The 25-mile route wound through the hills and countryside of the beautiful Santa Ynez Valley, ending with a delicious barbeque dinner under the oak trees at the charming Midland School. I always enjoyed going with my good friends, Jim and Marcia Wolf — except for one year. In 2014 they called to let me know they wouldn't be able to attend, so I went alone.

I stepped up to the registration table to fill out the paperwork at the same time as a man whose name I later found out was Dennis Forster. We chatted a bit and decided to ride together since we both came to the ride alone. Off we went carrying on a lively conversation as we rode along the country roads through miles of lush grapevines and fruit-laden orchards. I had been having a challenge at work with my new employer and Dennis proved to be a great sounding board, giving me some good advice.

We stopped for lunch at the beautiful Roblar Winery. We were both hot and tired by the time we returned to Midland School in the afternoon. It was too early for the group dinner to start, so we found cots in a couple of the cabins and each took a nap. Dennis and I were both quite hungry by the time the barbeque dinner got started. We sat around on the large log seats enjoying the delicious food, lively music and inspiring presentations. Dennis and I each climbed into our respective cars and headed home after a delightful, fun-filled day.

Dennis called me a couple of times over the next few days to find out how things were going for me with my new employer. It was clear that we both had enjoyed the time we spent together. I was feeling pretty lucky as I began to realize what a kind, thoughtful, generous, fun and smart guy Dennis was.

I've always been diligent about keeping a full, up-do-date calendar. I would routinely buy one of those large, laminated calendars from OfficeMax so I could plan out the entire year. I wanted to make sure that I planned some sort of outing for myself every quarter plus a two-week vacation every year. I was considering my empty calendar and wondering where I should go on my next quarterly adventure when I remembered that I had been wanting to make another trip out to the Channel Islands to go kayaking in the caves. So I decided to pick a date and make arrangements.

I called Island Packers at the Ventura Harbor to find out when their next trip to the islands was scheduled. They told me July 6. I signed up and sent an email to some of my girlfriends to let them know I was going and invite them along. They all seemed excited, but as the date got closer, each one let me know she had a conflict with the timing. I knew I would have fun even if I went alone; but then I remembered the guy I had met on the bike ride a few weeks earlier.

I called Dennis and asked if he would be interested in going out to the islands with me. He enthusiastically said yes; but when he called Island Packers they said there were no spots left — that trip was sold out. Dennis is a very persistent guy and, somehow, convinced them to let him go on the trip. I was pleasantly surprised.

It was a perfect summer day — with lots of sunshine and blue skies. We boarded the ship after collecting our rented kayaks from the vendor next door and launched out into the sparkling ocean. Hundreds of dolphins jumped out of the waves for much of the three-hour ride to Santa Cruz Island. It was thrilling and magical! Dennis and I ventured up to the bridge and the captain let Dennis drive the boat for quite a while — which he really enjoyed.

We anchored the boat just offshore, gathered up our gear and piled into the kayaks. The guide gave us a short safety talk and then we began to explore the dim caves with our headlamps shining through the darkness. Some were so narrow that we had to go through one at a time behind the guide and lean backwards to use our hands on the cave ceilings to thread ourselves through. We navigated large swells, which added to the fun and excitement as we paddled from cave to cave. I was glad I was such an accomplished kayaker.

We headed back to Ventura in the afternoon after lunch on shore and some afternoon paddling.

They use this boat for overnight scuba diving trips, so the lower floor has several built-in beds with dark green curtains for privacy. On the journey back Dennis asked if I wanted to take a nap. I'm not a fan of naps but I thought, "Poor guy, he must be really tired after all of that kayaking." I agreed even though I thought it was a bit strange. We climbed down the ladder to the bottom deck and crawled into one of the beds. As it turned out, a "nap" was not exactly what he had in mind. Let's just say I discovered that Dennis is a very affectionate and amorous guy.

Dennis called me several times and we went to dinner a couple of evenings during the next two months. One of our very memorable dates was at Cold Spring Tavern, where he told me he was married but that his wife was incapacitated — deeply affected by depression and various physical ailments for decades. (Eventually she declined to the point that she passed away.) He said he was trying to enjoy his life and do what he could to care for his wife of 50 years at the same time. I never thought I would date a married man, but he was charming and his rationale seemed to make sense. So we continued to enjoy each other's company.

We have both been long-time supporters of the local Council on Alcoholism and Drug Abuse (CADA) and I had served on their board of directors for six years. Every September they host a local hike at Elings Park, called the Summit for Danny, which raises funds for their work in honor of the founder's son, Danny, who died of a drug overdose. The hike is always a popular local event attended by many people we both know. We decided to go to the event together. We walked through the park to find our car after a really enjoyable hike, a delicious barbeque lunch and inspiring presentations about CADA's work.

Dennis tried to kiss me just before we got to the car. I was so surprised! We were out in the open and anyone passing by would be able to see us. So I pulled back and said, "No, we can't do that — someone might know." I was concerned that if anyone who knew him saw us, they would be scandalized. He just laughed and kept trying to embrace me. I finally conceded but made sure we were shielded behind a large tree trunk.

And that was the start of the most magical, loving and adventurous years of my life.

That secret kiss was September of 2014 and Dennis and I dated off and on during the next year — going out to dinner, dancing at SoHo and sharing happy hour with friends.

Dennis was president of the Santa Barbara Ski Club. I had never wanted to join that group because they did a lot of skiing on weekends and I only liked skiing on weekdays because of the crowded conditions on weekends. But Dennis convinced me to join and we began going on ski trips together with the group. I felt somewhat self-conscious whenever I was with the ski club folks because the members had all been friends of Dennis for many years and they knew he was married. I tried to make the best of it, but I always felt like an outsider and sure that they were judging me. Still, we had lots of fun in spite of my misgivings.

Our first ski trip with the club was to Snowbird Ski Resort in Utah during the week of February 3, 2015. It was a great trip and we quickly learned that we could ski together quite well, even though he skied faster than I did. In fact, his nickname in the club is "The Bullet" because he goes so fast down the mountain.

I thoroughly enjoyed the skiing and camaraderie. On that trip we both had the unusual experience of a strange sort of vertigo. We were enveloped in a thick fog soon after we emerged from the gondola and started to ski down the mountain. We couldn't even see our hands in front of our faces, we couldn't tell if we were moving forward or standing still, and we had no idea where we were or how to get down the hill. It was very scary. We finally made it past the fog, to our mutual relief, but it took a long time.

Our next ski trip with the club was to Mammoth Ski Resort in California later in February, where we enjoyed another great time on the slopes with wonderful people who were quickly becoming friends of mine as well as Dennis'. In March we skied at Steamboat Springs Resort in Colorado. We were actually there for my birthday week, so it was fun celebrating in such a spectacular place. Dennis made sure it was a very special event. And then two weeks after we returned from that trip we went back to Mammoth for several days of skiing. I'm so glad he likes to ski so much!

In early April of 2015 we started doing lots of hikes and bike rides to prepare for the international Summit for Danny hike, this time set to proceed along the famous Camino de Santiago de Compostela in Spain in mid-May. While CADA was a local Santa Barbara organization, it always organized an annual hike in an exciting international location.

Meanwhile I needed to leave Santa Barbara at the end of April to go to Sioux Falls for the six-month assignment as CEO for Girl Scouts in South and North Dakota. This necessitated a lot of schedule juggling, but Dennis and I were determined to enjoy each other's company as much as possible. Dennis called me every morning and every evening during my time in South Dakota. Thankfully I was able to come home for a few short visits during my tenure as well as take time off for some pre-planned trips, including the trip to Spain.

In Mid-May of 2015, Dennis and I joined 20 participants to hike 100 miles of the 500-mile trek along the spectacular Camino de Santiago (also known as "The Way of St. James"). The hike itself was 10 days long, but we arranged for extra sight-seeing before and after the hike, extending the trip to 21 days. Starting in Madrid, we danced to their rock and roll music at 2 a.m., marveled at the incredible flamenco dancers and enjoyed delicious meals and fine wines.

We visited the fascinating Guggenheim Museum in Bilbao, hiked through the drizzling rain in Roncesvalles, France, and I read scripture from the pulpit at the beautiful Iglesia de Santiago back in Spain. We also visited the famous city of Pamplona where they release six bulls to run down the narrow streets at 8 a.m. in the second week of July.

Each day of the international hike started with the group gathering around to hear one of the hikers read a letter written by one of the students in the Daniel Bryant drug abuse program. They are always touching and powerful. I had the honor of reading one of these letters on the first day of the hike.

One highlight of the trip was dining on fresh-caught seafood in the quaint town of San Sabastian overlooking the expansive Atlantic Ocean. The 100-mile hike ended at Finesterra, which some considered to be the end of the earth when it was thought to be flat. It was wild and windy that day and the rugged scenery was breath-taking.

We bid adieu to our fellow hikers and began the last portion of our trip in Barcelona. We decided this is one of our favorite cities. There were lots of colorful parades celebrating the recent soccer tournament, dancing to rock and roll music until all hours of the night and a bike tour through the very crowded main streets. We saw many elaborate cathedrals, including the Sagrada Familia Basilica, toured the Barcelona Olympic Village and took a bike ride through the beautiful harbor area along the Mediterranean Sea.

August is the winter season in Patagonia, South America, so we decided to go there for a two-week ski trip. We flew into Buenos Aires and headed to San Carlos de Barilochi to ski after enjoying a tour through the city. The magnificent ski resort there, Cathedral Patagonia, is the largest in South America. The ski operators went on strike after we had skied for just three days, so we went to the nearby Cerro Bayo Resort for more skiing. The view from the mountaintops over the enormous crystal blue lakes below was incredible. We turned in our rental equipment after a week of skiing and headed to Peru.

At the top of our list of sights to see was the imposing and mysterious Incan citadel of Machu Picchu. We started in Cuzco, which is 11,000 feet in elevation, and took a three and a half hour train ride to Machu Picchu, whose altitude is only 8,000 feet. The train took us along the Urubamba River in the Sacred Valley, with dramatic canyon walls on either side. Thankfully we arranged for a private guide so we could appropriately appreciate this iconic Incan archaeological site. The guide was so valuable — telling us the stories of all the ancient tribes that farmed the carefully tiered hillsides and making sure we didn't miss anything along the way.

A live band was playing on the train ride back to Cuzco, so Dennis and I danced our way through the trip. It's pretty tricky to dance while on a train winding through the canyons but we managed to have lots of fun and create a sweet memory.

Next we flew to Lima where we arranged for a four-hour culinary tour through the farmers markets, butcher shops and coffee houses. At the final stop we made our own pisco sour drinks and ceviche. What a taste treat! We ended the trip with dinner at the incredible Cala Restaurant overlooking the black-as-night ocean and the city to the enchanting sound of the waves crashing on shiny round black rocks below. We will never forget that evening — in fact we agreed that we would happily fly to Lima just to go back to that charming restaurant.

In October of 2015 I finished my work in South Dakota and came home. That month we rode our bikes in the Ski Club's Bike & Wine event, tasting wine at various wineries in the Santa Ynez Valley. It can be a little tricky to peddle a bike after indulging in libations, so we were particularly careful about our intake amount.

In November we headed to Belize where we stayed at the spectacular Chabil Mar Resort in Plascencia for 10 delightful days. It was as beautiful and magical as we imagined it would be. We took a nap as soon as we arrived because we were both tired from the long trip. A lively wedding reception was in progress when we awoke in the late afternoon. Folks were dancing to a great band, drinking bubbly champagne and having a fun time. We decided to join in. The young bride and groom were clearly delighted to have these groovy oldsters crash their party.

The next day we went for a long hike through the lush rain forest, spilling over with beautiful tropical plants and flowers at every turn. We were pretty warm from the exercise as well as the high humidity and temperatures, so a plunge into a cold pond below a waterfall felt exhilarating. A fun fishing trip was on tap for the next day. We met the small motorboat and its captain at the nearby dock early in the morning. We each caught two very large Jack fish after a couple of hours. The captain cleaned them when we got back to the dock and packaged them up for us to take with us. The resort kitchen staff prepared them in a delicious dish for our dinner that evening, which we enjoyed as we sat on our sweet patio under the swaying palm trees.

We had been wanting to take the resort's kayaks out for a paddle, but each day we were too busy or the sea was too rough. We were determined to go kayaking, but only one day was left on our trip, so even though the waves were big and boisterous, we grabbed two of the resort's kayaks and started pulling them into the ocean. Three staff members hurried over to tell us they were concerned about our safety and advised us not to go out into the roiling ocean. Dennis assured them that we are veteran kayakers, but they were unconvinced and remained worried.

Once we were in the water and had paddled out quite a distance, we looked back to shore to see most of the staff lined up on the beach watching us. It seemed like they were sure they would have to come rescue us before long. We were satisfied with our paddle adventure and agreed the waves were getting too big, so we headed back to shore — and made it safely, much to the relief of the staff. What an invigorating memory!

We finished the year with a week of Ski Race Camp in Mammoth in mid-December where we were paired with four or five skiers of a similar level and were assigned an instructor for lessons every day for five days. This is always a great way to get ready for the ski season.

2016 was full of exciting adventures in Italy, Croatia, Norway, Finland and Sweden as well as escapades in popular spots in the U.S. The first three months of the year included great ski trips to Mammoth, Jackson Hole, Wyoming, Mount Rose at Lake Tahoe and Banff, Canada. While in Wyoming we took a wild snowmobile ride through Yellowstone National Park, where we witnessed the fascinating Old Faithful Geyser. The Banff trip included a stay at the incredibly beautiful Banff Springs Hotel for my birthday. It was the height of luxury.

In April we drove down to Coronado, a charming island just offshore in the San Diego area to visit my son, Michael, and his family. We enjoyed walking around the beautiful harbor area and even rented bikes for a tour around the city. Neither of us is a "shopper," but Dennis was taken with a colorful dress displayed in a shop window as we walked along the boardwalk. We ended up buying it even though I would have never chosen it by myself. Over the years I have worn it to most fancy events — so now we refer to it as my "hot dress."

In May we decided to take a trip to New York, since neither of us had been there for a few years. We took an impressive ride in a helicopter touring New York City — which was my first ever helicopter ride. The next day we hired a fancy horse and buggy for a ride through Central Park which was fun and felt decadent.

Mid-June through Mid-July we joined a 16-person bike group, led by a local Santa Barbara cyclist, Frank Schipper, who is also a friend. We rode our bikes 250 miles through the beautiful countryside of Italy from Venice to Croatia. We arrived in Croatia and then boarded a boat which took us around to the various Croatian islands, where we rode another 100 miles. When passing from Italy to Croatia, we also peddled through a mountainous portion of Slovenia.

The temperature was a little too high for cycling comfort in Croatia but we persevered, knowing that when we got back to the boat every afternoon we would change our sweaty bike clothes for a bathing suit and jump off the back of the boat into the freezing and stunning Aegean Sea. What a treat! Croatia was so jaw-droppingly beautiful that one time I was too busy admiring the sights and fell off my bike when it hit a gravel-covered hill. I injured my leg and knee and had to ice and wrap it for a while, but I was lucky it wasn't hurt worse. So when we saw a Jet Ski rental vendor, we jumped at the chance to take a spin. I just propped my injured leg up on the front and off we went.

In August and September it was time for another Summit for Danny international hike — this time to Norway. We arrived a couple days early so we could tour the beautiful city of Oslo before the formal trip started. Then we met 23 fellow hikers, mostly from Santa Barbara, and climbed the gorgeous hills and valleys in Norway. We had to be careful because the frequent rain made the trails muddy and slippery. We got pretty dirty, but no one was injured and the challenge added to the delight. The bountiful rain also created hundreds of magnificent waterfalls, many of which we toured and walked under.

We all boarded a large ferry which cruised through some of Norway's 1,000 breathtaking glacier-carved fjords, with cliffs plunging to the sea. On another day, we toured the world-famous Norwegian Glacier Museum and learned that Norway has 1,600 glaciers. The Sognefjord is Norway's longest fjord, stretching more than 125 miles and measuring 4,291 feet at its deepest point.

After the hike, we decided to visit Stockholm, Sweden and Helsinki, Finland as long as we were in that part of the world. We first toured Stockholm — walking and biking through the iconic cobblestone streets along the Baltic Sea for two days. Then we booked a suite on the Silja Symphony, a large ship that sails from Stockholm to Helsinki.

We boarded the ship and settled into our very large and beautiful suite located at the back of the ship. We discovered that the ship held 2,500 passengers and made the round-trip voyage twice every day. Many of the travelers used the ship as a ferry for business transportation — as they live in one city and work in the other. We were continually amazed as we explored the multi-decked vessel to see the diverse collection of elaborate shops, live music venues and all sorts of restaurants — fancy and casual.

The ship left port in the afternoon and we were treated to magnificent views of the famous Stockholm archipelago before heading out to the Baltic. We enjoyed dinner at one of their upscale restaurants and then danced to a rock and roll band. Eventually we settled into our suite for the overnight voyage to Helsinki. We arrived at the Helsinki port mid-morning and enjoyed touring that beautiful city for two days. Finally, we took a cab to the Helsinki Airport and flew home after three glorious weeks of incredible travel.

2017 was highlighted by ski trips to Snowmass and Aspen in Colorado, Mammoth and Whistler in Canada (we spent the night at the incredible Fairmont Chateau in Whistler). This year also included biking and hiking tours of South Africa, Botswana, Italy, Prague in Czech Republic and Budapest in Hungary. In May we headed to South Africa for a three-week trip of biking, hiking and safaris with what has become our favorite adventure trip provider — Backroads — which always features premiere hotels and amazing culinary experiences. We checked into the elegant Mount Nelson Hotel in Cape Town, South Africa, and started out on a long hike at Table Mountain National Park progressing up the steep green hills overlooking the expansive Atlantic Ocean and the city of Cape Town. The next day we rode our bikes through Cape Point National Park, ending at the Cape of Good Hope, which is the southwestern most point in the African continent.

While we were riding and admiring the sparkling azure ocean below us, several very large ostriches burst out of the shrubbery that lined the road and began to run alongside our bikes. It was scary and fun at the same time because we didn't know what to expect from them, especially because they were taller than we were and had lots of energy. As it turned out, they just like to play this way and are notorious for surprising tourists like they did us.

After a few days in Cape Town, we hiked and biked at Bushmans Kloof Wilderness Reserve where we were able to view some of the incredible ancient Bushman rock art. Next we boarded a six-passenger King Air plane and flew to Mashatu, Botswana. Several open-top Land Rovers picked us up and drove us to our luxury camp-style hotel at the Mashatu Game Reserve. We were amazed at how remote and rural yet elegant it was. That night we were treated to a sumptuous dinner outside around a blazing fire, including a performance by a host of African dancers — with Dennis and I even joining in for a bit. The next day we were in for a big treat.

We rode mountain bikes along ancient elephant trails through the wilderness teeming with wildlife, including giraffes, big cats and hundreds of bird species. Our guide carried a rifle, which gave us pause, but also a certain level of comfort. Several members of our group chose not to participate -- either because it was too strenuous or a bit scary to think of riding a bike through the wildlife. But we loved it!

The back country terrain was so unpredictable that we had to pay attention constantly. We had to be ready to climb dirt hills, ride through deep sand and water on the river bottom and navigate through the brush. Thankfully Dennis and I managed to keep up with the guide.

The next two days we climbed into open-top Land Rovers for a series of amazing safaris through the reserve. We were thrilled to see so many large animals at close range, including elephant herds, giraffes, wildebeests, wild boars, zebras, lions, hippos, ibex, hyena and water buffalo.

One time we happened to see a large female leopard stretched out atop a Baobab tree. We crept closer to the tree until we were at the very base and peered up to get a better look at what the leopard was doing. Our binoculars revealed that three cubs were on a nearby limb eating on an emu. At one point one of the emu's legs fell out of the tree, so the leopard jumped down immediately to retrieve it and haul it back up to the top of the tree.

The guide explained that this was a highly unusual sight because the mother leopard would typically hide her cubs in a bush and bring the food to them so that the hyenas wouldn't attack them. The mother had taken quite a risk by bringing her cubs up into the tree. The guide further explained that the reason the leopard quickly retrieved the emu leg was so that the hyenas couldn't smell it and try to gather to eat it — finding the cubs in the process.

Every evening at sundown, after a safari, the Landie drivers would park on a cliff overlooking the bush, pull down the gate on their vehicles and serve us snacks and "sundowners" — which is their term for gin and tonic cocktails served at sundown. Standing out in the open in the middle of the bush while sipping our delicious drinks and tasting our snacks as we watched the sun slip behind the horizon was a really magical experience.

Next the Landies drove us to our luxury hotel, Summerfields Rose Retreat & Spa. There we toured the opulent rose gardens and saw lots of giant hippos bathing at dusk in the nearby river. Our final destination on this part of our trip was the most impressive. We checked into the famous Landolozi, an elegant game lodge on the Sand River. The accommodations, food, wine and entertainment there were unimaginable. There we saw lots of elephants and hippos and toured a school for local children. We were invited in to observe the students recite their schoolwork for us and then a local dance troupe entertained us outside with marvelous African dances — and yes, once again Dennis and I joined in.

We drove to Johannesburg after 11 wonderful days of safaris and memorable experiences. Our tour of this famous city included a trip to Soweto where we visited the Nelson Mandela home and the impressive Johannesburg Apartheid Museum. We learned that Nelson Mandela spent 27 years in a brutal prison for his efforts to rid South Africa of apartheid. When he was released he urged everyone to work together toward this worthy cause rather than being resentful. He was soon elected the President of South Africa and led the effort to rebuild the country in an inclusive and positive manner. Three days later we boarded the plane for the flight home. The airplane ride was enjoyable even though it was so long because we traveled in business class where our seats reclined into beds and we were constantly treated like royalty.

In late June of 2017 we once again joined the Summit for Danny international hike for a three-week excursion — this time to Italy. We arrived a few days early so we could explore the captivating city of Florence in the Tuscany region. Our tour took us to the iconic Duomo Cathedral with its bell tower designed by Giotto, to the Galleria del Academia where we viewed Michelangelo's inspiring "David" sculpture and the Uffizi Gallery where we marveled at Botticelli's "The Birth of Venus" and da Vinci's "Annunciation."

We met the Summit group in Bolzano for a week-long hike that would take us to Venice. We trekked through magnificent landscapes and picturesque villages, rode chairlifts above pine forests and storybook mountain huts, enjoyed lots of fine dining and marveled at views of the Cinque Torri stone pinnacles.

The part of the trip we will never forget is when Dennis and I rented electric bikes and rode up to the top of the gondola at the Cortina ski resort. The electric bikes helped us navigate the steep rocky dirt road but since it was such a sheer vertical incline, we had to pedal hard for a long time. If we lost our momentum or fell off the bike, the power assist would not be strong enough for us to continue up the mountain — we would have to ride down instead. So we just kept focusing on our pedaling and balance. Finally we made it to the top of the gondola but we got lots of inquisitive stares from locals who were hiking down the trail. Riding down was a little tricky because the bikes were heavy and the trail was steep and gravelly.

We had such a good time on the electric bikes that two days later we rented them again, however this time another couple came with us. We rode up another steep mountain trail, but the road ended at a cow pasture. We decided to keep going and explore the area, sometimes falling down into the soft loam of the meadow. We rode all over the area and eventually realized we were lost. Everyone had a different idea of how to get back to our hotel — which made for lots of laughs and extra miles. We finally made it back with only a tiny amount of charge left on our batteries.

Dennis and I took the train after a week of hiking with our Summit group and left for a four-day visit to the stunning Lake Como. We stayed at the quaint Hotel Bellagio, an upscale resort area known for its dramatic scenery, set against the foothills of the Alps. Our beautiful suite was high on a hill overlooking the sparkling lake — and we kept the French doors of the balcony open to allow the breeze to bathe us in warm delight.

We walked through the cobbled streets of the picturesque old town center, exploring all sorts of shops and restaurants. We enjoyed a glass of wine at La Punta restaurant overlooking the placid lake and watching the locals come and go in their colorful wooden boats. We definitely felt like we were in an enchanted place.

We walked to Villa Melzi to tour the beautiful botanical gardens, museum and chapel. And on another day we arranged for a private tour of the expansive gardens of Villa Serbelloni, owned by the Rockefeller Foundation. One day a ferry took us for a cruise around Lake Como, dropping us off at various spots so we could explore. At one of the stops we took a bus tour through the stunning vistas to the edge of Switzerland. Finally a large black cab whisked us away to catch our flight back home.

Once back home we jumped into our regular activities like dancing at the Thursday afternoon Concerts in the Park along the beach in Santa Barbara.

September took us on yet another Backroads trip — this time a three-week bike and barge trip on the Danube River. We started in Prague, the picturesque capital of the Czech Republic.

We walked through the charming countryside during the day and boarded the barge every afternoon for a brief rest and a sumptuous dinner. Our bike rides took us along the lovely Danube River, through bright fields of sunflowers, next to colorful Baroque buildings and Gothic churches.

It was thrilling to walk across the famous Charles Bridge which was built in 1402 and is lined with hundreds of statues of Catholic Saints. We also saw the renowned medieval Astronomical Clock with its animated hourly show. While sailing through Budapest, we climbed up to the top deck of the barge at night to see the stunning Basilica and Parliament buildings lit with bright lights against the dark sky, while we sipped an after-dinner aperitif.

Our trip ended in Budapest, the capital of Hungary. What a beautiful city it is, comprised of the hilly Buda area and the flat Pest section. Many years ago Buda and Pest were two separate cities, but now they are combined to form Budapest. Our layover in London was extended for several hours on our way home. So we hired a cab to drive us on a quick tour of downtown London — including Westminster Cathedral, Buckingham Palace and the Tower of London. We didn't have time to even get out of the cab or walk around, but we were glad to be able to see the sights from the cab window instead of just sitting in the airport.

Ski trips to Mammoth and Crested Butte, Colorado kept us busy the first three months of 2018. In April my grandson, Jarod Rocker, and his bride Ashley were married in a beautiful ceremony in the sweet town of Three Rivers near Fresno. Dennis and I were so glad we were able to attend and share in the touching celebration.

Dennis has always loved flowers, especially tulips, and he has long wanted to visit Holland to see these beautiful blooms. So we joined another bike trip in late April — this time to

Netherlands and Belgium. We arrived a few days earlier than the start of the official trip so we could explore Amsterdam. The number of people riding bikes there was astounding and we soon learned that there are twice as many bikes as people in this unique city. We had fun walking through this friendly town and savoring their delicious cuisine.

Dennis and I do love to dance, so one night after dinner we happened upon some live music at one of the charming outside restaurants. We immediately made ourselves at home and started dancing to the lively tunes, but before too long the manager chased us away saying dancing was not allowed. It was disappointing, but we had fun anyway. We also toured the renowned Van Gogh Museum and took a romantic boat ride on the Amstel River.

Our official adventure started in Amsterdam with a leisurely bike ride through the emerald-green fields, horse farms and windmills. Our hotel was a historic country estate situated within the Zuid-Kennermerland National Park. The timing of our trip could not have been planned better for optimum tulip viewing. We started at the famous Keukenhof gardens after riding for several miles past countless fields of bright, multi-colored tulips.

We were greeted by an explosion of color after parking our bikes in their huge bicycle parking lot. Keukenhof is one of the world's largest flower gardens, known as Europe's Flower Garden, and spans 79 acres. The gardens are only open to the public eight weeks each year, mid-March through mid-May. An average of 26,000 people visit Keukenhof each day during the eight-week window, for a total of 1.5 million visitors annually. Spending an entire day meandering through the amazing displays and unique configurations of tulips was beyond wonderful.

The next day we peddled through a landscape of dunes and seaside lanes on the way to The Hague, famous as the

International City of Peace and Justice. The Gothic style complex is the seat of the Dutch parliament. Continuing on our ride, we were amazed at the plentiful windmills. At one point, we got off our bikes and toured two of these iconic structures and learned that years ago they were used to drain the surrounding floodplain to keep the whole city from being engulfed in water. Today Holland uses steam-powered pumps to move the water between the plains. We cruised along the dikes and through the quaint villages on our way to Gouda where we sampled their world-famous cheese.

Beginning the second half of our trip, we biked over the border to Belgium on a scenic spin to the romantic city of Bruges. This town was like walking around in a fairytale. Our guide told us all about the secrets of this medieval city as we rode through their narrow cobblestone streets, past leafy forests and over rippling canals. The next day Dennis wasn't feeling well, so I joined a small group and peddled to the port city of Ghent where we marveled at their medieval monasteries. Their huge outdoor marketplace was teeming with visitors and locals alike. This university town impressed all of us with its lively spirit, ubiquitous canals and striking castles.

Dennis and I bid adieu to the group at the end of the tour and took a short train ride to Brussels to explore the capital of Belgium. We were amazed at the unique combination of modern steel and glass skyscrapers contrasting ancient architecture like the Grand Palace. We boarded a train back to Amsterdam where we toured the unique NEMO Science Museum that features five floors of interactive experiments, plus the Heineken Museum where we learned the history of this famous beer and even tasted a few samples.

We checked into the impressive Hilton Hotel for our last two nights in Amsterdam before heading home. One evening we ventured up to the Sky Lounge on the 40th floor to take in the expansive view of the city, have some snacks and listen to the upbeat DJ music. It's hard for Dennis and I to stay in our chairs very long when lively music is playing, so we decided to get up and dance. They didn't really have a dance floor — just a small space in front of the band. I asked the DJ if it was okay to dance (since I was remembering how we got chased away from another music venue just days before). He said, "Sure," and we were quickly up there boogying to the irresistible tunes.

In no time about two dozen young people joined us on the make-shift dance floor. What fun we all had! There were two hotel employees in the elevator with us when we rode back down to our room. They said, "You two are so much fun! No one has ever danced here before." What a night to remember.

Probably the most impressive part of this trip was our visit to the Royal FloraHolland flower auction located in Aalsmeer, Netherlands. It is the largest flower auction in the world and the whole operation is mind boggling. The building itself is the fourth largest building in the world, covering 128 acres. Flowers from all over are traded every day in this gigantic building, which sells around 20 million flowers daily. The auction is set up as a "Dutch auction" in which the price starts high and works its way down. Bidders get only a few seconds to bid on the flowers before they are sold and passed on to the new owner.

Dennis and I watched from the elevated viewing floor with other visitors as the automated little trucks, filled to the brim with different kinds of bright flowers, wound their way across the expansive floor to their next destination. The flowers are subjected to 30 quality checks so that they can be graded on a scale.

Our plane left from Amsterdam and, thankfully, it was an enjoyable flight because we were, once again, in business class.

My grandsons Jarod and Richard Rocker with
their newborn baby sons, Lukas and Atlas

At the Camino Finesterra, Spain, once believed to be
the Edge of the World

Dennis and I rode a snowmobile to Old Faithful
in Yellowstone National Park

Enjoying the slopes at Banff, Alberta, Canada

Ever self-sufficient, I easily snag dinner in Belize

Cooling off with D at a waterfall in Belize

Unique glimpses of nature in Botswana

With my guide in Botswana

I'm glad to say the animals are generally free to live
and roam and are well protected

Gorgeous views in Budapest, Hungary

Hiking in Cape Town, South Africa

This was once called the "Cape of Storms"
and presents quite the ordeal for sailors.
Nice view from land, though.

There is plenty of wildlife in South Africa. In the bottom shot, a leopard has hauled an emu into a tree to feed her cubs and avoid attracting hyenas.

Wave running and biking in...Croatia

Dennis took me to the Miramar Hotel in Montecito
to celebrate my birthday. Here we pose out front.

Bikes on our barge in the Netherlands

Awesome array of tulips in Keukenhof, the Netherlands

Dennis and I in New York's Central Park

America's most famous symbol of liberty and an iconic
welcome to those seeking a fresh start in life.
This was taken during our helicopter ride over Manhattan.
We have trouble living up to our reputation
as the world's inspiration for liberty and democracy,
but we must not forget what America stands for

Us again, this time in the fjords of Norway

Hiking in one of Norway's beautiful forests

From Norway (above) to Prague (below), in the Czech Republic

Machu Picchu, Chile and pouring a Pisco Sour

Skiing with Dennis in spectacular Patagonia

This location needs no identification, does it?

CHAPTER TWELVE
Traveling the World

Travel is the only thing you buy
that makes you richer.
– Sheryl Sandberg

Shortly after returning home from Amsterdam, we drove to San Jose for my grandson Jarod Rocker's graduation from the Fine Art School at San Jose State University. It was a proud and happy time for all of us. We all agreed that it would have been wonderful for his father to have been alive to witness this impressive milestone.

In June I went to Santa Fe, New Mexico, to attend a conference for the organization I was working for at the time, Community Action of Ventura County. I made the best of the opportunity by extending my stay for an extra two days. I had never been to Santa Fe or the surrounding area. I asked some locals about where I should go for a hike and they suggested Tent Rocks National Monument. So off I went in my rental car, determined to climb to the top even though the weather was really hot. It took a little over an hour of hiking, made more strenuous by the high temperature, and I took lots of photos and met some interesting visitors along the trail. After the hike I drove to Taos and Albuquerque since I had never visited those areas either. It turned out to be a delightful trip and a fun adventure.

In August of 2018, Dennis and I boarded an Icelandic WOW airplane (an Icelandic ultra-low-cost carrier) to take us to Reykjavik, Iceland, where we participated in another international Summit for Danny climb. Iceland is 600 miles from Norway and 180 miles from Greenland. This wild, untamed country has 3,700 miles of coastline and enjoys 20 hours of sunlight in the summer months. Iceland is the size of Kentucky (which has a population of 12 million), but has only 300,000 residents. Glaciers cover 11 percent of the land; the largest glacier is 5,000 square miles in breadth and 3,300 feet deep — bigger than Rhode Island.

Some of the 200 very active volcanoes are covered by glaciers and when the 2,000 Fahrenheit degree magma comes into contact with the frozen water, the result is called a *phreatic eruption*. When the lava hits the ice it causes an instantaneous evaporation of the glacier into steam, resulting in an explosion of steam, water, ash and rock as well as torrents of water and mud.

One of our excursions was to the fascinating Svartsengi Geothermal Power Plant. Thankfully I was so impressed that I took good notes during this visit so I can tell you all about it. Melting glaciers, abundant rivers and 177 inches of rainfall every year feed the enormous underground aquifers here, resulting in 600 separate hot springs, which provide one of the most concentrated sources of geothermal hydroelectric energy on earth. The 200 active volcanos in Iceland heat the underground water to 750 degrees Fahrenheit. Ninety percent of households in Iceland use radiant heat from the hot water and 100 percent of the electricity in the country is generated by renewable geothermal and water resources.

The water that seeps into the ground is heated up to 750 degrees Fahrenheit by the proximity of the magma just beneath the bedrock and the power plants dig wells to tap into the super-heated water to bring it to the surface. The steam from the water is then pushed through turbines that turn a generator which produces electricity. The 102-degree water is then transferred above ground in pipes that are so well insulated that on a 15-mile journey from power plant to city, they lose only three degrees of heat before reaching the buildings and homes.

Despite the fact that Iceland derives almost of its electricity and heat from renewable resources, the country only taps into about 17 percent of the total potential hydroelectric and geothermal energy available. The other 83 percent remains unused because Iceland is using all it needs and because the island is so far from anywhere else that it hasn't been feasible to export it.

Our group of 17 hiked through the surreal cinematic landscape, which is unlike anything I've ever seen before. Our trek took us over rugged coastal cliffs, onto black sand beaches and to a steaming valley where we were awed by the aqua hot pools and bubbling hot mud pots. We were constantly surrounded by breathtaking scenery on all sides. Sometimes the wind was so strong that we had trouble standing upright, much less climbing a hill.

Iceland has 10,000 majestic waterfalls and we were fortunate enough to walk by many of them — even venturing behind some to feel and hear the force of water pounding into pools below.

One morning Dennis and I joined a small, intrepid group to go horse-back riding on the unusual Icelandic horses. (I found it interesting that no other breed of horse is allowed in Iceland.) It was really cold, very windy and raining but we were determined not to miss this unique experience. It was exciting and miserable at the same time — even our underwear was wet. Climbing into the hot tub when we returned to our hotel felt really good! Dennis hung his bathing suit on the railing outside so it could dry out after we changed into our warm clothes. But the next morning we were astonished to find it frozen hard as a rock!

One of the most interesting animals we encountered was the Atlantic Puffin, which has a fascinating story. Ten million of these adorable birds with the bright orange beaks arrive each spring to breed and nest, forming the largest Puffin colony in the world. They spend the winter months entirely at sea, never setting foot on land. When spring comes, they return to the same place they hatched and find their mate. Puffins form life-long pairs and, despite not spending the winter together, they somehow manage to find one another in the mass reunion each spring. It's during breeding season that their beaks turn the distinctive orange and yellow.

When they've found each other, the pair will nest in an underground burrow — preferably the exact same one they used last year — and line it with grass, leaves, and feathers. The female lays just one egg and both parents take turns with incubation and feeding the puffling.

Once the chick is grown and fully fledged, it leaves the nest at night, following the moon out to sea, where it will spend the next five years before it's ready to mate and return to land. Some of the young birds confuse city lights for moonlight and instead of finding themselves safely out at sea, they crash land in town and have to be rescued by the Puffin Patrol — squadrons of families with young children who scout the streets during the month of August looking for wayward pufflings.

Bedtimes are ignored as children search long into the night for the lost and confused chicks. The rescued birds are kept overnight and then taken to the local aquarium where they are weighted and tagged before the families take them down to the beach to be released. The children hold the birds around their bodies so their wings are free to flap and they toss the pufflings into the air so they have enough momentum to make it past the breaking waves and out to their life at sea.

Our last excursion was to the popular Blue Lagoon, a geothermal spa with milky blue water located in a lava field. It is filled with water supplied by the nearby geothermal power station and attracts over a million visitors annually, making it the most visited attraction in Iceland. The water's milky blue shade is due to its high silica content which forms soft white mud on the bottom of the lake that bathers rub on themselves. The water temperature averages 100 degrees Fahrenheit and renews every two days. Dennis and I enjoyed our time in the water as well as having lunch overlooking the lagoon and all of the bathers. The next day we boarded our WOW airline and flew home.

2019 began with ski trips to Mammoth and Telluride in Colorado. We were all thrilled the next month to welcome my great-grandsons, Atlas and Lukas Rocker, born just two weeks apart — February 12 and 27 respectively. Atlas was born to my grandson, Richard Rocker, and his wife, Yer; and Lukas was born to my grandson, Jarod Rocker, and his wife, Ashley. Both boys are darling and healthy — sure to live fulfilling lives.

Dennis surprised me for my birthday with an overnight stay at the elegant Rosewood Miramar Resort in Montecito. We enjoyed our luxury suite, which opened onto the expansive beach, and hanging out at their Cabana Bar and Pool, sipping cold mimosas. We felt like movie stars in this chic setting!

Later that month Dennis and I flew to Nashville, Tennessee, to celebrate my Aunt Toni's 100th birthday. We had lots of fun dancing at the multitude of music venues, touring the Musician's Hall of Fame and exploring the Gaylord Opryland Resort. We rented a car for the two-hour drive to my aunt's house in Bowling Green, Kentucky. Over 100 friends and family members attended the lively celebration at my cousin Sandra Laughlin's beautiful home. Everyone marveled at Aunt Toni's high energy and good spirits; one would never guess she was 100 years old. What an inspiration she is!

Dennis proposed that he move out of the retirement home he had shared with his wife, and that I move out of my condo and join him at the beautiful home he had owned for 25 years, but had rented out for the previous 10 years. I loved the idea of living with this wonderful man I had come to love deeply over the previous five years of dating and traveling the world. Still, I felt somewhat insecure about leaving my sweet condo where I had lived for the previous 15 years.

After thinking long and hard about this, I finally took the plunge and agreed to his offer. I gave all of my furniture and sports equipment to my grandkids, and the movers came to pack up the rest of my belongings, delivering them to our new home. Dennis' movers brought his things the previous day. Combining our households was surprisingly quick and easy, especially with the expert assistance of our friend and decorator, Cheryl Fontana. We spent the next two months refurbishing the house, picking out some furniture and installing a beautiful hot tub on our deck overlooking the ocean and city.

At first I felt displaced and ill at ease living in someone else's house. Even though it was a beautiful place with an incredible view, it was still not my space. Dennis kept encouraging me to think of it as my home, so I tried hard to do that. Before long this charming place felt like home to me. Living together, working on projects to create beauty and just enjoying being in this incredible place are things we relish every day.

In June we traveled to Dennis' home state of Michigan to visit his family and some of our friends. July took us to Rancho Laguna to celebrate my daughter Pam's 60th birthday. I had sorted through my old family albums to find photos of Pam at the various stages of her life so I could send them to her daughter, Taryn Gluckman, who compiled a video presentation. It turned out great and Dennis and I were glad to join in with friends and family to share in this momentous occasion.

In August we were off on another grand adventure — this time for a cruise around the Greek Islands on the famous Windstar. We were excited to sail on this ship because it only holds 160 passengers — and its small size means it can navigate into ports that the larger cruise ships cannot. Our journey took us on excursions from one island to another, exploring the beautiful seaside scenery and ancient treasures. Every evening we enjoyed refreshing cocktails and delicious meals beneath the huge white sails on the open deck, and then we moved inside for entertainment and dancing.

Our most affecting memory of this trip was in the ancient city of Ephesus, Turkey — the only part of the trip that was not in Greece. Our ship was able to take us right into their tiny port because the Windstar is so small. The crew had arranged for a spectacular evening set in the middle of the ruins of the ancient Library, built by the Romans in 117AD. Elegantly decorated tables filled the ancient marble floor, waiters dressed in starched white uniforms served us a scrumptious seven-course meal and a string trio, positioned on the elevated wall, entertained us throughout the evening. It was magical — like stepping back into history. Not many people get to visit Ephesus or enjoy this type of experience.

We decided to combine two trips into one extended one because of the long flight overseas. The Windstar cruise around the Greek Islands was in August and the next Summit for Danny international hike was in Switzerland in September, so we planned to fly from Greece to Barcelona after the cruise, and then to take a short flight from Barcelona to the island of Mallorca, Spain. Then we would rent a car to drive through Spain and Portugal.

We rented bicycles as soon as we arrived in Mallorca. Our bike ride along the boardwalk in Palma, Mallorca, took us along the incredibly beautiful Mediterranean Sea. It was so hot that day that it felt exhilarating to plunge into the chilly sea after our ride, lay on lounge chairs on the beach and then dive back into the water when we got too hot.

We decided to rent a cab to take us on the hour-long ride inland to the famous Rafa Nadal Museum and Tennis Center. The facility was huge, with multiple displays of the outfits that Rafa wore in his Grand Slam tennis tournaments and the Olympics where he won a Gold Medal in 2008 and 2016, plus his shiny rackets and huge trophies. The Academy is also home to 26 tennis courts, a spa and several fancy apartments to house students who come for the tennis clinics.

We ventured downstairs where we saw lots of virtual experience machines. Dennis and I both climbed onto separate contraptions that simulated skiing. We put on the requisite goggles, pushed the start button and kept our eyes glued to the screens in front of us. It was so real — like we were actually racing down steep slopes, over crevasses and through narrow trails — but fast! I kept squealing out loud and Dennis was laughing. Every now and then I had to pull my goggles up on my head so I could get my bearings again, and then I would put them back on and race some more. What an amazing experience that was! We both agreed that if we ever saw another machine like that we would try it again.

While still in Palma, Mallorca, we feasted on the most incredible seafood you can imagine — huge lobster claws, the biggest shrimp we had ever seen, juicy scallops and thick pieces of fish — while sipping on excellent Chardonnay and enjoying the breezes from the Mediterranean Sea. We also toured several gilded, gorgeous cathedrals in Palma.

Then we boarded a small airplane that took us to Granada, Spain, where we rented a car and toured the elaborate Alhambra Palace and Granada Cathedral. We stayed in the exquisite Alhambra Palace Hotel overlooking the expansive city. Our next stop was Ronda, Spain where we stayed at an elegant hotel dramatically perched on top of a deep gorge.

And then on to Seville, built in the second century BC, where we stayed in the old part of town with streets that were built for walking — just marginally wide enough for cars to pass between the multi-storied, centuries' old buildings. This was one of the most hilarious and frustrating parts of our driving adventure because we drove around and around these incredibly narrow streets, trying not to damage the side mirrors of the car. We plugged the hotel address into our GPS but even the GPS got confused.

Finally, when it was obvious we would never find our hotel unless we changed our strategy, I spied a line of cabs along one of the wider city streets. I told Dennis to watch which cab I got into and follow it. My Spanish came in handy as I stuck my head into the open window of a cab and explained that we were lost and asked if he would take me to the hotel. He agreed. I gave him the address and watched out the back window to make sure Dennis was behind us. I was worried when I didn't see him. I found out later that, unbeknownst to me, he couldn't see which cab I got into and became concerned. Thankfully he figured it out and before long we were standing in front of our classic ancient hotel. It was like a cartoon and could have ended badly...but thankfully it all worked out fine.

We found Seville to be a charming city for walking around town, touring their gorgeous palaces, enjoying dinner on the river and admiring the beautiful buildings and sights. After a couple of days in Seville, we drove to the big city of Lisbon, Spain, where we walked all over town, strolled down to the Dao River and mingled with the hundreds of people visiting the fancy shops. After Lisbon we drove to Vidago where we stayed in an upscale hotel and went for a long hike up into the nearby mountains, enjoying the terraced vineyards that crisscrossed the verdant hills.

Our final stop on this incredible road trip was in Porto, Portugal, where we rented kayaks and paddled down the beautiful Duoro River. We explored the charming city and then boarded a plane to Zurich, Switzerland, and spent three days roaming around. We walked down to the harbor and hopped on a boat that took us on an enjoyable tour around Lake Zurich. We also toured the magnificent Swiss National Museum and watched a local craftsman making huge pots of Swiss cheese.

Now it was time for us to join our Summit for Danny group for its annual international hike, this time in the mountains from Interlaken to Zermatt. We hired a cab to take us to the gigantic Zurich train station — the largest train station in Switzerland — serving nearly 3,000 trains each day. Next we figured out how to find the right spot to stand (which was not easy) and boarded the train to Interlaken, Switzerland, to meet the group of 23 hikers (most of whom, once again, were from Santa Barbara).

We had intentionally arrived a couple of days early, so the first night we walked down the street of this tiny but bustling town and noticed a beautiful hotel with cocktail tables situated around a large, lush lawn. We walked up the pathway, sat down at one of the tables and ordered a gin and tonic from the waiter. We sat there enjoying the refreshing drink, listening to the live music from the large piano situated on a cement square in the middle of the rich green lawn – being played by a maestro in a tuxedo – as we gazed at the snow-covered mountains just across the street. It was surreal.

The next day we rented mountain bikes and rode along the river toward Stechelberg, one of the quaint alpine towns, in search of the renowned waterfalls. But we took a wrong turn. We both began to ride up a steep mountain trail, thinking we were going the right way. Dennis had an inkling that we might be going the wrong direction so he stopped to check his map, motioning for me to keep going. I kept peddling because the trail was getting steep and I was afraid of losing momentum. I rode and rode and rode until I couldn't pedal any further. I finally stopped and got off my bike, which was challenging because of the steep incline.

Dennis was not behind me. I waited and waited expecting him to come around the corner at any time. Soon I became worried — especially when I heard ambulance sirens in the distance. Had he fallen and hurt himself or had a heart attack or some other malady? I tried to ride down the trail but the steep mountain made it impossible, so I got off my bike and walked it down what felt like several miles. I finally found him waiting for me where I had left him.

We exchanged our stories, had a good laugh and then headed back on our ride to find the waterfalls. We rode through sweet towns and green fields beneath towering mountain peaks. Finally we found the majestic waterfalls, hiked up for a closer view and climbed behind them to experience the forceful water plunging down into the pool below.

By now the hikers had arrived and some of us decided to rent *trotties* and ride them to the bottom of the mountain, while others chose to ride down in a gondola. We had never seen anything like these trotties before — they are sort of a cross between a bicycle and a skateboard. We balanced ourselves on the middle section with one foot in front of the other and let gravity propel us down the hills. It got pretty hairy when we encountered a car coming the opposite direction. Good balance and lots of courage were crucial for success. Thankfully neither Dennis nor I fell off or got hurt or even lost our balance—but it sure was dicey at times.

On September 13 our group assembled to hear about our trip and to read the letter from one of the students at the Daniel Bryant Center. We gathered our hiking poles, hats, sunglasses, water and snacks and were off on a grand adventure. We hiked through rolling pastures flanked by imposing snow-capped peaks above the sweet little town of Adelboden, where we saw a parade of very large cows coming down the street. They had various sizes of bells around their necks and were decorated with flowers on top of their heads. On this, our lucky day, we had happened upon the celebration of milk and learned that the size of bell on each cow indicated the amount of milk it gave.

The next day we climbed a mountain up steep metal walkways that took us 400 feet above powerful waterfalls. A few in our group had a fear of heights, so they had real struggles climbing the sheer vertical catwalk.

That evening we were treated to a unique concert by three Swiss Alpenhorn players (the performer blows on a wooden cup-shaped mouthpiece at the end of a six foot long horn with a large cup at the bottom resting on the grass). The next day was a tough climb to a cheese farm where they demonstrated the process of cheese making. And then we set off on a train called the Glacier Express to Zermatt, where we got our first

Matterhorn view while enjoying Rosti and Bratwurst in a tiny alpine hamlet.

Our final summit day was met with lots of miles and big smiles as we toasted the week with Prosecco and Sorbet from the most scenic lunch spot in the Alps. As our final night drew to a close, we had to say goodbye to our friends and fly back home. Dennis and I will look back on this adventure with fond memories.

Two weeks after our return to Santa Barbara Dennis and I boarded a flight to Maui, Hawaii, for the wedding of my son, Michael. The day after the wedding, Dennis and I hiked the famous Iao Valley and then flew on an island hopper flight to the Hilo side of the Big Island to visit my brother, Kip Raiford, and his wife, Jane. We stayed at the magical Mauna Kea Beach Resort where we swam in the ocean and snorkeled over the coral reefs.

It was a busy time for us. The morning after we returned from Hawaii we climbed in the car and drove to Temecula for the enchanting wedding of my grandson, Marcus, and his beautiful bride, Marina. After the ceremony we had the honor of participating in the touching naming ceremony for my great granddaughter, Leah Gluckman. The next weekend we drove to Fresno for the graduation of my granddaughter, Stephanie, from pharmacy school. I am so proud of her and all she accomplished.

At that point our plans changed dramatically. I was scheduled to attend a party to celebrate my retirement from Community Action of Ventura County and we were all packed and ready to leave the following morning for a week of skiing at Mammoth's Race Camp. But that evening I began to experience abdominal pain and severe nausea. I tried to just wait it out, thinking the sick feeling would pass in time, but when Dennis came home and saw me lying on the floor just outside the bathroom (it made perfect sense to me because of the nausea) he insisted on taking me to the emergency department of Cottage Hospital. I reluctantly agreed — not wanting to go to the hospital for just a simple belly ache — and we climbed into the car and drove through the very dark, rainy night. I told him, "I've heard about these crowded emergency rooms and I'm not waiting in line."

We pulled into the emergency area, he got out to run through the rain and check out the hospital waiting area. It was packed. So he hurried back to the car and drove me to the Goleta Cottage Hospital where there was no line. They took me right away and the doctor determined I had appendicitis after conducting a couple of tests. They removed my appendix that night so it wouldn't burst. I spent the next three days in the hospital, missing my retirement party and our trip to Mammoth. I was thankful to Dennis for insisting that he take me to the emergency room.

By January of 2020 I was healed and eager for ski trips that included Snowmass and Aspen with our good friends, Bob and Patty Bryant, Steamboat Springs, Colorado, and Lake Tahoe to visit my daughter, Pam, and ski with my son-in-law, Jeff Hoffman, who is an excellent skier.

In early March we flew with the ski club to Montana for a week-long ski trip at the famous Big Sky Resort. It was a spectacular place with first rate accommodations. The first day of skiing was wonderful — with excellent snow and good weather. That evening, we were informed that the resort would be closed the following day due to the coronavirus. We were all pretty disappointed and will definitely return to ski there some day. But we had to scramble to figure out how to get our 68 members back home to Santa Barbara. We all agreed that it was a long way to go for one day of skiing.

True to his way, Dennis arranged for us to spend my birthday night at the elegant Bacara Resort in Goleta. He made reservations at their spectacular Angel Oak restaurant for my birthday dinner. When we arrived to check in, the attendant said that all the restaurants had just closed because of the recent coronavirus scare. She explained that just the day before the hotel had 100 percent occupancy booked, but that within the last 24 hours it had plummeted to only five percent occupancy, forcing them to close all of their eating areas. I casually mentioned that I was disappointed because we had planned to celebrate my birthday at the Angel Oak restaurant. She apologized and a large golf cart buggy drove us to our lovely suite.

The phone rang as soon as we entered our room. I answered and the director of client services said she had heard about our dashed birthday dinner plans and wanted to offer an alternative. She invited us to be their guests at the Executive Penthouse for a delicious meal prepared just for us by their culinary staff. She asked us for our entrée preference and we set a time for arrival. Dennis and I were escorted to the expansive penthouse at 6 p.m. where we found a mass of red rose pedals lining the elegantly set table overlooking the ocean. Two waiters attended to our every whim, serving a delectable salmon dinner. After our meal they invited us to sit out one the balcony just above the waves to enjoy a decadent chocolate birthday cake complete with rich vanilla ice cream.

We had planned a big party for Dennis' 80th birthday in April — dinner and dancing to live music on the Channel Cat as it sailed around the harbor — but the coronavirus forced us to cancel all of our plans. So to celebrate his birthday, on April 9, I went to the local fish market to purchase the ingredients for his favorite dish — Cioppino. We pulled a card table in front of our fireplace, made a fancy table setting and enjoyed this delicious fish stew in front of the blazing fire. Chocolate lava cake with vanilla ice cream finished off this special birthday dinner. I had never made either of these dishes but they both turned out great (she said modestly).

Closures, restrictions and fear of catching the virus impacted everyone's lives and dramatically changed our day-to-day routines. Dennis and I took lots of bike rides and went on hikes in an effort to stay busy, healthy and in shape. We often rode on the Rincon bike path down to have lunch at Shoal's restaurant sitting outside by the ocean. Social distancing and mask-wearing were now the norms and we tried to abide by the regulations.

However, eventually we began inviting one couple at a time over for cocktails or dinner on our deck where we could easily maintain distance in an outdoor setting. We were able to venture downtown for dinner when State Street closed to traffic allowing only pedestrians and bikes — and assorted restaurants built parklets and put tables on the streets for outside dining.

Finally, though, the dangerous spread of Covid 19 forced restaurants to close altogether, except for take-out dining. Restaurants were one of the sectors of society hardest hit by the pandemic and we feel so sorry for the proprietors and workers who have lost their income due to the relentless spread of the virus.

In July my granddaughter, Ashleigh, her husband, Tim, and their lovely family visited us from Fresno. We arranged for them to stay in a local hotel and we met them at outdoor venues (necessary due to the virus restrictions) like the Zoo and the Natural History Museum butterfly exhibit. It was delightful spending time with my three-year-old great-grandson, Simon, and his newly arrived sister, Hayleigh.

Also in July, my granddaughter, Jenelle Shapiro, gave birth to my ninth great grandchild, Amelia. Amelia's birth story is a bit like a Hollywood movie. Eighteen minutes after getting into the car to drive to Kaiser Hospital for delivery, Amelia decided she had waited long enough. Jenelle's husband, Yossi, pulled off on the side of Highway 101 and called 911 as Jenelle was delivering Amelia in the front seat of the car.

The 911 dispatcher asked Yossi if he had a shoelace on his shoe – and, thankfully, he had one! The dispatcher instructed Yossi to use the shoelace to tie off Amelia's umbilical cord. The Novato Fire Department arrived around 15 minutes later.

The paramedic instructed Yossi to cut the umbilical cord and then the crew loaded Jenelle and baby Amelia onto a gurney and drove to the hospital. Thankfully everything went smoothly...leaving Amelia with a very wild birth story.

Our friend, Fred Brander, began to have live music, taco trucks and of course wine in the outdoor courtyard at his Brander Winery. He followed all the mask and social distancing rules and Dennis and I enjoyed it all on many Saturday afternoons — even dancing while wearing our masks.

In September we decided to take a road trip for some outdoor activities. We drove to Zion National Park in Utah to hike the magnificent red rock formations. After a couple of days of hiking, we drove to Bryce Canyon National Park in southern Utah. Bryce is known for crimson-colored hoodoos, which are spire-shaped rock formations. The scenery was absolutely breath-taking and we enjoyed hiking all over the various trails.

After several days of exhilarating outdoor exercise, we drove to Page, Arizona, to visit the expansive and beautiful Lake Powell. We wanted to rent a houseboat or a speed boat but every single boat was already rented because so many people were trying to take outdoor vacations. But we were content to hike through the hills around the lake. The week-long trip was just enough for us to feel like we had gotten away for a bit.

Dennis and I feel so fortunate to have found a soul mate who enjoys the same activities, lives life at the same speed and sees the world in a similar manner. We have loved every minute of our hiking, skiing, kayaking, cycling and traveling. We have traveled to 27 countries in the past five years — sometimes with the trips being back-to-back. Our Facebook friends always joked that we were never home. We always wondered what it would be like to just stay home and enjoy our local area. We found out, as a result of the coronavirus shutdown, that we are tickled just to be at home, living together 24/7 and experiencing life in our beautiful space.

We read an article in the Wall Street Journal recently that said some people are naming their homes in response to the virus restrictions since they have to spend so much time there. We always feel like we are sitting up on a perch — because we are 450 feet above the city overlooking downtown Santa Barbara and the ocean — so we officially named our home the "Heavenly Perch." Neither of us knows how much time we have left, but one thing is for sure — we are enjoying every moment together and when it's all over we will slide into home base exclaiming, "Wow, what a ride!"

Getting away for some hiking in Santa Fe, NM

Dennis and I in Bryce National Park

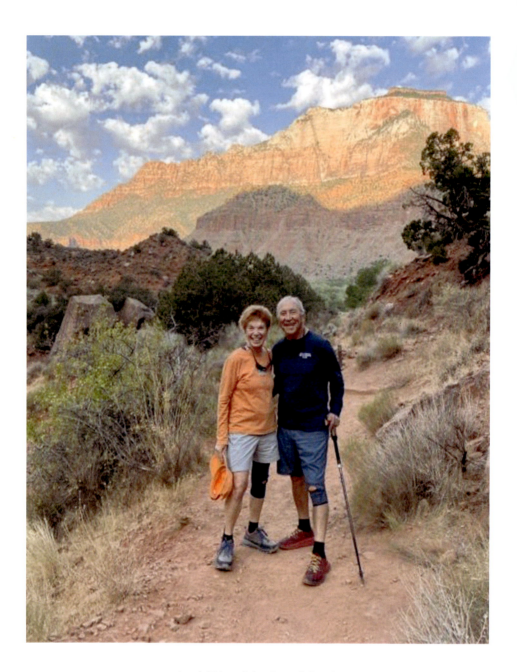

And Zion National Park

Cold but loving it in Iceland

The adorable Atlantic puffin

With my daughter Pam at her 60th

My Aunt Toni at her 100th birthday party

In Michigan, Dennis' home state

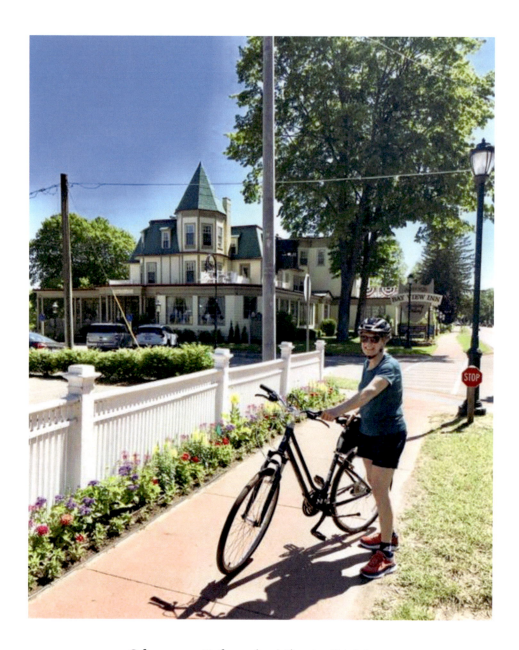

Of course I found a bike in Michigan

And managed to score a kayak
for the lovely Michigan lakes

Music and dining among the ancient ruins in Ephesus, Turkey

Hiking with the Summit for Danny crew in Italy

Sunshine and smiles in Switzerland with the Matterhorn
in the background

We witnessed a cow parade in Switzerland
that celebrated the milk giving ability of the cows.
The size of the bell each one wears
commemorates how much milk it gave.
Only two cows made it into this picture,
but trust me, it was a cow parade

We loved everything about Mallorca and had
the chance to see the views on our own
personal bike tour

Hiking in the Iao Valley, Maui

With my son Mike in Hawaii

Together with Mike's daughters (my granddaughters),
Koty and McKallah Rocker in Hawaii

Dennis brought me to the exquisite Bacara Resort
in Goleta for my birthday, but just that day
travel warnings due to the Covid 19 virus caused
so many cancellations that the resort closed
its restaurants.
When Dennis explained it was my birthday, Bacara
executives invited us into their executive penthouse where we
had a delectable salmon dinner and a decadent
chocolate birthday cake.

CHAPTER THIRTEEN
Ten Life Lessons

Life is not a journey to the grave
with the intention of arriving safely
in a pretty and well-preserved body,
but rather to skid in broadside
totally worn out and proclaiming
"WHAT A RIDE!"
–A paraphrase of motorcycle racer Bill McKenna

I've learned a great deal over the years, some by the tough lessons of life, some by trial and error, some by getting a little wiser with experience. I happen to be a voracious reader and over the years I have come across many excellent books that helped considerably in teaching me these lessons. I will share some of the excellent thinking from these books as I elaborate on some of the things I have learned that form important priorities in my life and have helped guide me through many challenges.

1. Persistence Pays Off. Once I set my sights on a goal, a project or something I want to achieve, it takes determination and persistence to succeed. But first, the goal must be worthy of my energy and fairly well-defined. I don't need to have all of the answers in the beginning, but I do need a clear focus.

For example, my end result was a little fuzzy when I founded KCAPS (chapter 1). I knew I wanted to do what I could to improve the lives of the farmworker children and their families, but I didn't have all the answers about how I would accomplish that. I kept my eyes, ears and mind open as I met with many of these families so I could identify my next steps.

The support I hoped for from community members and churches didn't materialize at first and, in fact, there were several naysayers who found fault with my ideas. I ignored them. I didn't waste my precious time and energy trying to convince anyone of anything. Thankfully many good-hearted supporters emerged in time.

In the meantime I was persistent and determined to reach my goals. I was also resilient in the face of indifference and criticism. I have heard the advice: "bless and release." I find that the practice of blessing someone in spite of their grumbling and releasing them from any expectations keeps my energy focused on the task at hand. I realize that if I do my best in any given circumstance I will never have reason to be disappointed in myself.

Henry Ford said that obstacles are those frightful things you see when you take your eyes off your goal. So it's important to be courageous and strong regardless of any disappointment you may feel in others. Don't even harbor any ill will toward them because it will distract your focus. The key is to continually move forward, which is why I have always loved this admonition from W.H. Murray, who was the leader of the Scottish Himalayan Expedition in 1953: "Until one is committed, there is hesitancy . . . the moment one definitely commits oneself, then Providence moves too. All sorts of things occur to help one that would never otherwise have occurred . . . whatever you do, or dream you can do, begin it. Boldness has genius, power and magic in it. Begin it now."

I have found that one necessary element in achieving my goals is maintaining a high level of energy. I seem to have been blessed with a lot of drive and vitality, but I believe everyone can intentionally increase their amount of oomph. For me, that means lots of exercise. I try to maintain a regular work-out routine and do some form of cardio every day. I believe that the more I work at keeping fit the more my feeling of liveliness increases — even though that might sound counter-intuitive.

In their very popular book, *Younger Next Year*, the authors opine that because life is an endurance, we must train for it. They recommend doing some form of exercise six days a week and doing serious aerobic exercise four days a week for the rest of your life. They advise that this consistently high level of exercise will result in more energy because it increases circulation. The authors explain that "circulation is the basic infrastructure of exercise. Steady aerobic exercise, over months and years, produces dramatic improvements in your circulation system, which is one of the ways exercise saves your life."

2. Continuously Choose Joy. One of my favorite books is *The Book of Joy*, which is essentially a conversation between the Dalai Lama and the Archbishop Desmond Tutu. I recommend this book to you and encourage you to pass it along to your friends and family. It contains many powerful messages to enhance your life. Archbishop Desmond Tutu says, "Joy is a way of approaching the world . . . our greatest joy is when we seek to do good for others."

The Dalai Lama explains, "The way we heal our own pain is actually by turning to the pain of others. It is a virtuous cycle. The more we turn toward others, the more joy we experience, and the more joy we experience, the more we can bring joy to others. . . the goal is to be a reservoir of joy, an oasis of peace, a pool of serenity that can ripple out to all those around you."

In his book, *Soft-Wired: How the New Science of Brain Plasticity Can Change Your Life*, Dr. Michael Merzenich opines that life should be about seeking and spreading joy. Many times we must consciously choose joy, especially when we don't feel especially joyful. If we can move beyond our current trials and tribulations for a moment, we can find joy by reframing our situation to reveal a new perspective.

For example, when my son, Rick, was dying of cancer I was consumed with grief (chapter 10). I couldn't even think of one joyful thought — until I looked around and noticed the heartache of my other children and grandchildren. I decided to choose joy by helping each of these dear ones cope with the sorrow of losing their father, husband and sibling. My changed perspective not only brought joy to them but also to me.

Sonja Lyubomirsky, who is a professor in the Department of Psychology at the University of California, Riverside, wrote a bestselling book called *The How of Happiness: A Scientific Approach to Getting the Life You Want*. In it, she talks about strategies backed by scientific research that can be used to increase happiness. I'd like to pass along this one thing she said because it really resonated with me: "The three factors that seem to have the greatest influence on increasing our happiness are our ability to reframe our situation more positively, our ability to experience gratitude and our choice to be kind and generous."

3. Find Other's Unique Gifts. Each of us is distinctive, bringing our own gifts and perspectives to the world. It is our responsibility to share our unique talents and also to intentionally recognize them in others. In the past I would often think about how an individual was such a good speaker or how another person was particularly proficient at analytical thinking or about how someone displayed good people skills — but I didn't say anything. Then one day I learned a valuable lesson.

I was completing the final portion of my Doctoral residency in Phoenix, Arizona (chapter 8). My professor for this class was Dr. Dora Johnson, whom I had never met prior to this mandatory in-person, week-long session. I don't remember the exact assignment she gave us, but I recall feeling particularly inadequate and somewhat embarrassed at my perceived shortcomings.

Dr. Dora (her preferred title) communicated her belief in me in a powerful way that picked me up, dusted off my rocky self-esteem, and sent me marching down the road — confident that I would make a difference through my research study and life work. She inspired me to rise higher and strive farther than I otherwise might have because she was convinced I could succeed.

How did she do this? She simply told me about the unique gifts she saw in me and why they were important. I failed to recognize these talents because they were simply an integral part of me that I couldn't even see until she pointed them out. Dr. Dora passed away a few weeks after this class from an invasive cancer that no one knew she had, but she left behind a powerful legacy by demonstrating the importance of letting others know that you see and appreciate their special gifts.

She showed how important it is for each of us to communicate our belief in others who cross our life path. Giving the gift of belief in others is perhaps the most important contribution we can make. It takes time and intention to do this effectively because we must take the time to notice and then to sincerely highlight each person's unique value. Dr. Dora lived her life in continuous appreciation of every person she met and I try to emulate that.

I find opportunities to practice this skill with wait staff in restaurants or clerks at retail stores. On many occasions I have pointed out an individual's obvious high emotional intelligence when I noticed them giving me particularly good customer service. And then I explain to them how good people skills will serve them well their whole life. I said something like this to a server at a restaurant recently.

The next Saturday I was picking out vegetables at Farmer's Market and she was staffing the stand. She excitedly asked, "Do you remember me? I met you at Oku Restaurant!" And then she turned to her co-worker and exclaimed, "This is the nicest lady. I was feeling tired and down at the restaurant last week and she told me what a good job I was doing. It changed my whole outlook."

I believe that each of us has unique gifts and talents and it is our job to enhance the lives of others by shining a light on their special attributes. I also believe that, once we learn about our distinctive talents, it is our responsibility to share them with others for the benefit of humanity.

That's why I love this quote by John O'Donohue in his book, *Anam Cara*: "To be born is to be chosen. No one is here by accident. Each of us was sent here for a special destiny. For millions of years, before you arrived here, the dream of your individuality was carefully prepared. You were sent to a destiny in which you would be able to express the special gift you bring to the world. There is a unique destiny for each person. Each one of us has something to do here that can be done by no one else. When you begin to decipher this, your gift and giftedness come alive. Your heart quickens and the urgency of living rekindles your creativity."

One of my favorite authors, Sister Joan Chittister, from the Sisters of Saint Benedict in Erie, Pennsylvania, echoes this idea by reminding us that, "What I have to give is always that one thing that is most needed in every situation because no one else can give it. The obligation is to pour it out like oil on the head of the universe."

4. Build Others to their Highest Potential. One of my favorite approaches to leadership is a concept created by Robert Greenleaf. His seminal work, written in 1970, is called *Servant Leadership: A Journey into the Nature of Legitimate Power and Greatness.* At the bottom of his philosophy is the scripture from Matthew 23:11 which says, "The more lowly your service to others, the greater you are. To be the greatest, be a servant." Greenleaf believes that successful leaders are the ones who help their people reach their highest potential and, in so doing, they create a stronger team and a more robust organization. In fact, he posits that the only truly viable institutions will be those that are predominantly servant-led.

Greenleaf's premise is that leadership can be bestowed or taken away from an individual; however, the one who is a servant at the core of their being is the best leader. That type of leadership can never be withdrawn. He goes on to say that "the secret of institution building is to be able to create a team of strong people by lifting them up to grow taller than they would otherwise be."

Frances Hesselbein is another one of my favorite authors and leadership practitioners. She was the national CEO of Girl

Scouts of the USA from 1976 to 1990. As a result of her work there, she earned the Presidential Medal of Freedom and was named the Best Nonprofit Manager in America by Forbes Magazine in 1998. Frances turned 105 years old in 2020 and is still traveling and sharing her passion for leadership. She proclaims that "to serve is to live" because it is the most effective way of building others up to their potential, which she believes is the highest calling of any leader.

Too many leaders ask the wrong question: What should a good leader do? Frances explains that "leadership is a matter to how to *be* — not how to *do*." We must first look inside ourselves and know what truths we hold dear and what our belief system looks like.

Next a leader must check to see that what they are doing matches what they believe. So even though good leadership is demonstrated by the end result of what a person does — building a strong team of people working at their highest potential — it must begin with who they are inside. I am grateful that, when I served as CEO for Girl Scouts of the central California coast, I had several opportunities to meet this beloved woman and hear her speak (chapter 7).

Patrick Lencioni is another leader who believes in building up others so they can reach their best and highest potential. He has written many books about this and I have read most of them. My favorite one is *The Motive: Why so Many Leaders Abdicate their Most Important Responsibilities*. Lencioni says that the most important job of an organizational leader is to build up each individual team member because the result will be a strong team and ultimately a solid organization.

This means leaders must be willing to have difficult conversations, to be sure their meetings are effective and they should frequently repeat key messages to all employees. He emphasizes that "leadership can never be about the leader more than the led...if we can restore the collective attitude that leadership is meant to be a joyfully difficult and selfless responsibility, I am convinced that we will see companies become more successful, employees more engaged and fulfilled, and society more optimistic and hopeful."

In fact, Lencioni says the best outcome would be that no one uses the term "servant leadership" anymore because they will understand that it is the only valid kind.

5. Find Ways of Adding Value. When I was working in wealth management at Santa Barbara Bank & Trust, I heard some terms I had not heard before — expressions like *value added*, *value proposition* and *value chain*. I soon learned this referred to clarifying services that set one company apart from another, describing the value a company will bring to their customers and ensuring that internal systems created the desired outcomes. I liked these ideas and, in fact, I taught my students about these concepts several years later when I served as an instructor in the MBA program at Antioch University, using Joan Magretta's excellent book *Understanding Michael Porter: The Essential Guide to Competition and Strategy*, as my text.

I also encouraged my students to consider their own personal value proposition by answering the question: How do you add value to your community, to your organization and to your family? And then I would invite them to create a statement describing what they do to add value in the various aspects of their life.

It can be challenging to generate such a declaration. So I asked them to first make a list of their own inherent gifts and talents — what they notice they are good at, what others say about their competencies and what they really enjoy doing for others (as described earlier in this chapter in item 3).

Next I told them to look around their community, their workplace and their family and make a list of what value is needed. I asked them to use all of these insights to put together their own personal value statement describing how they want to use their personal attributes and interests to bring joy to their world.

For myself, I noticed that I seem to have an aptitude for imagining possibilities that are unseen by others, infusing positive energy into situations, acknowledging the special gifts of others I encounter and bringing seemingly unrelated groups and individuals together to accomplish a common goal. I continually and intentionally watch for ways I can use these gifts to add value wherever I can.

For example, at one point in my career I brought together various businesses so they could trade best practices in philanthropy and corporate social responsibility. Then I combined nonprofits with the businesses so the conversation could be broader and deeper, with each one learning from the other.

I brought together representatives from all aspects of healthcare during the beginning of the Affordable Care Act so they could gain additional perspectives on this new movement that would dramatically affect them all (chapter 8). I also initiated a monthly roundtable discussion for nonprofit executive directors so they could address a variety of mutual challenges and also hear from local leaders in assorted fields.

I knew a farmer named Hank back when I was raising my children in the San Joaquin Valley. Hank ran a fruit stand on a country road. These roadside operations are not uncommon in this highly agricultural area of California. But for some reason Hank's fruit stand always had lots of cars lined up waiting to buy his fruit, and he consistently outsold his neighboring establishments.

One day I asked Hank why he was so popular. "Oh it's simple," he said. "I just add a few peaches to the basket." I was a little confused, so I asked him to explain. "After a customer buys a basket or two of peaches and pays for them, I add two or three extra peaches to their basket for no charge," he explained. "They are always surprised and happy so they keep coming back."

I've always remembered the lesson I learned from Hank and try to emulate his wisdom whenever I can. I look for ways I can exceed the expectations of people, whether personally or professionally.

My friend Penny Collins is a master at this practice. Penny is a realtor who was referred to me when I was looking for a house to buy in Santa Barbara. She seemed to anticipate my every need and question from the very beginning, but I was in for more surprises once I got to know her better. After I purchased my condo in Carpinteria, California, she asked if I needed a painter or a decorator or someone to tune the squeaky garage door opener. The people she recommended to me were equally as responsive as she was — in fact they were her friends. Regardless of what I needed she had an answer, sometimes even before I knew what my question was. And she never charged me any extra. She has become my good friend and I always enjoy watching others be surprised by the way she adds peaches to her customers' baskets.

6. Focus on the Positive. According to people who know me, I have always been a sunny side up type of person—an optimist. Sometimes I'm proud of it and other times I'm a bit embarrassed, thinking I might seem a little like Pollyanna. But after I read the 524 pages of David Landes' book, *The Wealth and Poverty of the Nations: Why Some are so Rich and Some are so Poor*, I became proud of being an optimist.

This is the conclusion Landes came to after spending years researching and studying this multi-faceted topic: "In this world, the optimists have it, not because they are always right, but because they are positive. Even when wrong, they are positive, and that is the way of achievement, correction, improvement, and success. Educated, eyes-open optimism pays, pessimism can only offer the empty consolation of being right."

Stephen Covey, in his popular book *The 7 Habits of Highly Effective People*, talks about the power of maintaining a positive attitude. He explains that we each have a Circle of Concern and a Circle of Influence. The first circle is comprised of things over which we have no real control and the second includes things we can do something about. Covey claims that the most productive people focus routinely on their Circle of Influence. As a result, this circle grows larger; however, a person's Circle of Concern grows larger when we spend our time and energy on it.

Covey further explains that, "Proactive people focus their efforts on those things they can do something about. The nature of their energy is positive, enlarging and magnifying, causing their Circle of Influence to increase." On the other hand, he says that, "Reactive people focus their efforts on the weakness of other people and circumstances over which they have no control. The negative energy generated by that focus causes their Circle of Influence to shrink."

A reactive mind would typically view a positive thinker as not understanding the gravity of a certain situation, not caring about it or not facing the facts. However, those who take a proactive view have actually taken a close look at a situation, analyzed it and determined the most productive path forward.

One of my favorite books is *The Art of Possibility: Transforming Professional and Personal Life* by Rosamund and Benjamin Zander. The authors show how embracing a positive outlook can reveal possibilities that naysayers would never notice. These cynics pride themselves on their supposed realism. However, the authors point out that, "It is actually the people who see the glass as half-empty who are the ones wedded to a fiction, for emptiness and lack are abstractions of the mind; whereas half-full is a measure of the physical reality under discussion. The so-called optimist, then, is the only one attending to real things, the only one describing a substance that is actually in the glass."

I had not heard the term *enrollment* until I read this book. The writers describe this term as "the art and practice of generating a spark of possibility for others to share." To illustrate this concept, they describe a time in the Middle Ages when lighting a fire from scratch was an arduous process. They relate that "people often carried a small metal box containing a smoldering cinder, kept alight throughout the day with little bits of kindling so they could light a fire with ease — because they always carried the spark." They proclaim that, "Our universe is alive with sparks. We have at our fingertips an infinite capacity to light a spark of possibility. Passion, rather than fear, is the igniting force."

I watched a spark ignite the imaginations of inmates at Duel Vocational Institute when I worked to encourage them in their art class. They were able to focus on the creative possibilities of their artwork rather than on their bleak surroundings for a few hours each week. (chapter 6) As a result, their spark, realized by the result of funds raised through their art sale, kindled increased possibilities for many abused children at the Child Abuse Prevention Council in Stockton.

7. Always Create Beauty. A bright orange sunset or sunrise can be incredibly gorgeous but it lasts a short while and is gone. I have seen lovely sandcastles constructed with artistic intricacy only to be destroyed by a crashing wave. Larry and I built a stunning setting at our ranch complete with horse stables, a riding rink, lush green pastures and a beautifully landscaped front yard highlighting a dry creek. It was quickly destroyed by the folks who bought the ranch after we left.

I have created a workplace culture multiple times — operational systems and strong staffing teams — only to see the next leader reverse everything I had worked years to build. I was heartened to learn that even Bill Gates and Jack Welch report disappointment at the demise of their carefully constructed business environments after they left.

It's only by looking back on these seemingly unrelated events that I came to realize that just because the beauty we create is (or can be) eventually destroyed, it does not mean that our creation has no value. Just because something does not last does not mean it has no benefit. Quite the opposite. I believe we must do our best to create beauty wherever we are — with our work, in our home or through anything in our life.

Create beauty with abandon—even though there are no guarantees it will endure. I have learned to put my best effort into everything I do because I know that, in the moment, those around me will benefit in some way. The message I take away is to always bring beauty to the present regardless of what the future may hold.

Christopher Columbus said, "you can never cross the ocean unless you have the courage to lose sight of the shore." It takes courage to venture away from the "shore" that we are used to and create something new and different. But I found that when I have a vision of what I want to do, only my best effort will satisfy my quest, even when there are no assurances of success or long-term advantages. I have also noticed that I learn from the very process of these endeavors and become emboldened by my own accomplishments. Many times remembering things I established in the past gives me inspiration to move forward with future projects.

For example, when I was worried about whether my traumatic brain injury would keep me from successfully delivering the keynote address at my Master's graduation, I reminded myself about how I learned to scuba dive even though I suffered from debilitating claustrophobia. I keep a photo taken during my speech as a reminder that I can do anything I set my mind to even when there are no guarantees of success.

8. Show up and Pay Attention. Many times in my life I have dreaded showing up at one event or another — like the time I had to give my first speech at a Rotary club, or when I was expected to represent my organization at a fancy gathering where I knew no one or the first time I had to pray out loud at a friend's funeral. I have experienced the magic of just showing up even when I don't want to.

I say "magic" because just being present speaks volumes to myself and to others. It's a sign of commitment. I signaled to myself that I had something of value to say to everyone in the room the day I tentatively stepped up to the podium at a Rotary club to talk about the cycle of child abuse and invite donations to the Child Abuse Prevention Council, where I was serving as executive director.

Just my presence communicated to event attendees that Girl Scouts was an active part of the community when I made my first formal fundraising soiree as CEO of Girl Scouts in Santa Barbara, even though I was nervous about not knowing a soul there.

I showed up at the funeral of my friend's son and ended up doing something I had never done before — I invited them to let me pray for them to bring some light to their intense grief. To this day they thank me for that whenever they see me.

Just being present can create more opportunities for ourselves and others because being in the right place at the right time can be key to success. I have made showing up a habit in my life because I have noticed that when I take the first step towards achieving an important goal, the rest of my journey doesn't seem as daunting. I end up feeling more confident in myself and better able to go after the things in life that will bring joy to me and to others.

Just showing up might be 90 percent of the battle, as Woody Allen was quoted as saying. But just as important is paying attention once you get there. I often go places with no preconceived agenda except to ask questions, listen and pay attention to what others say—and what they don't say. I have learned that if I can have patience, jewels of opportunity for connection emerge from the synergy of just being with others. But I can't be in a hurry. I must wait, listen, watch and trust that I will know how to respond when an opportunity arises to bring joy to others.

9. Find Your Heroes. I have always believed in the power of having mentors, role models and heroes. If I want to learn something new or improve in a certain area, I look around to find examples of others doing it well and learn from them. I travelled to Mendenhall, Mississippi, and to Miami, Florida to observe examples of thrift stores being used as a ministry to the poor. And then I was able to start KCAPS (chapter 1) in the late 1970s.

My long-time friend, David Peck, was always interested in how the brain works. He would challenge widely accepted concepts about such things as consciousness and the unconscious. David concluded there was no such thing as the unconscious brain because the brain was always conscious in one manner or another. I never knew if that was true, but his intellectual curiosity continually inspired me. David consistently challenged me to think more deeply and explore ideas with abandon. He set the example for me to complete my Master's and Doctorate degrees and to always use critical thinking.

I was 56 years old when I started my Master's program and when some of my friends heard I was beginning this arduous endeavor, they hinted that they thought I was too old. They asked, "How old will you be when you finish?" I said, "I'll be 58 or so, but I'll be that same age in two years whether I complete my Masters or not."

Education was important to me not because I thought it would result in an increased salary or more prestige, but because I have always been intellectually curious and I enjoy learning. I highly recommend finding ways to broaden one's scope and knowledge about a wide range of topics. I enjoyed the process of completing this degree so much that two years later I embarked upon my Doctorate. I am so glad I didn't let age or circumstances derail me from my goals.

David Peck's wife, Helen Cummings, also served as a role model for me. Her joy in applying scripture to everyday life, especially with the children in her school, was something I always tried to emulate. I also watched closely as she expertly convinced others to work toward achieving her own goals. Helen was a master and I learned so much from her.

I have found I must maintain a spirit of being coachable and open-minded with my mentors. And I need to pay attention and follow directions when I ask them for help. In 2012 I started my business, *Nonprofit Kinect*, and needed a website. I had no idea how to do this or where to start. Thankfully I was introduced to Michael Kramer who owned a website design company called Ameravant. Michael invited me into his office, asked lots of basic questions about my new business and gave me loads of homework. I quickly and diligently completed all of the assignments even though they were arduous. He was a little surprised that I finished so quickly and so completely.

That opened the door to the next steps in the process and soon I had a beautiful, compelling website as well as a clear focus of the goals for my business. Next was something called search optimization. I wasn't sure what that meant, but I did everything Michael told me to do — things like make a list of key words, use these words in the title of my blog articles and link my public articles back to my website. As a result of Michael's knowledge and my following of his instructions, my business consistently is found at the top of a Google search whenever my key words are used. People often remark about this and I always say, "I just do what Michael tells me to do and it works."

I have many heroes including Martin Luther King, Jr., Nelson Mandela, Sr. Joan Chittister and Peter Drucker, just to name a few. But the hero I want to tell you about now is Admiral Jim Stockdale who was the highest-ranking military officer in the "Hanoi Hilton" prisoner-of-war camp during the height of the Vietnam War. In his popular book, *Good to Great*, Jim Collins explains that Stockdale was tortured over 20 times during his eight-year imprisonment. He had no prisoner's rights, no set release date and no certainty as to whether he would even survive to see his family again.

When Stockdale was finally released, people asked him how in the world he was able to survive, not having any idea when or if he would get out. His response is now referred to as the Stockdale Paradox: Retain faith that you will prevail in the end, regardless of the difficulties and, at the same time, confront the most brutal facts of your current reality, whatever they might be.

Many people like to ask either/or questions — Is it this way or is it that way? Stockdale would say the answer is actually both. The best approach is to hold seemingly opposing realities at the same time. In this case it was a deep abiding faith in a positive outcome and, simultaneously, acknowledgement of the brutal facts involved. It's not easy, but whenever I am able to practice this strategy it proves immensely helpful.

10. **Trust Your Own Wisdom**. My astrological sign is Pisces, represented by two fish swimming in opposite directions. Many years ago I was exasperated by a difficulty in making decisions. The impediment was that I could usually see both sides of any issue or problem. I was able to notice the benefits of all choices. Finally, in frustration, I just said to myself, "If you can see the value of both decisions, then it doesn't matter which one you choose. Just pick one." Eventually I became proficient at making good decisions quickly.

I developed a process that seemed to work well for me. First I would clarify the decision to be made. If appropriate, I would invite input from trusted colleagues, research the topic and consider risks involved. Sometimes the best choice would clearly emerge; other times I would be stumped. Some leaders tend to overanalyze their choices resulting in "paralysis by analysis" which typically results in an inability to move forward. I didn't want to be like those individuals.

I am convinced that we know more than we think we do. I read an article once talking about the use of intuition in decision making. The author said it is sort of an inner wisdom we all have that is comprised of many things, most importantly an accumulation of all of our experiences over our lifetime. We often pit logic against intuition, but they both have an important role to play.

According to *Psychology Today*, "intuition is a process that gives us the ability to know something directly without analytic reasoning, bridging the gap between the conscious and nonconscious parts of our mind, and also between instinct and reason." Some people are uncomfortable with the idea of using our instincts as a guidance tool — or at least they don't want to admit it to others for fear of seeming undependable or bizarre.

The truth is that good decision making requires using three elements: reason, facts and research; input from trusted advisors and colleagues; and our own inner wisdom. So, when I am stumped about which decision to make after having researched the facts and solicited suggestions from others, I routinely check in with my inner wisdom. The combinations of these three essentials always serve me well. I don't demand to know all the facts before making a decision, I count on the feedback from colleagues and I trust my own intuition.

Once we become adept at this type of decision making we are ready to learn how to use creative tension to achieve our dreams. Peter Senge explains how this works in his seminal work, *The Fifth Dimension*, published in 1990. I became acquainted with Senge and this book when I worked for Girl Scouts. This is one of the earliest books that talked about learning organizations, mental models, shared vision and personal mastery. But I found the idea of creative tension particularly useful.

Imagine a rubber band is stretched between your two hands, one hand on top and the other on the bottom. The bottom hand represents your current reality whereas the top hand symbolizes your vision for the future. Notice the gap between the two created when you pull one hand further from the other. That gap is the source of creative energy that Senge calls *creative tension*. The more you spread your hands apart the more tension is created.

Tension always seeks release or resolution. There are only two possible ways for the tension to resolve itself: pull reality toward the vision or pull the vision toward reality. We often think of tension in a negative light, but if we use it in a creative way to bring our reality closer to our vision, we will be more likely to accomplish our goals. So I've learned to make friends with the creative tension so I can always move my reality closer to my dreams.

These are lessons that have particularly impacted me and hopefully the insights I've gained can be helpful to others.

The End

Because family is so very important
to me, I wanted to include
a few photos that show
family members,
some at major events and some
in just more casual settings.

My daughter Pam's wedding in 1981.
Top row: Baird, me, Larry, Peggy, Rick, Mike
and Jeff (all are Rockers);
Bottom row: Matt Rocker and the newlyweds,
Pam and Jeff Hoffman

Yossi and Janelle Shapiro at their wedding

Marcus and Marina Hoffman

385

Jarod and Ashley Rocker

Yer and Richard Rocker

Taryn and David Gluckman

Tim and Ashleigh Greene

Jarod Rocker at his graduation from San Jose State
University's Fine Arts program

Stephanie Rocker at her graduation from pharmacy school

Epilogue

Writing a book has always been at the top of my bucket list. Frankly, I never thought I would complete this dream—mainly because I had no idea where to start. Now that it is finished, I feel a great sense of accomplishment but, I also have gained a broader and deeper perspective of my life as I review the chapters.

Like most people I have asked myself several "what if" questions over the years. What would my life have been like if I had been raised by my actual birth father? What would be different if I had stayed at UCLA and pursued a career with the State Department instead of running off to Fresno with Larry? What if I had made different decisions along my life's journey?

In the end, I find myself impressed by all of the challenges that came my way and the incredible strength I found in facing them. Whether raising children at such a young age or being married to a dishonest man for so long, or experiencing the pain of losing my son or the ordeal of recovering from two separate traumatic brain injuries, resiliency has always been my steadfast companion. As a result, I have had a rich life filled with so many blessings and so much joy. Actually I don't think I would change a thing.

I feel so honored to have raised my five children and had the privilege of enjoying them as adults as well as relishing time with my wonderful grandchildren and now my great grandchildren. All of the organizations I served have brought me immense joy and a sense of making a difference in the world. Meeting Dennis and traveling the world with him has been an enduring blessing to me.

So what comes next? Of course, we never know what is in store for us, but reviewing the pages in this book assures me that I have what it takes to meet any challenge and to enjoy every opportunity that comes my way. I am grateful to all the people who have supported me and shared their wisdom with me over the years and I look forward to more adventures to come.

Editor's Note

Normally I wouldn't interject myself here, but meeting and working with Cynder compelled the need for me to say a few words.

It is too bad that Cynder waited until she was in her 70s to write a book – because she is an absolute natural at it. Had Cynder started in her 40s or 50s, I have no doubt that she would be on her 10th or 12th book by now.

When Cynder and I agreed to work on this book together, she did not quite know how to do it. She told me a bit about herself and I suggested that she start the book with a chapter about a turning point in her life that had a major impact on what would follow.

We agreed that her work in starting a thrift store for poor immigrant farm workers in California's Central Valley was the place to start her book. The work Cynder did in eliciting community involvement in the KCAPS thrift store, then creating the food bank, pre-school and Spanish-language church were wonderful accomplishments. They were tributes to her instinct to help others, her commitment to her religious values and her determination to set a goal and pursue it to completion.

After a couple of stabs at this first chapter and plotting out the subsequent chapters of *My Wild and Precious Life*, Cynder was rolling. She started producing chapters at an astounding rate. She knew what she wanted to say and just how to say it.

I've never seen anything like it. I've worked with many other people who wished to write their life story, but never a person who did it so prolifically and so well. Once when I was stunned that Cynder got a new section to me in record time, I said "Cynder, you are a fiendishly hard-working overachiever." And I could have said that many times.

Later chapters likewise chronicled Cynder's impressive achievements, continued dedication to helping others, her leadership abilities, voracious reading regimen and devotion to her family. Oh, and on the side she becomes a tireless outdoors person and bikes, hikes, skis and kayaks around the world with the love-of-her-life, Dennis Forster.

Cynder has led a most eventful life and does so well in describing it to us. I hope she writes more books because I sure want to read them.

–David Wilk

(Cynder writes a column about non-profit management
for the news service Noozhawk and we have included
a couple to illustrate what she covers and how)

Cynder Sinclair:
Use Scenario Planning to Create Your Nonprofit's New Normal

By Cynder Sinclair, Noozhawk Columnist
June 9, 2020

Our last article highlighted William Bridges' work with Transitions. He advised starting at the end rather than at the beginning so that we can let go of the old before we pick up the new. This period is followed by what he calls the neutral zone, where "old and maladaptive habits are replaced with new ones that are better adapted to the world in which the organization now finds itself."

After we analyze and learn from our ending and imagine possibilities in the neutral zone, it's time for our new beginning. In this phase, we will be developing a fresh identity, experiencing renewed energy and discovering our revitalized sense of purpose. Scenario planning will be an effective process for exploring the new beginning.

» **Scenario planning helps us imagine and prepare for various possible outcomes.**
Think of scenario planning as imagining numerous stories and how they might unfold rather than what might be the best- or worst-case scenario. With so much unknown, we need a higher degree of imagination than ever.

We are not trying to predict the future; we are developing an orderly way of thinking and making decisions. Instead of asking "what if" questions, we will be asking "what will we do if" questions.

So start with what you don't know. What unknowns are weighing on you most heavily? Think of what actions will have the greatest impact and require quick decisions. You can't tackle everything at once, so begin with what most supports your mission and achieves your core objectives.

» **Start with a diverse team.**
Scenario planning offers an excellent opportunity to gain feedback from a wide variety of stakeholders. Invite board members, staff, donors, collaborators and other supporters to a brainstorming session. Not only will they contribute new ideas, they will also feel like a valued part of the organization.

French philosopher <u>Emile Chartier</u> said it well: "Nothing is more dangerous than an idea when it's the only one you have." So, a team approach with diverse membership will yield the best and most creative results.

Of course, because of social distancing, the meeting won't look like sessions you have had in the past where everyone sits around at a table and someone writes on a whiteboard or flip chart. Hearing ideas from a cross-section of stakeholders is still important and possible in the new environment. For example, you can have a period of asynchronous brainstorming on a digital channel, followed by a couple hours of debate and refinement on an open videoconference.

» **Use your imagination to create the best scenarios for your group.**
Start by examining your mission. Ask yourself if your mission statement is still serving the original need. Get in touch with the real purpose of your organization and adjust the mission statement accordingly. The result, of course, will be your "North Star," guiding all current and future decision-making.

Now is the time to be creative but realistic. At first, narrow your focus on timely, essential needs. Ask yourself what impact your organization wants to have, how you are going to fund it, and ultimately what organizational capacity is needed.

Begin with just two or three scenarios based on your most urgent needs. It can be stressful and overwhelming to imagine more than that. Be sure to get input from those who will perform the work. Think through all aspects including program, financial, development, human resources and operations. After creating a couple of scenarios, evaluate each one to assess the likelihood of success. As more information becomes known, re-evaluate your scenarios and create new ones. This is an iterative process, not a once and done project.

Your goal should be to pick the scenario whose outcome seems most likely and to base a plan upon that scenario. You should also plan clear contingencies if another scenario begins to emerge instead.

» Budgeting for each scenario is essential.
Even though your newly imagined scenarios may turn out to be wrong, creating a basic budget for each one is still critical. Keep in mind, scenario budget planning is not a complete budget or a new strategic plan. It is an effort to paint a complete picture of your scenario using the information available to you in the moment.

Carrie Wanek, chief financial officer for the Foodbank of Santa Barbara County, offers insight into the process she uses: "Given the uncertainty of several key drivers, we have elected to develop a budget based on a base level, or target budget methodology. Our assumption was that FY21 would perform in a similar manner as FY20, with modest increases in donations and fairly flat to slight increases in operating expenses.

"The scenario planning approach was utilized by adding a column for each period (we broke ours down by quarter) specific to our COVID-19 activities, and then added the two data fields together, for each quarter. This allows us maximum flexibility to adjust our forecast as new information is gleaned every day.

"We can easily pivot the projections up or down with all remaining forecasts adjusted automatically using built-in formulas. For example, we assumed six months of current activity, but can shorten that timeline or increase it easily, along with adjusting the amounts."

The old nonprofit adage "no money, no mission" still holds true and reminds us that even when creating multiple scenarios, budgeting for revenue and expense is still an important part of the process.

» Remember you have a dual bottom line: mission impact and financial return.
The <u>nonprofit</u> business model is simply what we do (programs), why we do it (mission) and with what resources (finances). <u>Wikipedia</u> defines sustainability as "the capacity to endure." One of my favorite books, <u>"Nonprofit Sustainability,"</u> reminds us that "sustainability encompasses both financial sustainability and programmatic sustainability. Sustainability is an orientation, not a destination."

I highly recommend purchasing and using this book as an important tool to evaluate your organization's work and plan for future development. The authors recommend evaluating all of your programs according to two criteria: impact and profitability. Impact relates to whether the program is essential in achieving your mission; whereas profitability tells whether it is financially sustainable. Here are four possible program evaluation scenarios:

» High Mission Impact but Low Profitability. These are often activities that are popular with the community or staff. Often they are thought of as sacred cows — we've always had these programs, so we must continue. This can be a valuable evaluation because it gives you the opportunity to identify ways you can increase profitability if the beloved program is indeed essential to your mission.

» High Mission Impact and High Profitability. These are your star programs because they support and promote your mission and are also financially sustainable. You can keep these programs and maybe even think of ways to increase the profitability.

» Low Mission Impact and Low Profitability. You should probably stop these programs. They are typically things you've done for a long time, but they don't contribute to your mission or to your financial bottom line.

» Low Mission Impact but High Profitability. These are often fundraising events. Sometimes attendees have a great time but can't even remember which organization is in charge or what the mission is. But the organization continues to host the events because they are so profitable. If a program or event falls into this category, you can go ahead and keep it but find ways to enhance it so it is more in line with your mission.

» **Jump in and start your scenario planning today.**
Once you have identified the lessons learned from the pandemic's abrupt ending of your normal operations and spent time in the neutral zone imagining possibilities, it's time to start your new beginning. And even though all the unknowns make the way unclear, you can create and assess a few scenarios. For each one, you will pull together a diverse group of people to build a strawman budget and evaluate which programs will be included based on their impact and profitability.

I predict you will enjoy the process and be surprised and happy with your results.

— Dr. Cynder Sinclair is a consultant to nonprofits and founder and CEO of Nonprofit Kinect. She has been successfully leading nonprofits for 30 years and holds a doctorate in organizational management. She can be contacted at cynder@nonprofitkinect.org. The opinions expressed are her own.

Nonprofits

Cynder Sinclair: Recruit Your Best Nonprofit Board

By Cynder Sinclair, Noozhawk Columnist
May 30, 2017

A well-functioning board of directors is not only essential to meeting legal requirements but also critical in helping a nonprofit achieve its goals and mission.

The effectiveness of a board's performance depends on strategically identifying the skills, expertise and contacts the board needs to achieve its goals, and then recruiting board members who reflect these characteristics. Recruiting the right board members takes hard work, much of it done weeks or months before new board members are invited to join the board.

The key is to create an intentional recruitment plan that clearly defines the kind of board members the organization needs and outlines a recruitment and orientation process carefully matched to the group's programs, operations, goals, and resource needs.

Board governance committee

Ideally, board recruitment should be an ongoing process. The organization should always have a candidate pool where individuals move through various stages of cultivation, which can include serving on board committees.

When a vacancy occurs, it is easier to rekindle communications than to start from scratch.

While every board member should be involved in identifying potential candidates, the chief executive should act as a valuable partner with the governance committee in the search for new board members.

The governance committee's task is to find the best candidates, convince them of the benefits of board service, present candidates to the full board, and after the final nomination, make sure new board members are well-equipped to do the best possible job.

The governance committee's first question to consider as they start to formulate their board recruiting plan is: What are our key strategic priorities, and what new skills or expertise might we need on our board to help us achieve those priorities?

Creating a simple grid to categorize the various expertise areas needed on the board will provide a quick answer to this question. Keeping this grid up-do-date will ensure you don't have to start from scratch every time you recruit more board members.

Recruiting for diversity

Be sure to include all considerations in the board profile grid such as age, ethnicity, geography, skill set, community connections, experience, and other categories you want to consider for a well-rounded board.

Depending on the domain in which the nonprofit operates and the beneficiaries it serves, the board may want to include specific areas of expertise, perhaps functional or geographic.

For example, an organization focused on healthcare issues may want a few board members with expertise in that area.

Similarly, a nonprofit primarily serving underprivileged families in India or Africa will likely want to include board members who are either from the area served or who have a deep knowledge of the area.

Dedicated board members typically bring more to the table than their expertise in a given area. A member's value isn't only what's in his/her head, it's also the networks and reputational capital they bring that allow them to contribute to the organization.

The most effective boards are those that are able to bring together a diverse group who bring a range of thoughts, experiences, knowledge and perspective. Diversity should be an integral part of the recruitment process rather than tacked on at the end.

Diversity goals for the board can include representation from communities the organization serves. Consumer representatives can add a unique perspective to the board's work.

Involving people who are served by the organization is not just a good thing to do; it can be the pathway to making the organization's services higher quality.

Identifying great candidates

After an organization has evaluated how the composition of its board can advance its strategic priorities and has identified the board roles it needs to fill, it can begin identifying potential board candidates.

Research other organizations with similar missions; look at who is serving on their board. These are typically people who are passionate about your cause as well.

Perhaps some of these people are finishing their board term or maybe they can suggest others who are aligned with your organization's mission. One sure fire way to find high-quality board members is to encourage every board member to use his/her network to constantly identify potential candidates.

When board members attend events or community meetings, they can look around the room watching for individuals who might add value to the board.

Having informal side conversations with these people about the organization will begin to lay a foundation for future board recruitment. This intentional networking can be richly rewarding.

Be sure these conversations focus on the organization's mission rather than how prestigious the board position may be. The best board members are passionate about the cause rather than eager to promote their personal agenda.

Conducting due diligence

As part of its early due diligence, the organization should ask board candidates some key questions:

» Can you fulfill our board's fiduciary and legal oversight responsibilities?

These responsibilities can include approving financial plans, monitoring the organization's financial health, ensuring financial controls are in place, ensuring there are independent audits, managing key risks, and ensuring all legal requirements are met.

Specific duties will vary based on the organization's size and complexity, and may change over time as an organization grows.

» How have you already demonstrated a passion for organizations like ours?

People familiar with high-impact boards said passion for the mission can be shown in many ways.

It could be as straightforward as previous nonprofit board or volunteer experience for a similar organization.

It also could be that the candidate grew up around the Boys & Girls Club or YMCA, for instance, and believes deeply in the value of youth-serving organizations.

» Do you fundamentally have the time to serve on our board?
People familiar with nonprofit board service said those who are new to the sector often underestimate the amount of time required to be an effective board member.

In fact, the time commitment for many nonprofit boards can be substantial and should not be minimized to attract board members.
All board members must be able to meet the basic requirements of board service.

At most nonprofits this means, at a minimum, preparing for and attending monthly board meetings, serving on at least one board committee, working on special projects, and advocating on behalf of the organization.
If, for example, a candidate already serves on many boards, she/he most likely will not have adequate time to devote to yours.

No matter how enticing a potential board member may seem, if she/he can't devote adequate time and attention to your organization do not recruit them. Lack of a single board member's participation discourages the whole board.

Can you meet the board fundraising expectation?

The role of fundraising by board members varies widely within the nonprofit sector.

Boards that have a revenue strategy based on raising funds from individuals and businesses often need board members who are able to personally make substantial financial contributions and who are willing to solicit donations from others.

For other nonprofits, such as organizations that rely heavily on government grants, fundraising may not be a significant board responsibility.

The key is to be clear about your organization's board fundraising requirements before recruiting begins. Then explain those requirements to potential board member as part of the recruiting process.
You want board members who are fully engaged with your board activities, including fundraising.

At the other extreme, organizations that make the ability to raise funds the sole qualification for board membership can actually diminish their board's overall effectiveness.

It can be de-motivating for hard-working board members when other members are allowed to simply write a check and show up for luncheons. If someone is fully invested and also able to write a check, that's great; but don't go after them just because of wealth. Disengaged board members can make the board dysfunctional. Strong boards have one thing in common: Everyone is engaged.

Ensuring cultural fit
In addition to determining whether a board candidate meets specific requirements, it is important to determine whether the candidate will be a good cultural fit with the rest of the board and the organization itself. Look for people whose motive is to advance the mission rather than their own personal gain; people who are good listeners and who ask probing, thoughtful questions.

After talking to a board candidate, the governance committee should hold a debriefing session to discuss how the candidate would fit in with the board culture and identify the specific board role the candidate could play.

Remember, it's a partnership

It is important throughout the recruiting process to be clear about board member responsibilities and to make sure that candidates truly understand the organization's expectations before they commit to the job.

You might want to create a <u>Statement of Understanding</u> to spell out what the board member is agreeing to do as well as what the CEO and board chair agree to provide.

Being crystal clear about what everyone can expect from the partnership is an important element of board recruitment strategy, enabling you to build strong relationships with board members so everyone can work toward accomplishing the organization's strategic goals as partners.

— Dr. Cynder Sinclair is a consultant to nonprofits and founder and CEO of <u>Nonprofit Kinect</u>. She has been successfully leading nonprofits for 30 years and holds a doctorate in organizational management. She can be contacted at <u>cynder@nonprofitkinect.org</u>. The opinions expressed are her own.

(I love poetry and have included some of my favorites in the main body of this book where it seems they applied to the content. Following are portions of a few more of my favorites...)

A Few of My Favorite Poems

Fluent by John O'Donohue
   "I would love to live like a river flows,
   Carried by the surprise of its own unfolding."

When Death Comes by Mary Oliver
   "When it's over I want to say: all my life I was a
bride married to amazement.
   I was the bridegroom taking the world into my
arms.
   When it's over, I don't want to wonder if I have
   made of my life something particular and real.
   I don't want to find myself sighing and frightened or
full of argument.
   I don't want to end up simply having visited this
world."

Prayer by Mary Oliver
   "May I never not be frisky,
   May I never not be risqué.
   May my ashes, when you have them, friend,
   And give them to the ocean,
   Leap in the froth of the waves,
   Still loving movement,
   Still ready, beyond all else,
   To dance for the world."

A Summer Day by Mary Oliver
"So, tell me, what is it you plan to do with your one wild and precious life?"

In Blackwater Woods by Mary Oliver
"To live in this world you must be able to do three things:
To love what is mortal;
To hold it against your bones knowing your own life depends on it;
And, when the time comes to let it go, to let it go."

The Way it is by William Stafford.
"There's a thread you follow. It goes among things that change. But it doesn't change. People wonder about what you are pursuing. You have to explain about the thread. But it's hard for others to see. While you hold it you can't get lost. Tragedies happen; people get old or hurt or die; and you suffer and get old. Nothing you do can stop time's unfolding. You don't ever let go of the thread."

Inuit Indian Song
And I thought over again
    my small adventures
    as with a shore wind I drifted
    out in my kayak
    and thought I was in danger.
    my fears
    those small ones
    that I thought so big
    for all the vital things

I had to get and to reach.

And yet there is only
    one great thing
    the only thing:
    to live to see
    the great day that dawns,
    and the light that fills the world."

Unconditional by Jennifer Wellwood
    Willing to experience aloneness, I discover
connection everywhere;
    Turning to face m fear, I meet the warrior who lives
within;
    Opening to my loss, I gain the embrace of the
universe;
    Surrendering into emptiness, I find fullness without
end.

    Each condition I flee from pursues me;
    Each condition I welcome transforms me,
    And becomes transformed into its radiant jewel-like
essence.

    I bow to the one who has made it so, who has
crafted this Master Game;
    To play it is pure delight;
    To honor its form—true devotion."

Beanacht by John O'Donohue
"On the day when
the weight deadens
on your shoulders
and you stumble,
may the clay dance
to balance you.

And when your eyes
freeze behind
the grey window
and the ghost of loss
gets into you,
may a flock of colours,
indigo, red, green
and azure blue,
come to awaken in you
a meadow of delight.

When the canvas frays
in the currach of thought
and a stain of ocean
blackens beneath you,
may there come across the waters
a path of yellow moonlight
to bring you safely home.

May the nourishment of the earth be yours,
may the clarity of light be yours,
may the fluency of the ocean be yours,
may the protection of the ancestors be yours.

And so may a slow
wind work these words
of love around you,
an invisible cloak
to mind your life."

The Journey by Mary Oliver
One day you finally knew what you had to do, and began,
though the voices around you kept shouting their bad advice—
though the whole house began to tremble and you felt the old tug at your ankles.

"Mend my life!" each voice cried. But you didn't stop.
You knew what you had to do, though the wind pried with its stiff fingers at the very foundations, though their melancholy was terrible.

It was already late enough, and a wild night, and the road full of fallen branches and stones.

But little by little, as you left their voices behind, the stars began to burn through the sheets of clouds and there was a new voice which you slowly recognized as your own,
that kept you company as you strode deeper and deeper into the world,

determined to do the only thing you could do—determined to save the only life that you could save."

A Few More Favorite Quotes

"To be fully alive, fully human, and completely awake is to be continually thrown out of the net. To live fully is to be always in no-man's-land." Pema Chodron

"Success is never final, failure is never fatal. It's courage that counts." John Wooden

"I steer my boat with hope in the head and fear in the stern." Thomas Jefferson (when faced with grave personal turmoil)

"Logic will get you from A to B. Imagination will take you everywhere." Albert Einstein

"Spread love everywhere you go. Let no one ever come to you without leaving happier." Mother Teresa

"Our lives begin to end the day we become silent about things that matter." M. L. King

"Where we stand determines what we see." Juan Luis Segundo

"But it's the having not the keeping that is the treasure." Jack Gilbert (The Lost Hotels of Paris)

Some Family History

Births — Children

Pamela Jo (Rocker) Hoffman Santa Barbara	3/30/59
Richard Ernest Rocker Santa Barbara	7/19/60
Michael Gordon Rocker Santa Barbara	9/29/62
Douglas Baird Rocker Fresno	6/2/68
Matthew Clay Rocker Kingsburg	3/26/76

Births — Grandchildren

Jenelle Artema (Hoffman) Shapiro	1/14/86
Taryn Parser (Hoffman) Gluckman	9/6/88
Marcus Henry Hoffman	2/10/93
Stephanie Ann Rocker	8/15/79
Ashleigh Paige Rocker Greene	4/26/83
Richard Nathaniel Rocker	5/27/86

Jarod Henry Rocker	5/12/89
Koty Lynne Rocker	1/23/96
McKallah Jo Rocker	8/2/99
Sarah James Rocker	11/21/04
Ashley Ann Rocker	1/9//06
Mellissa Rocker	10/29/10

Births — Great Grandchildren

Hanna Shapiro	9/28/17
Amelia Shapiro	7/22/20
Jack Gluckman	7/7/17
Leah Gluckman	9/3/19
Simon Greene	10/27/16
Hayleigh Greene	2/3/20
Atlas Rocker	2/12/19
Lukas Rocker	2/26/19

Weddings — Children

Pam & Jeff Hoffman	8/30/81
Rick & Peggy Rocker	8/4/78

Mike & Amy Rocker   6/1/96

Weddings--Grandchildren

Jenelle & Yossi Shapiro   8/23/14

Taryn & David Gluckman   6/26/10

Marcus & Marina Hoffman   10/12/19

Ashleigh & Tim Greene   2/26/15

Richard & Yer Rocker   10/21/17

Jarod & Ashley Rocker   4/7/18

Acknowledgments

Bridges, W. (1980). *Transitions: Strategies for coping with the difficult, painful, and confusing times in your life.* Cambridge, MA: Perseus Books.

Chittister, J. (2019). *Dear Joan Chittister: Conversations with Women in the Church.* New London, CT: Twenty-Third Publications.

Collins, J. (2001). *Good to Great.* New York: Harper Collins.

Covey, S. (1989). *The 7 Habits of Highly Effective People.* New York: Simon & Schuster.

Edwards, E. (2009). *Resilience.* New York: Broadway Books.

Greenleaf, R. (1977). *Servant Leadership: A Journey into the Nature of Legitimate Power and Greatness.* Mahwah, NJ: Paulist Press.

Hesselbein, F. (2002). *Hesselbein on Leadership.* San Francisco: Jossey-Bass.

Lama, D., Tutu, D., Abrams, D. (2016). *The Book of Joy.* New York: Penguin Random House.

Lencioni, P. (2020). *The Motive: Why so Many Leaders Abdicate their Most Important Responsibilities*. Hoboken, NJ: John Wiley & Sons, Inc.

Landes. D. (1998). *The Wealth and Poverty of the Nations: Why Some are so Rich and Some are so Poor*. New York: W.W. Norton & Company.

Lewis, C. S. (1950). *The Lion, the Witch, and the Wardrobe (The Chronicles of Narnia)*. United Kingdom: Geoffrey Bles.

Lyubomirsky, S. (2007). *The How of Happiness: A Scientific Approach to Getting the Life You Want*. New York: Penguin Press.

Magretta, J. (2012). *Understanding Michael Porter: The Essential Guide to Competition and Strategy*. Boston: Harvard Business Review Press.

Merzenich, M. (2013). *Soft-Wired: How the New Science of Brain Plasticity Can Change Your Life*. San Francisco: Parnassus Publishing.

Murray, W.H. (1953). Leader of the Scottish Himalayan Expedition. https://en.wikipedia.org/wiki/W._H._Murray.

O'Donohue, J. (1997). *Anam Cara*. New York: HarperCollins.

Senge, P. (1990). *The Fifth Dimension*. New York: Doubleday Currency.

Stone, I. (1961). *The Agony and the Ecstasy: The Biographical Novel of Michelangelo*. New York: Doubleday.

Whyte, D. (2015). *Consolations; The Solace, Nourishment and Underlying Meaning of Everyday Words*. Langley, WA: Many Rivers Press.

Zander, R. and B. (2000).*The Art of Possibility: Transforming Professional and Personal Life*. New York: Penguin Random House.

The Living Bible. (1971). All scripture references. Wheaton, Il: Tyndale House Publishers.